SAINT FRANCIS OF ASSISI

IVAN GOBRY

Saint Francis of Assisi

TRANSLATED BY
MICHAEL J. MILLER

IGNATIUS PRESS   SAN FRANCISCO

Original French edition:
Saint François d'Assise
© 2003 Tallandier Éditions, Paris

Cover art: Detail of Saint Francis (ca. 1320–1325)
from the fresco *Saint Francis of Assisi*
painted by Simone Martini
© AKG Paris

Cover design by John Herreid

Contents

PART FOUR

THE PURE PATH OF THE
SOUL'S JOURNEY TOWARD GOD

PART FIVE

THE SUBLIME PATH OF ETERNITY

PART SIX

THE PATHS BY WHICH SAINT FRANCIS IS KNOWN

Who, then, O greatest of the saints,
could imagine and explain to others the ardor of your soul?

— Thomas of Celano
(First biographer of Saint Francis)

Showered from his birth with favors from heaven,
filled with the spirit that inspired the prophets,
all aflame with the burning fire of the seraphim,
he is the one symbolized by the angel who rises
up from the East and bears the sign of the living God.

— Saint Bonaventure
(Doctor of the Church)

In the twelfth century, love burst onto the scene with
extraordinary force, and Saint Francis was its champion.

— Hippolyte-Adolphe Taine

By imitating Jesus Christ, Francis became
the most perfect copy and image of Our Lord that has ever existed.

— Benedict XV

Preface

The French publishing house Tallandier asked me to write a new life of Saint Francis of Assisi.

My first reaction was to refuse. What good would a new biography do? In the French language alone, more than a hundred were published between 1800 and 1930. Everything has been said on the subject. And by what pens! I have in my hand the marvelous work by the Danish author, Johannes Jörgensen,[1] one of Saint Francis' converts. When I bought this volume, sixty years ago, it was already in its 125th edition; it is a rare combination of historical scholarship and literary style, brought to life in the French language by the talent of Teodor de Wyzewa. A few years later *Saint François* by Abbot Omer Englebert appeared,[2] which is just as charming and always a pleasure to reread. Could I ever expect to replace these masterpieces?

My editors insisted on a principle that they claimed was paramount: the more important a personage is, the more the public is disposed to read an account of his life. The reason that Saint Francis of Assisi has inspired more biographies than any other saint is that his fascinating personality continues to attract readers.

The argument was decisive, because it appealed to my deepest desires, and I was convinced, in my inmost heart, that Francis himself was urging me by the mouth of these editors. My familiarity with this spiritual genius and his religious family, with the historical sources of his life and his spirituality, persuaded me that I could undertake this task joyfully and diligently. He had been introduced to me when I was an adolescent by an unexpected middle-man: a Jesuit. It happened in Troyes in 1941, during the first year of the German occupation. I cared little about anything supernatural and had become passionately devoted to literature. I had read and reread, I don't know how many times, all the seventeenth-century classics, all the Romantic authors. I could recite, with feeling, whole acts from *Phèdre* [a tragedy

---

[1] *Saint François d'Assise*, translated from Danish into French by Teodor de Wyzewa (Paris, 1909). T. O. O'Connor Sloane (New York: Longmans Green, 1912).
[2] *Vie de saint François d'Assise* (Paris: Albin Michel, 1947).

by Racine], entire poems from [Victor Hugo's] *Légende des siècles*, but also cantos from the *Divine Comedy* and some sonnets by Petrarch. I sensed, however, a certain emptiness, which called for another form of enthusiasm and culture. One of my classmates encouraged me to meet with a religious from the Society of Jesus who was highly esteemed both as a confessor and as a retreat master: Father Butruyle. I went to see him, and I figured that there was every reason to begin with the master of that admirable man. I asked him to recommend for me a biography of Ignatius of Loyola.

He looked at me for a moment, as though he were trying to establish a connection between my soul and the souls of those who would inspire me in the future. Then he decided, with an impartiality that surprised me: "Saint Ignatius? No. For you, Saint Francis of Assisi."

I did not try to argue: the man of God was ordering me to discover Saint Francis of Assisi. I went into the first bookstore along the way and bought the biography best suited to my wallet: *Le saint des temps de misère, saint François d'Assise*, by François Duhourcau.[3] I found this account dull and stereotyped. But, far from dissuading me from pursuing my quest, this disappointment drove me to find something better; I could sense, through those chapters that were devoid of enthusiasm, that elsewhere there was something to satisfy me—not my curiosity, but my soul; not the discovery of historical facts, but a meeting with an ineffable being with whom I would communicate intimately. That was when I found Jörgensen; then, through him, the firsthand sources from the thirteenth century: Thomas of Celano, *The Three Companions*, the *Legenda antiqua*, the *Mirror of Perfection*, and the *Fioretti* [*Little Flowers of Saint Francis*]. I had arrived: from then on, I enjoyed a close friendship with Saint Francis of Assisi. In 1943 I was admitted into the Third Order Franciscans.

And I plunged so easily and so joyfully into these accounts and these reflections, as an everyday routine, that the personalities of Francis of Assisi, of his disciples, and of his spiritual descendants became familiar to me, to the point that I rediscovered them at Assisi as though they were my contemporaries and friends. They belonged to my interior world, where Racine and Hugo had formerly been enthroned.

---

[3] François Duhourcau, *Le Saint des temps de misère, saint François d'Assise* (Paris: Éditions "Spes", 1936).

In 1956, Paul-André Lesort, aware of my research and my enthusiasm, asked me to compose a *Saint François d'Assise* for [the publisher] Éditions du Seuil,[4] as part of the series of "Spiritual Masters" that was under his direction. The volume appeared the following year, and eventually sixty-five thousand copies were printed. Two years later, my book devoted to the Franciscan mystics was published by Éditions Franciscaines; the work is now out of print. In 1982, for the eighth centenary of the birth of the saint from Assisi, I published a study on his teaching and his spirituality, based on his writings and his words.[5]

Given that momentum, could I now refuse to write a biography of Saint Francis of Assisi for Éditions Tallandier, which had just published five of my historical works? Of course, it would be more than a history. But is that not the case with every book on history, especially if it is hagiography? I had had some glorious predecessors, whom I could never hope to equal. The important thing was to forget them and to say again in turn, in my own way, what they had said so well; certainly not by improvising or by saying something else, but by following in their footsteps, along the same lines. By carrying the same flame, although it now lit a new torch.

The nineteenth-century historian Renan said one day to Rev. Paul Sabatier, a Protestant minister: "You? You will be the historian of the Seraphic Father. I envy you. Saint Francis has always smiled upon his biographers." That, ultimately, is my ambition: to have Francis of Assisi smile at me.

---

[4] *Saint-François d'Assise et l'esprit franciscain*. The same work, without the illustrations, has been included since 2001 in the series *"Points sagesse"* by the same publisher.

[5] *Saint François d'Assise, le héraut du grand Roi* (Tequi, 1982).

Feeling quite unworthy and unequal to the task,
I would never have dared to write this life,
which deserves to be imitated in its entirety,
had I not been encouraged
by the affectionate fervor of my brothers
and constrained by the devotion
that binds me to my saintly father, Francis.
How could I escape?
I would sorely fear being accused of ingratitude
if I refused to bear witness in praise of him.

—Saint Bonaventure

PART ONE

THE LONG PATH OF CONVERSION

1182–1209

1. Assisi

Francis is from Assisi in Umbria. He was born in Assisi; he spent his youth in Assisi; he founded his religious order in Assisi; he died in Assisi.

An unimportant town, according to the geographer and the economist. The intellectual and commercial activities there are of little interest. Besides, it numbers now, at the beginning of the twenty-first century, only twenty-five thousand inhabitants: What is that, compared with Milan and Naples? Furthermore, it was never the capital of a duchy or of a principality, and even today it is not a county seat.

It does, however, have a long history. Certain Latin authors say that it sprang up well before Rome. Conquered in the fourth century before Christ by the Etruscans, it joined with them in fighting against the Romans when they invaded its territory; yet its troops were defeated at Santino (295 B.C.), and it became a Roman city. Within its walls was born the poet Propertius in the year 46 B.C. The inhabitants had built a temple there in honor of Minerva, which can still be seen on the town square (Piazza del Comune) in the middle of the city, although it has become the Church of Santa Maria della Minerva.

Christianity, according to an ancient but misty tradition, is said to have been brought to Assisi as early as the year 58 by a certain Crispolitus, whom the Italians call Crispolto, a disciple of Saint Peter; but it seems much more likely that he evangelized this region at the beginning of the third century and died as a victim of the persecution by Diocletian. There appears to be more real evidence for other apostles of Umbria, martyrs during that same period: Saints Victorinus, Sabinus, and, above all, Rufinus, devotion to whom has persisted in that locality. According to the tradition, the latter perished by drowning in the Chiascio, a tributary of the Tiber River that flows three kilometers away from the walls of Assisi. After the town converted to Christianity, his body was recovered and buried in the middle of

the settlement, and a large Romanesque church—later a cathedral—
was constructed on that site thirty or forty years before the birth of
Saint Francis. We can still admire this shrine with its austere Umbrian
façade and its sturdy bell tower.

Christianity had taken root in the region, which, with its deep
forests and its grottos, became a choice location for hermits, who
frequently gathered their disciples into monastic communities. This
might have been the case with Saint Benedict: his parents lived in
Rome in a palace on the Trastevere, but they owned an estate in Umbria where they went to spend the summer months, which were unbearable in Rome; this was in Norcia, the Latin name for what we call
Nursia, located 600 meters above sea level in the Sibillini Mountains,
about thirty kilometers east of Spoleto. It was there that Abondantia,
whose name tradition has preserved, would bring forth her son and
daughter. Benedict knew the area, therefore, and when he fled in secret so as to live a solitary life, he might have sought refuge in the
surrounding forests, where hills rose to heights of 1,700 and 1,800
meters and where unexplored caverns were carved into their sides.
But instead the young Benedict preferred to establish his hermitage
in Subiaco, in the region of Latium, perhaps in order to throw off
pursuers. This did not prevent him from receiving the usual title of
Benedict of Nursia, which makes him an Umbrian just like Francis.

But there were many other hermits and monks around Nursia.
Right nearby, since the end of the fifth century, there was a monastery,
the name of whose founder has not come down to us. In 528, upon
the death of their abbot, the monks elected the hermit Eutychius, who
lived not far from there with his disciple Florentius. He accepted the
office and governed this fervent community for ten or twelve years.
At his death, miracles multiplied at his tomb, and he was venerated as
a saint. But Florentius had remained alone, and he implored heaven to
send him a companion. Scarcely had he finished his prayer when he
found at the door to his chapel a big bear, whose humble, submissive
attitude showed him that it had been sent from heaven. Florentius
trained it, to the point where the animal diligently played the role of
a shepherd, leading the flock to pasture and bringing it back at the
appointed hour.

This idyllic scene was played out around ten kilometers to the north
of Nursia, in a place which today is called San Eutizio. At the same

distance to the west, toward Spoleto, where modern-day Campoli is located, there was another monastery then; the abbot, whose name was Spes, had been sightless for forty years, yet he governed his community with wisdom. In Spoleto itself, during the fifth century, there were several monasteries; one of them had as its abbot Eleutherius, who was an acquaintance of Pope Saint Gregory the Great. A little later on, we find there Saint Lawrence the Illuminator, so called because he had restored sight to a blind man; he became bishop of Spoleto, but resigned from the office to go build the famous Abbey of Our Lady of Farfa in the Sabine region, between Rome and Rieti.

There were yet dozens of other monasteries in Umbria. Still, even though they found a place in contemporary writings, they were destroyed by the barbarians, along with the houses that they mentioned. Central Italy was in effect occupied in turn by two Germanic peoples that professed Arianism, the Ostrogoths and the Lombards. Theodoric the Great (d. 526), leader of the Ostrogoths, extended his dominion over all of Italy and was proclaimed the king thereof. Emperor Justinian sent to the peninsula one of his best generals, Narses, who routed and killed the last Ostrogoth king, Totila (536): Umbria came under Byzantine rule. But only for a short time—thirty years later, the Lombards invaded Italy, expelled the Byzantine Greeks, and sacked the places of Catholic worship. Most of the monasteries in central Italy were demolished. The new occupiers created a duchy in Spoleto, to which Assisi belonged, and oppressed the population there. The Lombard monarchy was an elective office; in 653 the throne went to Aribert, who was a Catholic, as were his successors. Catholic worship flourished again everywhere; the bishops regained their sees, and monastic life revived. This renewal was evident especially in Lombardy: in Pavia (the capital of the Lombards), in Como, Vercelli, Parma, Milan, Piacenza, but also in Tuscany and in the duchy of Benevento, south of Rome. In Umbria there was scarcely any sign of it, but we must assume that this territory harbored many recluses who were unknown to the multitudes. Belatedly, however, we see the Benedictine monastery of San Michele di Limigiano appear not far from Assisi, built twenty-three years before the birth of Saint Francis.

During this period, lay activity and political life reached new heights in Assisi. The tenth century saw the construction of the first cathedral, Saint Mary Major, in the pre-Romanesque style, next to the bishop's

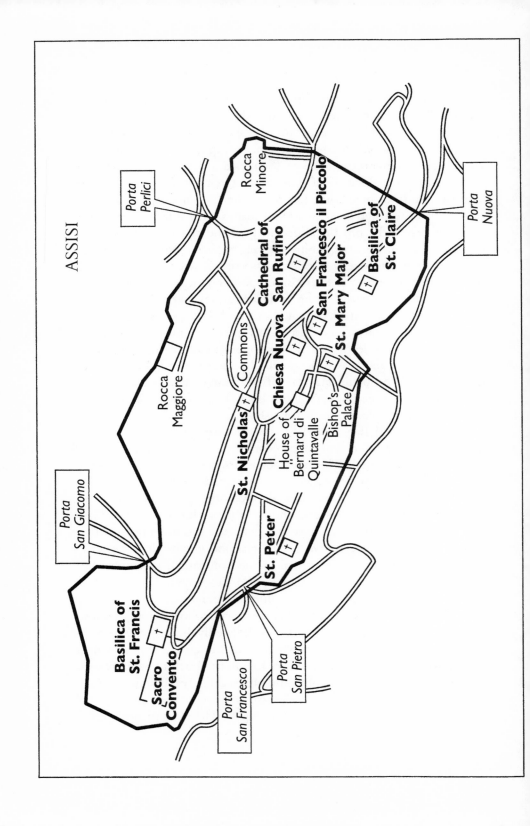

ASSISI

Porta Perlici

Porta Nuova

Rocca Minore

Cathedral of
San Rufino

San Francesco il Piccolo

Basilica of
St. Claire

St. Mary Major

Chiesa Nuova

Commons

Rocca
Maggiore

St. Nicholas

House of
Bernard di
Quintavalle

Bishop's
Palace

Porta San Giacomo

St. Peter

Basilica of
St. Francis

Sacro
Convento

Porta
San Francesco

Porta
San Pietro

palace; the eleventh century, especially, added monumental gates and handsome secular residences, but this was also the century in which they built the new cathedral of Saint Rufinus, and then in succession, while Saint Francis was still just a child, the churches of Saint Peter, Saint Nicholas, and Saint James. This was a prelude to Franciscan art.

Although the geographer has little to say about Assisi, the tourist, in contrast, is overwhelmed. First of all by nature itself, which is simultaneously exuberant and charming, abundant and delicate. Umbria, situated in the middle of the long Apennine chain, which forms the spinal column of the Italian peninsula, is of course quite similar in its landscapes to those that one finds just about everywhere in this romantic mountainous region, from the northern part of Tuscany, at the border of Lombardy, down to Calabria, at the southern extreme or "heel" of the "boot": 1,000 kilometers of an uninterrupted spectacle, composed of sheer cliffs, dense forests, and, around the towns, charming groups of cypresses, pines, and olive trees. But Umbria has a charm of its own, in which the lofty character of the Apennines is present in a tempered form. The Gran Sasso, nearby in the Abruzzi, rises to the north of Aquila, a massive mountainous wilderness extending over fifty kilometers and culminating in the 2,900-meter-high Monte Corno. But Umbria has no peak higher than 2,000 meters; furthermore they are, as it were, tamed, their ardor mitigated; Assisi unfolds at the foot of Mount Subasio, which does not reach a full 1,300 meters.

All of these Umbrian villages perched on a hillside resemble one another from a distance; all of these towns that scale a rock face, Spoleto, Todi, Gubbio, Narni, are sisters in their appearance. But Assisi, which extends upward from below, as they do, with a certain nonchalance, has something more. First of all, viewed from above, from the fortress of the Rocca Maggiore, which was built at the end of the twelfth century by the German invader, the town appears quite dense, with its narrow streets drawn tightly along the houses, its sanctuaries incorporated into the habitat. Viewed from below, for example, from the road that arrives from *Santa Maria degli Angeli* (Saint Mary of the Angels), it appears to be annexed to the formidable Sacro Convento, which extends toward the west, dominated by the double Basilica of Saint Francis. This marvelous, eye-catching monastic complex is outside of the town, and yet it upstages it; it is lower down, and yet it looms over it, so that the tourist and the pilgrim, drawn toward it as though by a lover, cannot help rushing toward it, with a joy mixed with reverential fear.

The reality does not disappoint their high hopes, and even far surpasses them. For this majestic monument, which was built to shelter the body of the saint, contains an accumulation of masterpieces from the period, in an atmosphere of recollection. The upper church, in a soaring, luminous Gothic style, displays, on the two walls of the nave, the major work of Giotto: the life of Saint Francis in twenty-eight tableaux, inspired by Saint Bonaventure's biography of him. Above them are scenes from the Bible produced by the Tuscano-Byzantine school: to the right, fifteen Old Testament scenes, and to the left, sixteen scenes from the life of Jesus. The transept is decorated with an abundance of other paintings, which can be attributed with certainty to Cimabue and Cavallini.

The lower church, evidently constructed before the upper church, with its lower vaults, bathed in a sacred shadow, is much more complex: it includes, besides the nave with three bays [travées] and the choir, two transepts and nine chapels; all of it, including the vaulting, is ornamented with sumptuous frescos painted by a legion of artists, including Cimabue, Martini, Lorenzetti, and students of Giotto. It would take a book to describe these marvelous works, and it would be worth it.[1]

Finally, beneath the lower church, the visitor descends to the crypt, where the tomb of Saint Francis is venerated.

Indeed, though the traveler may rush to the mighty basilica that attracted his attention from afar, upon arriving in it he finds only the conclusion of the life of Saint Francis, his glorification. But if he were to manage his time wisely, he would probably go there by way of the places that marked the stages of the saint's life. He would begin his visit, then, in the middle of the town, with the Chiesa Nuova [new church], built on the spot where his father's house stood, and perhaps, according to one tradition, on the same place as Francis' own room (although the latter could not have been so spacious as to suggest the floor plan for a church). Very close by, the visitor would not miss

---

[1] The severe earthquake of September 26, 1997, damaged many of these works of art, but they are being restored.— ED.

the chance to slip in to the chapel of San Francesco il Piccolo, which in its original form is supposed to have been the stable where Francis was born.

Then the traveler would make his way, with a few strides, to the cathedral, the Duomo San Rufino, where the baby was baptized. Retracing his steps, he would then be interested in seeing the house of Bernard of Quintavalle, the first disciple of Saint Francis, located along the street that bears his name. Then he would have to go only a few paces in order to stand in front of the bishop's palace, which was the scene of Francis' renunciation of his goods and his rights; and he would then visit the little chapel of Saint Mary right next-door to the bishop's palace. Finally, heading east, he would go down to the Basilica of Santa Chiara (Saint Clare) constructed in honor of the foundress of the order of Franciscan nuns. From there it would be easy for him to leave the town through the nearby Porta Nuova [new gate] and walk outside the walls down to the charming convent of San Damiano, where Francis received from Christ the revelation concerning his mission.

But why follow this chronological order, at the expense of those twists and turns and detours? Didn't the marvelous two-story Basilica of Saint Francis give the visitor the key to his subsequent sightseeing? Hasn't it acquainted him, in painted scenes rather than in learned commentaries, with all the phases of the saint's life, which bathes the entire town in memories? To begin one's visit to Assisi with this sanctuary, which is quite intimate and at the same time dazzling, is to discover the stages of this spiritual epic, without bothering about the precise dates, and to be imbued with the spirit that, over the course of the following visits, will help the visitor not only to know, but also to understand in an interior way, in the depths of the soul.

2. Ardent Youth

The man whom we are accustomed to calling Francis of Assisi, and who actually was referred to in that way during his lifetime, bore another name entirely at his birth: Giovanni Moriconi. His paternal grandfather was originally from Lucques, in the northwestern part of Tuscany, and was known by the surname of Bernardone: "big (or fat) Bernard". He belonged to a family of cloth merchants, and since there were two brothers in competition to acquire a fortune, he found it more expedient to go and open a shop elsewhere. Elsewhere was Assisi, and he was not mistaken: his business thrived.

He married on the spot an Umbrian woman, by whom he had a son, Pietro, who greatly expanded his father's business and became one of the richest men in the town. During a business trip to Provence, Pietro met a young woman "adorned with all the graces", whom he married. Her name was Pica, and she brought with her a rich patrimony of legends and songs.

From that union was soon born, in 1182 (probably on September 26), a boy who was immediately brought to the baptismal font. His father was away, still traveling on the far slope of the Alps, in the region of Provence, where he had found the woman of his life. But there was no question of waiting for his return before proceeding to the rites and festivities of the baptism: according to the custom Catholics hold dear, Pietro's newborn son had to be made a child of God.

Subsequently, this birth was embellished with piquant legends. One of them portrays the mother seized with labor pains without managing to bring her child into the world; who should enter the house then but a stranger, a pilgrim with the air of a prophet, who declares that the pregnant woman will not deliver until she goes to the stable and stretches out on a bed of straw; she obeys, and no sooner is she set up on her rustic bed, than Pica gives birth to her baby. This is an excellent way of showing that Saint Francis, from the first hour that he saw the light of day, was conformed to Jesus Christ. Later on, this stable was transformed into a chapel and was consecrated under the name of San Francesco il Piccolo. In order to commemorate the miracle, two verses were engraved there which elaborated further on the similarity to the Infant Jesus:

> *Hoc oratorium fuit bovis et asini stabulum,*
> *In quo natus est Franciscus mundi speculum.*

> [This chapel was the stable of an ox and an ass,
> Wherein was born Francis, the mirror of the world.]

This intervention by a pilgrim at the moment when the predestined child was born may have some foundation in truth, because according to a local legend this was the man who brought the new Christian to the baptismal font in the Cathedral of San Rufino, where we can still see it today. The story is also told that, after the ceremony, he took him in his arms, like Simeon of old in the Temple, to prophesy his future glory. And the witnesses asked one another afterward, "Could this pilgrim have been an angel in human form?"

When Pietro di Bernardone returned home, he found his firstborn son there. And he showed some displeasure that they had given the child a name without consulting him. Why Giovanni (John)? The vain clothier tried to imagine his son as Saint John the Baptist, eating locusts and wearing camel's hair. Was this an appropriate image for the offspring of the richest dignitary in Assisi? He had just returned from Provence, the inhabitants of which, although politically subject to the German Empire, were known to be Frenchmen. People with such grace, such elegance, such exquisite manners! Should not the son of Moriconi, in the middle of Umbria, assume the same charming ways as a French squire? And he decided to change the name Giovanni to Francesco.

This, at least, is the explanation of Saint Bonaventure, who entered the Franciscan order twelve years after the death of Saint Francis, a time when the legends had begun to proliferate. But could one change a baptismal name like that? Quite on the contrary, this name, assigned sacramentally and placing the child under the patronage of a revered saint, would have been treasured as the Christian's identity. It seems, rather, that Francesco was not a different name, but a nickname that was given to the boy later on; this occurred not by imagining the future manners of a baby in the cradle, but rather by observing the actual manners of an elegant, charming fop. The accounts of the biographers agree, indeed, in reporting that the young Moriconi, being the son of a French mother, was fond of that language, and that during his adolescence he used to sing merrily the poems that she had brought along from that much-admired land. It was therefore certainly not Pietro Moriconi who *changed* his son's baptismal name; it was the latter's circle of friends, hearing him converse effortlessly in the French language, who gave him the nickname "French". And the nickname stuck, even when he had become a ragged, miserable fellow.

No doubt Pietro Moriconi wanted to give to this graceful child, who was to make his lineage famous, not just a start in the family business, but also enough culture so that he could appear respectably in society. He therefore sent him to study at Saint George school, not far from the family's residence; there was a group of distinguished clerics there, perhaps canons regular, who both officiated in the church and instructed the youth; the Church of Saint George has since disappeared and been replaced by Saint Clare's. It is difficult to determine the level of the education imparted to these sons of knights and bourgeois shopkeepers. Whereas in Milan, Bologna, Ferrara, and perhaps Perugia, they made humanists out of these boys, the course of studies offered in the little towns of central Italy did not go very far. What we do know is that young Moriconi, who enthusiastically kept on improving his French on the side, attained a respectable command of the Latin language, as did his classmates; no doubt he used to translate Plautus, Tacitus, and Virgil. Yet, as his writings would show later, he also acquired a substantial knowledge of the ecclesiastical language, especially in canon law, since the priests of Saint George hoped that a certain number of their pupils would embark on a clerical career. It was likewise necessary, for a well-educated man, to understand administrative Latin without difficulty; not only the bishop used that language in writing, but even more often the podesta, the political and military leader of the town; furthermore the senators, an administrative caste, also carried on their deliberations in Latin.

Francis received, therefore, a mediocre intellectual formation. If it had been otherwise, no doubt his biographers would have hastened to tell us about it. Maybe some of his classmates were more brilliant than he; but that was not where the father's ambitions lay; what his oldest son had to learn was how to conduct business and amass a fortune. And so he left school in short order and became an associate of the industrious Pietro.

At this juncture, the tone of the biographers changes. Francesco (maybe this was when they pinned this moniker on him) may not have been the model student, but he became the perfect squire, a peerless man of the world. He quickly made himself the center, the guide, and the model of gilded youth. And there were two good reasons for that: his good manners and his fortune. *The Legend of the Three Companions* tells us:

> He gave himself over to amusements and songs and liked to stroll day and night through the city of Assisi with comrades of the same age. In his expenditures he was so liberal that he wasted on parties and other merry-making everything that he might own or acquire. . . . Always generous, even prodigal, he also lacked moderation in the way that he dressed: he had suits tailored for himself that were much more elegant than his status demanded.

How far did this dissipation go? Thomas of Celano, intent on showing us that his master's conversion was a miracle of grace, paints the young man's conduct in the darkest possible colors and likens it to that of his entire social class:

> Among those who bear the name of Christians a baneful custom has taken root, together with a pernicious doctrine that they all obey as though it were a law. It demands that parents raise their children, from the cradle onward, in luxury and pleasure. They do not yet speak, they can scarcely lisp, and yet these infants are taught shameful and abominable things by word and action. And when the time has come for them to be weaned, they are compelled to pronounce luxurious words and commit voluptuous deeds. . . . When they have crossed the threshold of adolescence, carried away by the whirlwind of pleasures of every kind and free to do what they want, they indulge ardently in every sort of vice. . . .
>
> Such was the wretched apprenticeship in life begun already in childhood by this man whom we venerate today as a saint, because he really is one. He wasted his life in this lamentable way until his twenty-fifth

year. He even surpassed in sinful vanity the young men of his age, inciting them to wickedness and vying with them in folly. Everyone admired him, and he strove to be preeminent in pomp and vainglory. He
loved games, jokes, pranks, and effeminate, flowing garments; wealthy
but prodigal, he squandered his fortune instead of hoarding it. As the
proud and magnificent head of this perverse band, he made his way
through the squares of Babylon.

Quite a different image of Saint Francis during this period of his
life is presented to us by *The Three Companions*:

> When he had grown up, the young man, who was endowed with a keen
> mind, plied his father's trade as a merchant. Yet he acted in a much
> different way: he, the son, was much more generous and carefree. He
> was courteous in his manners and speech. He had resolved in his heart
> not to say a harmful or coarse word to anyone, and, while remaining
> a dissipated, joyful young man, he had decided to make no answer to
> those who said unseemly things to him. These natural virtues were the
> steps that divine grace employed to raise him to nobler ideas.

It seems likely that this very simple portrait reveals a greater truth,
and that Celano, a learned man, is giving in to a literary impulse,
whereas the three humble friars, who were with Francis continually
from the earliest days of his conversion, are telling quite simply what
they learned from him. Then, too, they are the ones who report a
thought that occurred to the young clothier at that time and which
he alone could have confided in them. Realizing that his generosity
toward his friends, who were rich or well-to-do, was not enough,
he said to himself: If you show largesse and courtesy to men from
whom you receive only vain and passing favor, it is only right that,
for the love of God who is so generous in his benefits, you should
be courteous and generous to the poor.

From that moment on, Francis loved to visit the poor and give them
alms in abundance. One day, though, as he was in his shop, a poor
man who was aware of his good intention came to request an alms
for the love of God. No doubt annoyed at being disturbed while at
work, he sent him away without mincing words; then, immediately,
he rebuked himself for his lack of consideration.

He realized that if the poor man had asked him for something in the
name of a great man, a count, or a baron, he would have responded
to the request favorably. Should he not have done it for the King

of Kings and Lord of Lords?! Henceforth he decided never to refuse anything to someone who asked in the name of God.

Saint Bonaventure, echoing this little incident reported by other witnesses, adds that Francis, in his shame for having refused the alms requested for the love of God, ran after the poor man and pressed into his hand an unusual sum for a beggar.

Of course the resolution never to refuse alms to anyone—a resolution that he certainly kept with perseverance and generosity—spread throughout the town. The shop of Master Pietro became the meeting place for the destitute and the vagrants, who always found something to live on there. When his father was away, the young prodigal would have an abundant table prepared, as though his father and even invited guests were going to take part in the meal. But these dishes were intended quite simply for the hungry, who did not fail to hammer on the door at mealtime.

This munificence and the kindness of the young merchant earned him a good reputation in the disadvantaged sectors of the town. One good-hearted man, whom Saint Bonaventure describes as simpleminded, had the custom, whenever he met Francis in town, of spreading his cloak beneath his feet, as the Jews of Jerusalem did for Jesus on Palm Sunday. Giotto attempted to recreate this scene in his first tableau in the upper church in Assisi. The background, which is not meant to be accurate, juxtaposes the Church of Santa Maria della Minerva and the Cathedral of San Rufino; the simpleton, about fifty years old, bearded, and rather dirty, is on his knees, extending a grayish cloak in front of Francis, who, not wishing to make a show of humility, is about to tread the garment underfoot. Two bourgeois couples are watching the scene: the one pair, on the right, are looking on disapprovingly, with furrowed brow; the other couple, on the left, smile understandingly, while exchanging a glance. Is it a look of approval for this homage rendered to the prodigal son of a great merchant? Or of sympathy for that poor man who is not afraid to express his reverence in this way?

As for Saint Bonaventure, he sees in this act a prophetic homage: the simpleton recognizes in this young rich man an individual who will accomplish great things someday, and who will deserve the veneration of all believers. It would be better, no doubt, to interpret this homage, not as an inspiration from heaven, but as a token of gratitude toward the benefactor of an entire social class.

3. The Hand of God

This carefree life led by young Francis, in which poetry combined with a lively faith, and festivity with charity, might have continued for many more long years, if it hadn't been for two successive trials that the amiable troubadour had to go through.

First it was prison. Not the judicial prison that punishes criminals, but the political prison that chastises the defeated. The inhabitants of Assisi, after being under the yoke of the German occupier, yielded to that of their Umbrian neighbors: civil war followed international war. Emperor Frederick Barbarossa, continuing the policy of his ancestors Henry IV (1050–1106) and Henry V (1081–1125), had spent the greater part of his reign (1152–1190) subjugating the northern Italian cities. He found that he was confronting a determined adversary: the Lombard towns, and to a lesser extent the towns of Tuscany and Umbria, by their hard work and skill in commerce, had attained a level of affluence that assured them of a salutary independence, while at the same time arousing the covetousness of the German nobility. The imperialism of the emperors was both political in nature—they wanted to rule Italy as far as Rome—and also economic—they were intent on imposing the tribute on those wealthy cities. The weak point of the latter was their political isolation: each one was governed by a plutocratic senate, a product of the hard-working bourgeoisie, which would elect two or three consuls who were responsible for exercising the executive power. Thus the only way that they could offer resistance to an invader was by sending out the local militia, which was often inadequate, despite its bravery. The military solution was in the union of the cities against their common enemy. This was difficult to achieve, because they were economic rivals, in fact or potentially; yet desperate circumstances forced them to establish an alliance, without which they would fall prey to the conqueror, one by one.

Faced with the threat of an attack by Barbarossa, the cities of the

north united in a Lombard League, which, contrary to all expecta-
tions, crushed the imperial arm at Legnano in 1176, which compelled
the defeated party to recognize the rights of the victors. Nevertheless, he had established, in the Diet of Roncaglia in 1158, podestas in
the towns of Lombardy and Umbria—representatives of the emperor
whose duty it was to assert his rights. The defeat of Caesar and the
peace treaty concluded with Alexander III had allowed a certain number of cities, among them Assisi, to regain their communal rights and
government by their consuls. But after the death of Barbarossa, his
son, Henry VI, who ruled from 1190–1197, resumed the policy of
domination, and appointed Duke Conrad of Irslingen to govern the
duchy of Spoleto. After Henry's death, while the candidates to the
throne were shifting the hostilities to battlegrounds within German
territory, the Sacred College of Cardinals elevated to the Holy See an
energetic, thirty-seven-year-old pope, Innocent III, who resolved that
the rights of the Church should triumph. Feeling that he no longer
had the support of the imperial authority, Conrad went to kneel at
the feet of the Pope to do him homage.

The situation was immediately exploited by the cities in the duchy
of Spoleto. The middle-class inhabitants of Assisi armed themselves
and set out to attack the fortress on the Sasso Rosso overlooking the
town, which quartered the puny garrison that had the almost symbolic task of imposing imperial authority on the city. They seized it
and, in their rage, destroyed it. When the Pope's envoys arrived to
take possession of it in the name of their master, they found nothing
but ruins. Then the inhabitants of Assisi, more concerned about their
own autonomy than about their submission to the Supreme Pontiff,
hastened to use the pile of stones that they had heaped up in that way
to build a fortified wall around their city, the remains of which we
can still admire today.

This twofold and highly successful enterprise of taking the fortress
and building ramparts made the bourgeoisie realize their own importance. Were they not the true masters of the city? Why, then, was
the senate composed, in the large majority, of noblemen, who produced nothing, did not trade, and were content to pose as defenders
of the town, whereas until then they had only collaborated with the
occupying forces and, in return for that ostensible service, levied a
burdensome tax in order to maintain their life of leisure?

A gathering of middle-class men, stirred up by the most virulent among them (why not the father of Francis Moriconi?) turned into a mob. They rushed out and attacked the fortified mansions in the city where the lords resided and the castles that they had built on the heights. The occupants defended themselves doggedly; there were casualties on both sides. No doubt Francis, who at that time was eighteen or nineteen years old, participated, along with his younger brother, in this little civil war, since he was the son of one of the leading bourgeois citizens of the town.

But the affair didn't stop there. In that year, 1202, a group of noblemen, having escaped from their residences, galloped to Perugia, the rival city, which was always inclined to humiliate her neighbor. They made an agreement with her: if the Perugian militia, which was strong and well-armed, helped the aristocracy of Assisi to defeat the bourgeoisie and regain mastery of the city, the restored government would proclaim its dependence upon Perugia. For the latter, this was an extraordinary chance to impose its supremacy. Its senate sent an ultimatum to the bourgeois authority, which imprudently turned away the delegates with disdain. But it knew what this refusal meant: war —something that in those days was not uncommon between rival cities, and for which the communal militias kept themselves ready at all times.

Assisi intended to take its enemy by surprise. Without delay it mustered an army that was inspired with a warlike ardor and included two sorts of combatants: the cavalry, consisting of the part of the nobility that was allied with the bourgeoisie and that admitted certain members of it into its ranks, because of their financial clout—thus the Moriconi boys were numbered among them—and the infantry, which consisted of the foot soldiers, who were more numerous and less respectable. This army, determined to outmaneuver the enemy, took a path to the north of the city, marched four leagues, and found itself very close to Perugia, on the bank of the Tiber River; thus the attackers were counting on the advantage of surprise.

The enemy force, alerted to this intrusion, was already advancing on the other bank of the river. It numbered among its combatants not only the nobility of Perugia with its armed men, but also a part of the nobility of Assisi, including the Offreducci—the family of the future Saint Clare. Although it was plain that their adversaries were more numerous, the militia from Assisi confronted them on the Ponte San Giovanni, a bridge connecting the two riverbanks. The battle seems to have been short: a number of the combatants fell; the men of Assisi who could, fled, while the others were surrounded by the Perugians, who captured them. Francis was one of these.

Two prisons were set up: one, hastily improvised, for the peasants; the other, with more comfortable accommodations, for the noblemen. Given his membership in the bourgeoisie, Francis was treated the same as the nobility and found himself a prisoner with them. They were hardly inclined to be cheerful: besides the shame of defeat they had to deal with anxiety as to their fate. Were their lands going to be confiscated? Would they be asked to purchase their freedom with a large ransom? In any case, one thing was certain: they would be politically subject to Perugia and would have to pay a heavy tribute each year.

Francis, on the other hand, did not seem to share all these cares; he maintained the good humor that he had always displayed in Assisi. "While the other captives were lamenting," *The Three Companions* relates, "he was merry and joking and showed no sign of sadness."

Annoyed, one of his companions reprimanded him, "You'd have to be a fool to be cheerful in prison!"

In a playful tone of voice, Francis replied, "What do you take me for? Know that one day I will be famous throughout the world."

To be sure, it was not a reputation for sanctity that the young man foresaw, but rather the glory of his military exploits. For this adventure in which he experienced only disappointment did not cure him of his plans to be a warrior, but only spurred him on. When you are twenty years old, a defeat and imprisonment are not the last word on the subject. This captivity was long though, lasting over a year. Negotiations between the two senates plodded on. Finally, in November 1203, they arrived at a lasting peace, and the prisoners were released.

Once he was set free, Francis thought that he was going to accomplish the chivalrous deeds that he had daydreamed about in those idle hours in prison. But then he was struck down by an illness and remained bedridden for many long months. Had he caught cold in jail? Had he fallen victim to a virus that was unknown to the medicine of the time? Celano, who reports the fact, provides us with no explanation.

He simply states that "God attempted to bring back his wandering mind by besetting his soul with anguish and his body with sufferings." Indeed this trial, far from being a source of distress for him, became an opportunity to meditate on the frailty of human affairs.

Finally, healing came. One day the sick man felt strong enough to get up; leaning on a cane, he strove to walk again the paths that he had strolled along so often, hoping (always the poet) to find some consolation in the spectacle of nature. But the beauty of the trees, the charm of the flowers, the song of the birds had no power to speak to his soul. Everything had become insipid and unimportant to him. And yet, instead of complaining about this dryness of his feelings, he drew a lesson from it: Why become attached one day to everything in life that is charming, when soon there will be nothing left of it?

Nevertheless, the dreams of glory had not been extinguished. But they took on a more spiritual tone. Francis had read the romances about chivalry and hoped to become a gallant knight, an ardent servant of the noblest causes. The contemporary situation offered him many occasions to do so: the struggle between the Germans, on the one side, and the Holy See and the Normans of southern Italy, on the other, had started up again. The German emperor, Otto IV of Brunswick [Braunschweig] (1174–1218) had attempted to conquer the lands of southern Italy, which belonged by inheritance to the son of Henry VI, the future Frederick II (1194–1250), who was then still a child. To counter the incursion, Pope Innocent III had entrusted the command of the papal army to a valiant and loyal captain, Count Walter III of Brienne in Champagne. And the entire peninsula resounded with the exploits of Walter, who carried off one victory after another over the German forces in Apulia [Puglia] and Campania. Many young men of Tuscany and Umbria were looking forward with anticipation to fighting the detested emperor once more, so that they might enlist and take orders from this hero.

And now the news spread through Assisi: a nobleman of the city, whose name is not mentioned by the biographers, was making ready to leave to join up with Walter and was enlisting volunteers to serve under his orders. Francis immediately went to find him, offered his services, and was accepted. His joy was immense. The following night he had a marvelous dream, which is related for us by *The Three Companions*:

A man appeared to him, calling him by name, and led him into an enormous, charming palace filled with the weapons used by knights. Hanging on the walls were gleaming shields and other items of military gear. Full of joy, he wondered curiously what it all meant. Finally he asked the question: To whom would these dazzling weapons, this marvelous palace belong? The answer was: "All these weapons and this palace are for you and for your knights." He awoke the next morning with his heart glowing. Interpreting what he had seen as a worldly individual who had not yet tasted the fullness of the Spirit of God, he believed that the dream foretold that he would have princely honors. Thinking therefore that this vision was the herald of a great fortune, he immediately decided to leave for Puglia so as to be knighted there.

Of course, the ostentatious merchant's son intended to be the most lavishly dressed of these warriors on the point of departure. He had garments tailored for himself that were worthy of his reputation and of his father's. Several days before putting them on, however, he learned that another enlistee, who really was of noble heritage, had only one worn-out set of clothing to his name. Francis was deeply moved by this and could not tolerate the difference any longer. He arranged to meet his companion in a secluded place and presented him with his sumptuous wardrobe. This act of generosity impressed Giotto so much that he made it the subject of the second scene of the life of Saint Francis in the upper church in Assisi.

At last, one day in the year 1206, the lord who had recruited them gave the signal to depart. We have no information about the size of this little detachment, whether there were enough soldiers to undertake that long journey of more than 600 kilometers without an unfortunate encounter, or whether they had to join up with a more numerous troop one or two days into their march. The itinerary of these soldiers, however, seems to have been simple enough. Foligno six leagues down the road; then Spoleto after the same distance again; from there to Terni, to take one of the routes leading to the Adriatic coast.

In Spoleto, where this company was stopping over, Francis fell ill. No doubt it was nothing serious: a simple bout of fever. He was stretched out and half-awake, with his mind wandering, when a voice resounded in the silence: "So, Francis, where do you plan to go?"

There was no one else in the room. Accustomed to supernatural events, however, he was certain that the invisible interlocutor was from heaven. "To Puglia," he replied, "to be armed as a knight and to serve under Walter's orders."

"Who, though, can bring you the greater benefit, the servant or the Master?"

The answer was easy: "The Master."

"Then why are you abandoning the Master to serve the servant, and the prince to serve his vassal?"

Then he understood that this voice was the one that had spoken to Saint Paul on the road to Damascus; and like Saint Paul, he asked, "Lord, what would you have me do?"

"Return to your birthplace. There, someone will tell you what you should do. For you must understand the vision that you had in an entirely new way."

Thus, the beautiful dream, in which he gazed at the weapons that were to be his, was not a promise that he would participate in a carnal war, but in a war of another sort, which he vaguely guessed. He remained immersed in wonder and, at dawn, taking leave of his companions, he took the road back to Assisi, his only ambition, as the biographers say, being "to comply with the divine will".

As you might easily guess, Francis' reappearance in his hometown was not a glorious one. Full of enthusiasm, he had left to confront the enemy, battle, and conquer. And now, after three days, there he was, a piteous sight, unable to explain to those who ridiculed him why he had given up the prospect of glory. If the questioner insisted, he simply replied: "I decided that it is better to accomplish great things in my own birthplace."

What great things? He himself did not know, since the voice had not revealed them to him. Although he did not know how to discern them, he kept himself ready. While waiting, he was once again surrounded by his old drinking buddies, who urged him to resume his position as their ringleader. He had no desire to do so, disillusioned as he was now with the restlessness of the world. Yet, as Celano notes, he was not unaware of the fact that his popularity was at stake; his generosity was well-known, and these squires expected to see him cover all the expenses. And so as not to appear stingy, he decided to throw a big party, which he hoped would be an opportunity to say farewell.

When it was over, all of the guests went outside and dispersed in the streets of Assisi, some of them shouting, others vomiting, still others collapsing in a stupor on the nearest bench. Francis, to whom they had restored the scepter of his supremacy, was deep in thought and walked away from them without noticing. That was the moment that God chose to rush in on him. As *The Three Companions* tells it: "A marvelous sweetness filled his heart, to the point where he could neither speak nor move. He found it impossible to feel anything besides that sweetness, which estranged him from the sensations of the flesh. And he himself declared later on that, if someone had tried to cut him to pieces, he would have been incapable of making a single move to escape."

His companions spied him then and went to meet him, while crooning a drinking song. But they found him a quite different man from the one they had just left. What on earth had happened during that brief moment?

"Well," said one of them, "what are you thinking about, all alone?"

"Taking a wife!" exclaimed another.

Francis was startled but went along with the joke: "Yes, I tell you, I am thinking of becoming engaged. But she will be nobler, more beautiful, and richer than any woman you have ever seen."

A chorus of ridicule greeted his remarks. But he, no longer able to stand their company, left them and took refuge in his room.

Now, any free time that he had after working in the shop, he would spend in church, immersed in prayer. One incident occurred then that only Celano relates. Among all of those superficial friends, Francis discovered a young man of the same age who was sensitive and reserved and capable of recognizing the ways of heaven. He did not have superior intelligence, however; and so he understood in a material sense what his friend confided in him one day: "I have discovered a wonderful treasure."

Then he led him to a grotto located at a distance from the town, left him outside, and withdrew into it for a long time to receive the infusion of divine grace. When he came back out, his appearance was so preternatural that his companion understood what the treasure was: that it was not hidden in the grotto, but in the soul of that lover of God. "He burned so intensely with the divine fire that he could not prevent the ardor that filled his heart from appearing on the outside.

He repented of having offended God so seriously. And so, when he rejoined his companion, he was so broken-hearted with sorrow that the man who had entered previously was no longer recognizable in the one who emerged."

That was when he decided to make a pilgrimage to Rome. He began, obviously, with a visit to Saint Peter's in the Vatican. As he walked past a grating where the faithful were throwing their offerings, he noted that they were not very generous. "The Prince of the Apostles", he thought, "should be honored in a magnificent way. Why are all these people donating such small sums in the church where his body rests?"

Partly as a sign of protest against such stinginess, partly in order to provoke the pilgrims to greater generosity, he took out his purse, drew out a fistful of coins, and tossed them through the grating, where they chimed merrily, to the astonishment of the bystanders.

Upon leaving the shrine, he noticed how many beggars there were on the square in front of it, and he was seized by a desire to experience true poverty, that of the destitute. In a secluded spot, in return for ready money, he exchanged his bourgeois clothing with the rags worn by one of them and began to hold out his hand, begging alms in French. Then, when the time for the experiment had passed, he changed clothes once again. We must assume that he paid the beggar at that moment, and not when he clothed him in his own finery; otherwise it would be a sure bet that he would not have recovered it.

Back home, Francis reduced the number of hours that he devoted from then on to his father's shop so as to increase the amount of time that he spent in the grotto. His father, who was as avaricious as Francis was prodigal, was not happy with the decrease in productivity. But the son's assiduous attention to prayer, after all those banquets and parties, had one consequence that was very advantageous for the merchant: his expenses were cut back considerably. Of course, this son was still giving a lot away as alms and in purchases of food for the needy, but this charitable budget was still on a much smaller scale than what he used to spend on vanities. For the moment, therefore, Signore Moriconi, the father, did not try to assert any authority over this strange son, who was abandoning the good life for almsgiving and pomp for prayer.

What the young man wanted most now was to know the will of

God. Hadn't the voice in Spoleto promised that, if he returned to Assisi, he would know what heaven wanted of him? Months had gone
by since then, and God had not said a thing. This silence was for
him a source of deep anguish that crushed him and snuffed out the
great joy that he had experienced from that revelation; restlessly, he
awaited a new one.

Now God was expecting from him a still greater detachment. One
day, in the depths of the mystical grotto, he was immersed in prayer,
and the divine voice, the voice of Spoleto made itself heard: "Francis,
everything that you have loved and desired to possess, according to
the flesh, you must now hate and despise, if you wish to know my
will. When you have begun to do this, what once appeared charming
and delightful to you will become unbearable and bitter; and in what
formerly horrified you, you will discover a surpassing peace and an
infinite sweetness."

Mysterious words, but how comforting they were! For at last the
Lord was emerging from his silence, and although he was not asking
for anything specific for the moment, he would surely not hesitate
to make his demands known. Buoyed by this hope, the young man
returned to his horse, which was waiting patiently at the entrance
to the grotto. And as he was riding slowly back to town, deep in
thought, he felt his horse rear. And with good reason: a leper had
just crossed the road ahead of it.

Leprosy at that time was a constant scourge not only in the East,
but throughout the Western world, where it had been introduced at
the beginning of the Middle Ages. In Saint Francis' time there were
at least fifty thousand lepers in France alone. The Church was concerned about them, not only because they were her suffering members, but also because, according to one interpretation of a verse from
the prophet Isaiah, they were the image of the sorely wounded and
rejected Savior. However, because the illness was deemed contagious,
lepers were kept in isolation, dressed in black, and equipped with a
rattle that announced their approach.

A religious order specially dedicated to the care of lepers was
founded in the early twelfth century in Jerusalem and then gradually spread through the West. This was the Order of Saint Lazarus, in
memory of Lazarus, the friend whom Jesus had raised from the dead,
and who, as one tradition related, eventually died of leprosy. That is

why, in French, these sick people were commonly called *ladres*, and the houses that sheltered them were called *lazarets* or *ladreries*. There was one right near Assisi, and that is why Francis was not surprised to find along his path that oozing creature, whose nauseating odor usually announced his presence from afar. He was even less surprised that day, since God had just warned him that he now had to change all of his likes and dislikes.

Indeed, until then lepers had horrified him, as they did all his contemporaries. But that day he knew what to do when he met up with one of them providentially. He jumped to the ground and walked toward him. The other man, expecting an alms, stretched out his shapeless hand. But the squire was not content to slip a coin into it; he planted a kiss on it. And then, as it says in the *Companions*, "he realized the truth of the divine promise: what had been bitter to him before, that is, the sight and touch of lepers, had changed to sweetness."

According to Celano, the young man, after getting back into the saddle, looked around and no longer saw anyone—giving the reader to understand that the leper had been a supernatural being. He is no doubt confusing this anecdote with the one related by Saint Gregory the Great. One day a monk by the name of Martyrius, upon meeting a leper who was exhausted with hunger and pain, wrapped him in his own cloak and brought him to the monastery; and behold, the unfortunate man turned into Jesus, who said to the monk: "Martyrius, you were not ashamed of me on earth; I will not be ashamed of you in heaven." But Celano ought to have recalled that Saint Martin, at the gate of Amiens, had given half of his cloak to a real, suffering poor man, who was not suddenly transformed into Jesus; the Lord, however, subsequently appeared to him in a dream in order to praise that good deed.

The biographers of Saint Francis are not the only ones who recount this startling incident; he himself also alludes to it in his "Testament": "The Lord permitted me to begin my conversion in this way; while I was still living in sin, I could not endure the sight of lepers without experiencing repugnance. But the Lord led me among these unfortunate souls, and I acted toward them with compassion."

Indeed, on the day after that occasion—which was uniquely memorable, since even the protagonist admits that it inaugurated the conversion that until then he had only glimpsed—Francis retraced the path leading to the leper house. When he had been allowed to enter it, the poor people who happened to be there (and who no doubt had heard a description of him from their companion, who the previous day had received a double sign of affection) rushed toward him and stretched out their hands, which were partially consumed by the sickness. The odor was so fetid that the young man was at a loss this time and had to hold his breath for a moment. But he very quickly overcame his disgust, opened the purse that he had brought, and courteously distributed the silver pieces, as though he were dealing with personages from high society.

4. Builder

Shortly after that incident (still in the year 1206), Francis received a new clarification concerning his vocation. He was walking down the little path that led from the Porta Nuova to Spello and was passing in front of an old, half-ruined chapel that was dedicated to Saint Damian. Urged by an interior prompting, he went in. Everything there was in shambles, but over the tottering altar loomed a beautiful image of Christ in the Byzantine style, which dominated the narrow sanctuary by its majestic height. The place was so secluded that the young man did not hesitate to kneel down immediately to speak to this hieratic Savior. And, in the uncertainty in which he still found himself as to his vocation, he sent up to him a prayer that he was fond of repeating, which was at the same time confident and anguished: "O great and magnificent God, my Lord Jesus Christ, I implore thee to enlighten me and to dispel the darkness of my soul. Give me a strong faith, firm hope, perfect charity. And grant to me, O Lord, to know thee well enough to be able to act in all things according to thy light and in keeping with thy holy will."

He remained in this suppliant and contemplative attitude before the beautiful icon of Christ. And suddenly a voice resounded—a voice, as Jörgensen relates, that was "perceptible only in the young man's heart". That is not at all what the early biographers report: "The image of Christ crucified", writes Celano, "spoke to him with its painted lips." And Saint Bonaventure insists: "He heard with his ears of flesh the voice that came down from the crucifix." This voice said to him: "Francis, do you not see that my house is falling into ruins? Go, then, and repair it for love of me."

Immediately he replied with ardor: "Lord, I devote myself to the task with all my soul." Bonaventure specifies: "He made ready to obey and to take the steps required to restore that material church. But the Church that the voice was pointing out to him was the one that Christ purchased for himself by his blood. The Holy Spirit taught him this later on, and he himself revealed it to the brethren."

He left the chapel quite upset, prey to a keen emotion that was not something momentary but rather remained intense for the rest of his days. Here again, we should read Celano:

> From that hour on, compassion for the crucified Christ was imprinted on his holy soul, and one may piously suppose that the sacred stigmata were then deeply engraved in his heart, before being engraved in his flesh. From the moment when he heard the voice of his Beloved, his soul melted with love. He could not henceforth contain his tears and he would moan aloud over the Passion of Christ, which he seemed to have unceasingly before his eyes. He made the byways echo with his lamentations, and while meditating on Christ's wounds he refused to be consoled.

Nevertheless he was convinced that Jesus had called him, forcefully and perceptibly, to be a restorer of churches. That was his vocation. He had begged so much to know it! And now, behold, it had been revealed to him. There was no longer a second to lose: after so many days of waiting, he ardently desired to get to work.

Glancing around the place, he realized the magnitude of the task: the cracked walls, the holes in the ceiling, the rickety altar, the uneven pavement, the empty oil lamp. He would never have the resources with which to restore in a dignified manner this chapel that the Lord himself wanted to have beautiful and prayerful. He would have to have funds. Where could he find them? Where else but in his father's fortune? It was not a question of dipping his hand into the coffer, which would be carefully kept under lock and key anyway. But Francis was his father's partner; he shared in the business and the profit. The pieces of cloth that were stacked in the rear of the shop were, in part, his property, and he was honestly entitled to sell some of them for a pious work.

His father was away—on a business trip again. Carrying off the piece of cloth was that much easier. Where should he sell it? It was market day at Foligno; Francis knew this from having gone there often and having received considerable sums of money there. So he set off for that town immediately at a gallop. He sold not only the entire bolt of fabric, but the horse as well. A productive day! Of course, he had to return on foot. But what difference does walking five leagues make when you are twenty-four years old? And when you are light-hearted?

He did not go home directly: the money had to be set aside right away for the church of San Damiano. But how should he do this? Divine Providence would manage to show him. He didn't even have to make a detour to get to the church: it was along the way. When he arrived at the holy place, he was reassured: he found a priest sitting there who was as run-down as the building—no doubt a curate who was not in the best of health and had been assigned to a shrine that no parishioner attended. Francis genuflected and kissed his hand. Then he took out from the fold of his garment an enormous purse crammed full of gold pieces.

"Here, Reverend Father," he said to him, "is a donation to help repair your church. Don't be surprised: the Lord himself assigned this task to me. Since you are the curate of this holy place, it is your responsibility to use this considerable sum of money; with it you can buy all the necessary materials. As for me, since the Lord has commanded me to set my hand to this venture, I ask you to take me in under your roof. I will live with you in prayer and poverty, and I will ask nothing of you except to celebrate the Holy Sacrifice."

The poor priest was alarmed by the enormous purse. Should he accept it? He knew that this devout young man was the son of a man who was rich and hardhearted; the richest and perhaps one of the most hardhearted in the town. Would his father not come and dispute his claim to this gold? Or demand it back? And accuse him of complicity in the theft? The son was so charming, so sincere, so pious! He would be happy to live with him; it would brighten his residence with a gleam of youth. He therefore accepted half of the proposition. "My friend, I welcome your company. But I refuse to take your gold."

Disappointed and unwilling to keep this fortune that was not meant for him, Francis threw the purse into the opening of a window. He had no reason to fear thieves: the Christ who had spoken to him was the guardian of the place. And he followed the kindly curate into his residence.

No biographer has described for us Francis' routine during his stay with his new companion: their activities, their devotions, their conversations. It seems that during the day the young man hardly stayed at all in the little parsonage, but spent many hours instead in the grotto, which he continued to visit regularly. Furthermore we don't notice him undertaking any masonry work during that time, and we can only suppose that he was waiting for or seeking an opportunity to use the sack of gold that was slumbering in a corner.

Besides, Francis' stay with the curate was a short one. This was because the elder Moriconi, upon returning from his travels, found at home neither his son nor his piece of cloth, nor one handsome horse from his stables. The son, who was half-mad and no longer very helpful in the business, he could do without. But the price of the cloth and of the horse—that was what mattered, and he was intent on getting it back as soon as possible. Where was this worthless son, then? A certain number of his fellow townsmen knew. And, for a rich merchant, tongues loosen quickly. The moment that he learned the answer, he decided to lead an expedition. He summoned his menservants, rallied his neighbors: "An unworthy priest has made off with part of my fortune! Let us go settle accounts with him!"

The armed band made their way across the town, passed through the Porta Nuova, and arrived at San Damiano. The priest was there.

"Where is my son?"

Francis was praying in the grotto; but the curate was not obliged to know that.

"Where is my gold?"

That was the more important question, which was burning on the merchant's lips. The priest raised his arm and pointed to the opening of the window, where the fat purse was still resting. What imprudence! One manservant climbed up on the shoulders of another and retrieved the precious object. What remained to ask about now? Without his son, but with his gold, Pietro had nothing else to do but turn around and go back, triumphant and at the same time ashamed.

Thus began a somber period in the life of Francis. His father had spared him, but he no longer returned to the town; Christ himself had commanded him to repair his church, but he was burrowed in his grotto. He was depressed, disoriented, and no longer knew what he should do. "He zealously went to work", Celano relates. But we don't find that in his first biography, which was composed two years after the death of his master and in which he does not say a word about the matter; it appears in the second, the *Vita secunda*, which was written sixteen years later and in which he confuses the sequence of events somewhat. *The Three Companions* reports them precisely: "Francis remained *hidden* for a whole month in his grotto." Hidden: he did not go into town, he did not even come out to repair the altar or the pavement of the church; he lived in such seclusion that his retreat was known "by only one person in his family", who brought him his food in secret. His brother, perhaps? Or a devoted servant? What was he doing in that grotto all day? Again we must look to the *Companions* for the answer:

> His face streaming with a torrent of tears, he was constantly praying to the Lord to deliver him from this persecution that hindered his plans, and to grant to him as a privilege, out of his loving-kindness, the grace to accomplish in full the pious resolutions of his soul. Thus, in fasting and weeping, he begged the Lord fervently and perseveringly; relying neither on his own virtue nor on his skill, he resolutely placed all his hope in the Lord who, in the midst of the darkness, had inundated him with an inexpressible joy and enlightened him with a wonderful clarity.

Clearly, the knight of Christ no longer dared to come out of his haunt. He was so afraid of the persecution of men that he gave up doing the will of God. And instead of relying on God's grace to sustain him in his task, he was waiting for that grace to lend him some sort of enigmatic assistance. And this fear, this paralysis lasted, not a few days, but an entire month. This privileged soul, who had heard Christ speak to him personally and distinctly—a favor that left him with a soul on fire and an ardent resolve—was hiding and waiting for a new sign that he should obey the orders that he had received.

And then, one morning, he was ashamed of his cowardice. If God was remaining silent toward him, it was because of his own faintheartedness. God had spoken. Why should he have to repeat himself? In Spoleto, when he had commanded, "Return to your country", the adventurer had promptly made an about-face, despite the embarrassment that he experienced. And now that this same God was demanding that he be at his service (Francis could still hear the reproachful question: "Whom is it better to serve? The servant or the Master?"), he was seized by fear and human respect. Let's go! The moment had come to demonstrate that he was the Master's servant, unhesitatingly and uncompromisingly.

Francis emerged from his grotto and headed toward the town. The biographers do not tell us what his plan was at that moment. He was not engaged in his masonry work: we do not see him gathering stones and mortar, as he would do later on. The most likely explanation is that, in order to punish himself for his cowardice and to show God his determination, he decided to face and accept the contradictions that come from one's fellowmen. He was well aware that his appearance was both grotesque and repellent: the gaunt face, ravaged by constant weeping, the bare feet, the tottering body clothed in rags. Despite their devotion, his compatriots would not understand his distress.

And he was right. No sooner had he entered the gate of the city than the urchins, confronting this miserable man whom they mistook at first for a beggar, let loose with insults, mockery, and threats. But it was much worse once they had recognized him: this shaggy, stumbling vagrant was the quondam king of the carefree youths, the elegant son of the wealthy Pietro di Bernardone! For most of the spectators, there could only be one reason for such a drastic transformation: madness. The shouts redoubled, the insults became even cruder; they threw pebbles and filth at the crazy man. "But the knight of Christ walked like a deaf man amid all this outcry; no insult could discourage or move him: he continued to give thanks to God."

He walked up the street that is today called the *Via Borgo Aretino*, which led to the middle of town. The shouts were getting even louder and were spreading now to the adjacent streets. Pietro Moriconi stepped out onto the threshold of his shop. What on earth was it that was leading his fair city to the brink of an uprising? At last he spied the reason for the ruckus: a poor devil, filthy and dressed in tatters, that the crowd was ridiculing. Tut-tut! A fine amusement! Those people ought to be working instead! But his neighbors called to him, "It's your son, Pietro! It's Francis!"

The father was startled. His son, dressed like *that*?! His son, being booed? What a disgrace! He hadn't been heard from for a month, and now he was heaping ridicule on the entire family! The merchant waded through the crowd, in a dreadful temper, grabbed the accursed creature by the neck and pushed him back into his shop. Once inside, he dragged him to the most remote corner of the house, where there was a dark, malodorous closet that they called the dungeon, and he vehemently threw him into it. Then he closed the door and turned the heavy key, leaving the condemned man to meditate in the company of the rats and the spiders.

Meditate. For the fierce merchant was not trying so much to punish his son as to bring him back to his senses. Indeed, to him such conduct seemed irrational, mad, just as it had seemed to the unthinking crowd that jostled the penitent. He was completely unaware of what was on his son's mind: the revelation by Christ at San Damiano, the sorrowful tears in the grotto, his determination to become a knight for the Lord. What he saw was his son's appearance, which nonetheless resembled so strongly the Man of Sorrows foretold by Isaiah. What infuriated him was that poverty, that emaciated frame, that weakness, that renunciation of the opulent world that had been promised to him, his separation from everything in the city that was respectable, his abandonment of the rules and prerogatives of his social status. Obviously a passing aberration. A few days and a few nights down in that cold, uncomfortable corner, with nothing but bread and water, would help bring him around to another way of thinking. From time to time the father stooped to look into the dungeon and addressed his uncouth son in words that he tried to make both kind and stern. But the son, if he heard the father at all, did not heed him. From then on nothing could bend his will. We'll wait, the father would say; this obstinacy will have to give way someday.

But the father had to go away. There was always another business trip to make. During his absence, he supposed, the boy would have plenty of time to return to his senses. He entrusted the key to Pica, since it was still necessary to make sure that the criminal didn't die of hunger or thirst. But to give the key to a prison cell to a mother who suffers to see her son imprisoned is to liberate the prisoner. For the first few days, following orders, the mother pleaded with her son in moving exhortations, but the tone of voice was wrong—she didn't feel at all like a jailer. If she were to set her poor child free, how angry would her husband be on his return? And wouldn't he be seized again anyway and punished even more severely? Dismissing such thoughts, however, and noting that neither the deprivations nor the threats and supplications had had any influence on her son's soul, she opened the door for him. He fled and went back to his cavern. There is no record of the farewells spoken by the mother and the son. What is mentioned in just a few words is something that can be guessed easily: Moriconi's fury at finding the dungeon vacant. Why hadn't he known that Pica would no longer tolerate the sight of this proud young man as a captive and a criminal, being treated more severely than he had been by the Perugians? But it was not a question of his understanding maternal love or of accepting the escape of his unworthy son. Since Francis refused to obey his father, who was the natural authority, he would have to obey the communal judges, who were the civil authority. Pietro did not hesitate to denounce his rebellious son to the town councilors.

The consuls were obviously quite embarrassed to admit such a complaint, but that was their job, and besides, they could not refuse to register a complaint filed by the richest man in town, and who was its benefactor besides. Then, too, they were wealthy, highly respected men, and they sympathized with the sorrow of this father who had been scoffed at in public by a senseless son. What was the father demanding? That his prodigal son give back every bit of his father's fortune that he had in his possession and, if he persisted in his extravagance and his refusal to work, that he be disinherited.

And so the herald of the commune, the spokesman for the consuls, went to the residence of the curate of San Damiano and had the good fortune of finding the delinquent there. Solemnly, he read aloud the order that summoned him to appear before the consuls. Francis, unmoved, replied, "Let the venerable consuls know that I am consecrated to God. You see me living here at the service of a church under the authority of a priest. Therefore I do not answer to the civil authorities."

The herald bowed and went off to bring the response of the accused to the magistrates. They were very glad to hear it and conveyed it to Moriconi. "His status as a man consecrated to the service of God", they explained to him, "places him outside of our jurisdiction."

Pietro di Bernardone did not give up his pursuit. So his son was in the service of God, was he? Then he answered to ecclesiastical justice. He would lodge a complaint with Guido, the bishop of Assisi. And the latter summoned the young man, who willingly agreed to appear before him.

The session of the episcopal tribunal was held in public. The parties presented themselves to the Lord Bishop, who was seated on his throne: on the one side, the plaintiff who, we may suppose, was clothed in his most sumptuous garments so as to manifest his dignity; on the other side, the worthless son, looking pitiful in his tattered tunic. Behind them, their relatives, friends, and the curious. No doubt there were many of them, given the scandal that this confrontation caused. It was expected that the bishop, who represented authority and who in his own way was a wealthy man, would side with the humiliated father and would admonish the rebel youth severely. But he had had the time to find out about Francis' conduct, and he admired his courage. And so he spoke to him kindly, with little regard for the plaintiff's temper. "My boy, you see that your father, who is present here, is very angry with you. He even claims to be scandalized. For he declares that you still have money that belongs to him. Therefore, if you want to consecrate yourself to the service of God, give the money that you have back to him, without keeping any of it. For it is possible that this part of his fortune may be ill-gotten goods; in that case it would be unjust for you to consecrate it as Church property. God will not allow you to put ill-gotten gains to a good use, or to keep, even for a pious intention, the fruit of sins committed by your father. Surely, he is upset by his great anger, but it will subside when he has received what he considers to be his property. Act therefore like a man, Giovanni, and put your trust in God. Fear nothing, because God is your support, and it is he, your Father in heaven—and not your father on earth who is attached to mammon —who will bestow upon you abundantly whatever is necessary for the work of his Church."

This was certainly a judgment in favor of the plaintiff, but the speech was harsh to his ears and full of gentleness for the delinquent son. The ruling of the clever prelate had a twofold effect: he insisted that justice be done, but at the same time, having been informed of the dealings and abuses of the richest merchant in his episcopal city, he discredited him in the eyes of his peers. He declared publicly that the act committed by the accused had been a peccadillo that did not deserve the least punishment, and that the true sin was probably that of the plaintiff, who was more interested in money than in the love of his son, whose virtue and vocation he misunderstood.

Was the merchant aware that he had just been insulted in public, from the very lips of the man he had chosen to be the judge? The biographers say nothing about it. But we can guess that the only words heard by that miser were the ones in the sentence "Give him his money back!" Now there was a bishop who was really worthy of esteem!

The Three Companions tell us that Francis was consoled and gladdened by the bishop's words. Having resolved to submit to this merciful justice, he asked permission to go and bring back the treasure from its hiding place. The audience was recessed for the time that it took the young man to go to San Damiano and return. There was still another purse on the window sill, no doubt containing the last savings of the apprentice builder. To the son's way of thinking, it hardly required a ruling by a bishop to make him return it: if the merchant had known where his treasure (his heart!) was concealed, he would quickly have laid hands on it. Finally, the father must have been relieved to discover that his son had not been lying; the miser could now stop pursuing the thief, since he was recovering what he loved most.

Francis, however, did not immediately bring the second purse to the bishop; he was planning an even more significant scene. For returning the money was nothing, or not much at all; he wanted to go the whole way and give back *everything* that he had received from his father. Not to annoy or ridicule him, but because, as the bishop had declared in his decision, it was now up to God, to whom he was consecrating himself, to provide everything. Of course, he injected a bit of humor into the plan, since he was never lacking in that. We should note that, legally, Francis, having worked with his father for six or seven years, could have made a claim to a salary, either in money or in kind. But then his new life would have been dependent upon those worldly goods, which perhaps had been acquired unjustly. He was intent on divesting himself of them, immediately and publicly.

What did he have left besides the money? His clothes. He returned them. Religious art has accustomed us to seeing Francis taking off his clothes, or what remained of them, in front of an assembly of onlookers. It is certain that he said, "Your Excellency, I wish to return willingly the money belonging to my father, and even the clothes that I am wearing." But then, as *The Three Companions* emphasize, he withdrew to the bishop's chamber to take off his garments. After that he returned to face his accuser and his judge, holding that bundle. But he was still clothed in a hair shirt, which he had certainly not obtained from his father's shop. He put the heap of clothes on the ground and the purse on top of it.

And it was his turn to speak, in a loud, elated voice: "Listen to me, now, all of you, and understand correctly what I have to say. Until this moment, Pietro di Bernardone was the one I called my father. Now that I am consecrated to the service of God, I am giving back to him the money that was tormenting his soul, along with all the clothes that I had from him. From now on, I will no longer say 'my father, Pietro di Bernardone', but 'Our Father who art in heaven'."

The merchant, more furious than ashamed, did not hear this lesson; he hastened to gather up not only the purse, but also the rags—which perhaps the young man's mother had donated to a poor man. And he left without commenting, without caring about the impression made by his hardheartedness, without noticing that his avarice made the men snicker and the women weep. All of the witnesses, the biographers assure us, were indignant at his comportment and filled with pity for his son.

Then the bishop—no longer a judge, since his sentence had been carried out, but now a father, since the convicted man, in his nakedness, was consecrated solely to the service of the Church—opened his arms wide and pressed Francis to his heart. And he covered him with his own mantle. Thus, even without an investiture, or clothing ceremony, the new servant of the Church had an episcopal mantle upon his shoulders. The first thing that he did was to make over it the sign of the cross.

Giotto, with his customary sobriety, depicted this scene in the fifth fresco with which he decorated the upper church in Assisi. This artist does not show us a naked Francis disdainfully throwing a bundle of clothes at his father's feet, but rather an inspired Francis who has joined his hands and raised his eyes toward his Father in heaven, while the bishop hides his nakedness with an unidentifiable piece of cloth. The father, facing them, has already snatched up the robe and the pants and, with a menacing scowl, seems ready to attack the guilty party, but he is held back by an assistant, probably his second son, who notes that he has compromised himself enough in public opinion.

And so Francis was consecrated to God and to his Church. An inebriating experience. Before getting to work for a good cause, he had to pour out his heart, shout with joy, and call as his witness all of the luxuriant and peaceful nature that surrounded him. He did not take again the road to San Damiano, but the one leading in the opposite direction: the road to Gubbio. In order to do that, he had to walk through the town. There is no record of how the crowd along the way reacted—no doubt with respect, and even veneration. The story about the bishop's judgment had already spread throughout the city. And so old Pietro, that hardhearted, contemptuous miser, had been told off, humiliated. And his older son had made a sublime gesture in front of everyone. The bishop had clasped him to his heart and had clothed him and had recognized him as an ascetic consecrated to God. Who would have dared to utter a single insult to him or to throw the tiniest pebble at him?

But Francis scoffed at the respect shown him by the crowd, just as he formerly cared little about their insults. He was with God, he gave thanks to God, he rejoiced in God. And he walked now along the road, singing his heart out: some French songs, the ones that his mother had learned from the troubadours of Provence. And suddenly, from behind a bush along the road, jumped two thieves, who seized him. He was an easy prey: he was alone, unarmed, and seemed quite harmless. Yet he had an ecclesiastical mantle on his back, but he had no cincture, no headgear, and no shoes. They wanted to know what sort of a fanatic this was.

"Who are you?"

He, without a trace of fear, looked into those ferocious faces and proudly said, "I am the herald of the great King."

They searched him. He had no purse, no jewels, nothing to steal. Furious, they threw him into the ditch, where there was still a layer of snow.

"Take that, miserable herald of God! That's where you belong, so stay there!"

Once the robbers had gone off, Francis climbed out of the ditch, dusted himself off, and stamped his feet, shivering in the cold. The best way to warm up was to continue walking and singing. But night was falling. Turning back was out of the question; he was too far from the town. Ahead of him loomed the church of a Benedictine monastery. The biographers do not identify it, but it was probably the Abbey of Vallingegno, twenty-three or twenty-four kilometers north of Assisi.

He knocked at the door and asked for hospitality. The prior consented, provided that he earn his keep. No one is idle in a monastery; Saint Paul had written, "He who does not work should not eat." They sent him to the kitchen, where he was assigned to do menial chores. But the monks went farther than Saint Paul: he worked but received no food. He was reduced to drinking the greasy water with which he had washed the pots. Exactly the situation of the prodigal son in the Gospel.

This was not the sort of humility and poverty that he was looking for. He preferred to continue his journey, leaving his name with the porter. Several years later, when this name was being repeated throughout Umbria as the name of a great saint, the prior was seized with remorse. One can get away with treating any poor devil unfairly, with contempt, but a saint! He went to find the man whom he had mistreated and begged him, on his knees, for forgiveness.

Francis knew that the place that he had reached on his journey was closer to Gubbio than to Assisi. Now, in Gubbio he had a great friend, perhaps that confidant who used to help him right after his conversion, when he was staying in his grotto. He noticed, indeed, that the bishop's mantle was not enough to clothe him properly, and the monks had refused to give him any tunic at all. The friend was at home and gladly gave him some decent clothing. But Francis did not want to remain in his company; this was not the place for his vocation, any more than the Benedictine kitchen had been. It was time now to go back to San Damiano.

He was not unaware, however, of the fact that there was a leper house right by the market town. For him this was a call. He did not want to set out again without first helping these humiliated, suffering brothers; this side-trip was not inconsistent with his mission. Celano mentions this sojourn without specifying how long it lasted: "He stayed with them, serving them in every way, with the utmost zeal, and for the love of God he washed their sores, wiping the pus from their ulcers."

Ultimately, though, the little church of San Damiano was awaiting him. It was time to go back. He found the curate seated in the same place. Had he heard the latest news? Francis repeated to him what the bishop had said, to convince him that he was henceforth a cleric, and at the service of this chapel. The priest, taking his companion seriously now, clothed him in the robe worn by hermits, which had been traditional in the Church since antiquity.

Well, now, how was he going to complete this task, which appeared so arduous? Cracks ran through the church building on all sides; some walls would have to be demolished and entirely rebuilt; some sections of the paving had disappeared, leaving holes in the floor. He had sold the piece of cloth and the horse in order to make these repairs, but now that he had returned the proceeds of the sale to his father, he did not even have a penny with which to buy materials.

Actually, the Lord had not told him: "Have my house rebuilt", but rather: "Rebuild my house." It was up to him to take the trouble to do it. With what materials? With whatever he could collect by begging. So it was settled: the new mason would go through the streets of Assisi, asking for what he needed to repair the house of the Lord. And so, on the squares of the town, people again saw the troubadour of yesterday and the fool of today, who had now become a certified hermit; he was still singing pleasantly, in the beautiful voice that used to set hearts aflutter, "Give me stones! Anyone who gives me a stone will receive a reward. The one who gives me two stones will receive a double reward. The one who gives me three stones will receive a triple reward."

Everyone laughed, but they contributed stones. He transported them on his own shoulders, regardless of how heavy they were, and set them down in his stone yard, waiting to see how he could assemble them, despite the differences in size. At last, when he decided that there were enough of them, he started the job. It looked as though it was going to be a long one. But already curious townsfolk were coming to watch, wondering how this apprentice was going to manage. He called to them:

"Who wants to work with me? Who wants to rebuild the church of good Saint Damian?"

Some shrugged their shoulders; others allowed themselves to be persuaded; and Francis became the boss of the construction site. Were there any skilled craftsmen? It is quite likely, because there are some techniques that you don't just invent or master on one's own. Gradually the renovated building took shape, to the surprise and joy of the populace.

The curate was one of the happier ones. His bishop had assigned him to this unattractive ministry, which he carried out through obedience, although it distressed him daily. Every time that he offered the Holy Sacrifice of the Mass, he was obliged to watch carefully where he put his feet; the missal that he read from at the altar rocked back and forth on its wooden stand, and the rodents had the run of the place, going so far as to drown in the holy water font. He saw the slow transformation of the building, which had been so inhospitable to the Lord and to himself, and it inspired in him a deep gratitude toward the young man who was so enterprising. Then too, witnessing the hard labor that he was doing, he was afraid that he would see him collapse from exhaustion, so he prepared choice foods for his meals.

This solicitude continued until Francis himself put a stop to it. One day he went so far as to ask himself this question: "Are you going to find such a kindly priest, then, everywhere you go? Is it fitting for a truly poor man to have someone feed him in this way? If you want to practice holy poverty, it is your job to obtain your food, by begging for it door to door. That is how you must live voluntarily, for the love of him who was born poor, who lived in the world as a poor man, and who hung on a gibbet, poor and stripped of everything, and was buried as a poor man in a borrowed tomb."

So it was: he would beg for his food, as he had begged for the stones. Grabbing a bowl, he would show up at the first door of the first house that he came to and would continue in that way until the bowl was full. The citizens of Assisi were not generous: he received, first, a spoonful of one dish, then another from a second dish, then the crumbs from a third. The result was such a repulsive conglomeration that, when he started to taste it, he felt his stomach turning. Would he ever manage to continue? He went on eating, overcome with an insurmountable disgust. He continued. And suddenly the disgust turned into sweetness, the bitterness was transformed into joy. Grace came to his aid. This sort of menu was his daily diet.

One man was furious to see him walking again through the town: his father. Even though many people now admired that heroic young man, he, whose pride had been injured, could not lay eyes on him without becoming enraged. Soon, every time that Francis passed in front of the shop, Pietro came out to the threshold and uttered a curse. It is a serious matter for a son to be cursed by his father. What sort of defense could he put up against such imprecations? He devised a charade that, to tell the truth, was childish, but still meaningful. Every time that he had to pass in front of his father's house, he joined up with a beggar who had learned his lines.

Pietro would come out on the threshold and shout, "May you be accursed!"

Francis then knelt before the beggar and humbly asked him, "Father, bless me!"

Then the man, making the sign of the cross over the young man's head, would declare solemnly: "I bless you, my son."

And playing a part in this comedy earned him a share of the alms that Francis collected.

Soon, thanks to young Moriconi's courage, thanks to his persuasive confidence, thanks to the good will of the benevolent masons, the church of San Damiano, to the great joy of the curate, was entirely renovated, combining in a picturesque fashion new stones and old. The magnificent Byzantine Christ was more radiant than ever above the altar. The church was solemnly consecrated by the bishop in a ceremony attended by most of the populace, and public opinion was won over by sheer admiration.

Had the vocation of Francis, the poor man, come to an end? But how could that be? When God entrusts a mission to you, can it be considered finished from one day to the next? The year was 1207. Francis was twenty-five years old. He had just discovered the true life, and he had many years ahead of him. Since the splendid Christ of San Damiano no longer spoke to him, it was easy to understand that the repairs had to continue at other churches.

Right at the entrance to the city, facing the Porta San Pietro (on the other side of town from the Porta Nuova that led to San Damiano), there was another dilapidated church, Saint Peter's. We see it today in good condition, within the city limits. Back then it stood outside the ramparts. He transferred his workplace to there. He made this choice, Bonaventure tells us, "because of the special devotion that he had for the prince of the Apostles". Did he ask for permission from some ecclesiastical authority? It seems that the church was abandoned, to such an extent that the liturgy was no longer celebrated there, and so he did not have to seek the approval of a curate, as he had done in the previous case. We must suppose that the team that he had formed was effective there, too, because in a short time the church of Saint Peter was repaired.

And now what? Within the town, all the churches, whether they belonged to parishes or to religious communities, were carefully maintained: the clergy made sure that they were preserved. But Francis knew that only one league away from town, if you went out by the gate of Saint Peter, alongside the little road that runs parallel to the Chiascio and leads to Bettona, there was a chapel, even smaller than San Damiano, dedicated to Saint Mary of the Angels, also called the Portiuncula (in Italian, *Porziuncola*). It belonged to the Benedictine Abbey of Monte Subasio, which didn't care to keep it up. Francis, who had a tender and deep devotion to the Mother of God, fixed his choice upon her; and to that place he brought his team of masons. A few months later, the tiny chapel had been restored and was ready again for worship.

But then what became of the hermit builder's vocation? The Lord would see to it, once again, that he knew the next step to take.

PART TWO

THE EXCITING PATH OF A FOUNDER

1209–1216

1. The First Disciples

While waiting to be enlightened as to the will of God, Francis lived in the shadow of the Chapel of Saint Mary of the Angels [or Santa Maria degli Angeli]. Why did he prefer it to San Damiano? Because it was the second shrine chapel that he had repaired?[1] Because it was farther away from the town, and he reckoned that there he would be less of an object of curiosity? Perhaps all of the above. But we must suppose that the most decisive reason was the relative peace and quiet that he found in that remote locality. He had been invested in the livery of a hermit and wore it constantly: a dark-colored robe with a leather belt, sandals, and a staff.

Of what did his daily life consist, during those final months of the year 1209? It is easy to imagine it. He divided his waking hours between faith and charity. His faith was oriented especially toward the Eucharist, and therefore toward the churches that housed the Body of Christ. In his testament, which he begins by telling of his conversion, he mentions first his ministrations to the lepers. Then he adds:

> Then the Lord gave me such faith in the churches that I simply prayed in these words: We adore you, Lord Jesus Christ, in all your churches throughout the world; and we bless you, because by your holy Cross you have redeemed the world. Then the Lord gave me, and continues to give me such a great faith in the priests who live according to the rules of the Holy Roman Church, because of their sacerdotal character, that even if they persecute me, they are the ones to whom I want to have recourse. I act this way because in this world I see nothing of the Most High Son of God that is perceptible to the senses, except his most sacred Body and Blood, which they receive and of which they alone are the ministers. And I want these most holy mysteries to be honored

---

[1] Santa Maria degli Angeli was the third building that Francis repaired, but perhaps only the second *sanctuaire* or shrine chapel because Saint Peter's was a former Benedictine conventional church.—TRANS.

and venerated above all else, and housed in places that are exquisitely decorated.

From then on, the curate of San Damiano, who had become very devoted to this convert, ascetic, and restorer of his church, came every morning to Santa Maria degli Angeli to offer the Holy Sacrifice of the Mass there. He did not ask Francis to come to his church; he was the one who made the extra effort. No doubt he was careful not to walk through the town, taking instead the little path south of it that connected the two shrines.

But Francis, who had begged his sweet Savior so much to enlighten him as to his will, still had not received a message. He had obeyed conscientiously by repairing three churches, but he had the vague feeling that that was not his real vocation. And he was waiting for Christ to manifest himself, as at San Damiano.

On February 24, the feast of Saint Matthias, the priest was reading at the altar, for the Gospel of the day, the passage from chapter ten of Saint Matthew, which records the words of Christ as he was sending his apostles out on their mission:

> And preach as you go, saying, "The kingdom of heaven is at hand." Heal the sick, raise the dead, cleanse lepers, cast out demons. You received without paying, give without pay. Take no gold, nor silver, nor copper in your belts, no bag for your journey, nor two tunics, nor sandals, nor a staff; for the laborer deserves his food. And whatever town or village you enter, find out who is worthy in it, and stay with him until you depart. As you enter the house, salute it. And if the house is worthy, let your peace come upon it; but if it is not worthy, let your peace return to you.

Francis was not the best Latinist. He understood the gist of the reading, however, and experienced an intense emotion that he was not expecting. But he wanted to be sure of his translation, so, after the Mass, he asked the priest to confirm it for him. The priest complied and confirmed, word for word, what he had understood.

Then he cried, exultantly, "This is what I want! This is what I desire with all my strength to undertake!"

At last he had understood the message of Christ at San Damiano: the Church that he had to rebuild, by preaching the Kingdom of God, was not a church of stone, but the Mystical Body of Christ, which was crumbling because of heresy, lucre, and violence. His masonry work had certainly been pleasing to the Lord, but that was only a prelude and a prefiguration. Joyfully he put aside his staff and his sandals and found a gray tunic made of a coarse material, which he tied at the waist with a cord. In that attire he would truly be the herald of the great King.

And he went about preaching. When he entered the town, he chose as the place for his first sermon Saint George's Square, in front of the school where he had learned Latin and religion twenty years earlier. As soon as he began to speak, men, women, and children gathered around him. No one dared to laugh or joke or shrug their shoulders. They listened to him seriously. He had not prepared his speech: he let the inspiration pour out. He began by this invocation, which he had to repeat frequently afterward, "May the Lord grant you his peace!"

The rest was a commentary on this peace that ought to rain down on the city, which had been distressed for so many years by rivalries, feuds, and civil wars. And the fire with which he spoke inflamed their hearts. It mattered little that the one who uttered these moving words was the son of the merchant Pietro di Bernardone and who not long ago was making a fool of himself by begging stones. These words were the words of Christ; they were redolent of divine mercy. "Thanks to him," Celano says, "many enemies of concord and of their own salvation embraced peace with all their hearts, and, with God's help, they too became sons of Peace and seekers of their eternal salvation."

The speaker, who in the eyes of the populace had become the man of God, returned each day to the city, often changing the place where he preached. On one occasion his words unsettled the soul of a rich young burgher named Bernard of Quintavalle. This was not the first time that he had admired Francis; he had been watching him in action for two years and was convinced that his humility, his poverty, his patience, serenity, and kindness were the result of divine grace. And so he was quite ready to receive his message and to take him as a model. He decided, however, to observe him more closely and devised a stratagem to that end. He invited him to his house one evening, to the domicile that can still be seen on the Via Antonio

Cristofani, beside the bishop's palace; he offered him dinner, a light meal, during which they spoke about the things of God, and the host was mightily edified by the spiritual knowledge of his guest.

But night drew on, and Bernard said to Francis: "I ask you, my friend, not to return home, but to spend the night in my house."

Francis accepted the invitation, and his host had a bed prepared for him in his own room, a gesture that in those days was a sign of respect. After praying, each one lay down on his bed, and Bernard pretended to go to sleep by snoring like an pipe organ. Then Francis got up in silence and, on his knees, passed the rest of the night with his arms extended, praying and shedding many tears.

When morning came, Bernard had decided to leave the world and follow Francis. He still had some misgivings, however: Was that really the path for him? Would the ascetic accept him as a companion? He did not confide in him right away, but asked to meet with him again so as to make his final decision in the presence of God. Francis invited him to morning Mass at the Church of Saint Nicholas the following day. When it was over, Francis asked the priest for the Gospel book. "Here", he declared, "is where we will find out the will of heaven for you."

He knelt in front of the altar and opened the volume at random. Random, as far as his hand was concerned, but not for Providence, which was being invited to supply the answer. The verse lay open before their eyes: "If you would be perfect, go, sell what you possess and give to the poor, and you will have treasure in heaven."

But this was not conclusive. Even if one admits that divine grace can manifest itself by a single answer, it is advisable to look for another. Francis opened the book a second time and read: "Take nothing for the way. . . ."

This was the passage for the Feast of Saint Matthias, the one that had decided his own vocation. But, after all, God is triune, and it is a hallowed custom to invoke him as a witness three times. Francis opened the Gospels a third time. And he read: "If any man would come after me, let him deny himself and take up his cross and follow me."

This was a new revelation for the Poverello, the little poor man of Assisi: a suggestion of a sort of life in community that would endeavor to model itself on the evangelical counsels. And since Bernard was proposing to join him, he decided, as though there were many of them, to institute this new life: "Here, my brothers, is the life and the rule that we will follow, we and all those who will come to join us."

But for now, although the brethren were not numerous, there were two of them. For Francis and Bernard had been accompanied in their reading of the Gospel by a canon who seemed to be deeply disturbed by the whole scene. He was a cleric and a lawyer, and his name was Pietro di Cattani (Peter of Catanio). (French translators have unanimously called him "Pierre de Catane", as though he were originally from the great city in Sicily; but in that case his name would have been *da Catania*.) We must assume that this surname, like that of *Quintavalle*, came from some named place, because it does not correspond to any geographical location in Italy. [In this translation he will be referred to by the name commonly given him in English, Peter of Catanio.]

Francis had said: *the rule*—the same expression used for the regulations that had been governing the difficult life of the monks of Saint Benedict for six centuries, and which had proved its effectiveness for hundreds of monasteries and tens of thousands of religious. Without calculating, reflecting, or choosing, he had used the word that applied to a community that had been tested and approved by the Church. He foresaw—at the same time, and quite spontaneously—that he would be followed, not by one disciple (not his own, of course, but a disciple of Jesus Christ), but rather by a group, by a crowd, by a multitude of disciples.

For the moment, Bernard, who was convinced and resolved, made haste to put into action the counsels that Jesus had just presented to him so extravagantly. They were clear. He went home and put his mansion up for sale, along with his furniture and his lands. He added that astronomical sum to the amount that was slumbering in his coffers; then he inquired of the bishop, the curates, the consuls, and the charitable matrons about the poor people in the surrounding area. He divided his fortune into two major parts: one for the monasteries, the hospitals, and the leper houses; the other for the needy, the widows, and orphans. Then, aided by admirers who had placed themselves at his service for such a praiseworthy undertaking, he gave away his fortune, down to the last penny. Having responded to the first Gospel precept with strict obedience, he hurried to comply with the second: he went to join up with Francis, who was placed before him as the image of Jesus Christ. And he merited, as Bonaventure remarks, to be called "the firstborn of our blessed father".

Moreover, he holds an important place in the history of the Franciscan order; for, as the *Fioretti* [*di San Francesco d'Assisi* (*Little Flowers of Saint Francis of Assisi*)] note, "he attained such great sanctity that Saint Francis had a deep respect for him and often praised him." At the time of his own death, Francis called for him and gave him a special blessing.

Bernard was soon followed by Peter of Catanio, who gathered together the few belongings that he owned and quickly divided them up among the poor. Thus the firstborn had a brother who was almost his twin. Francis clothed both of them in hermit's garb. So there were three of them who placed themselves under the evangelical rule, forming a community that, although reduced to the smallest possible size, had the privilege of reciting the Divine Office as a canonical entity. This recitation would take place in the narrow nave of Santa Maria degli Angeli, which was later called the Portiuncula, the mother church of the Franciscan order. But these three penitents would have to find lodging somewhere. A stone house—perish the thought!—would be too worldly for them. They built themselves a hut, right beside the oratory, out of branches and mud.

The departure of the rich burgher and the learned canon—men who were quite different, but equally edifying—from the town of Assisi provoked abundant commentary, but also, among some people, a lively admiration. At any rate these were the sentiments of Egidio, or "Giles", a young man from a good family. Eight days after Bernard, he came to Francis, knelt before him and asked to be admitted among his brethren. We know the date of this event: the Feast of Saint George, that is, April 23, 1209. We find this detail, and many others, in *The Life of Blessed Giles*, written by someone in Saint Francis' inner circle, Brother Leo, who died in 1271 and who knew both individuals well.

Francis answered the postulant: "My dear, dear brother, God has given you a great grace. If the emperor came to Assisi and wanted to make some citizen his knight and private chamberlain, would not the man have to rejoice over this honor? How much more, then, must be your joy, since God has chosen you as his knight and his dearly beloved servant, so as to practice perfection according to the holy Gospel! And so, remain firm and constant in the vocation to which God has called you."

Indeed, the good brother remained firm and constant in his vocation, since until his death he was considered as one of the most wonderful disciples of Saint Francis and merited the privilege of being beatified. His wisdom became so proverbial that his contemporaries memorialized his words in an anthology, *The Sayings of Blessed Giles*, which was handed down to posterity.

At the moment, it was necessary to clothe the new hermit in the tunic proper to his state of life. But there was no more cloth in the hut of the brethren. Francis called Giles to bring him to town to purchase material with which to make a habit. Along the way, they encountered a poor woman who asked them for an alms, for the love of God. They had nothing to give her. But Francis said to Giles: "My brother, give your garment, therefore to this poor woman."

The postulant quickly and joyfully did so, without caring that he would have to go into town in his undergarments. Then, when the tunic had been made, Francis solemnly clothed his new brother in it. He wanted to teach him humility and the art of preaching. And so he took him along for a grand tour of northern Umbria, going as far as the Marches of Ancona. They always talked about the same themes: the love of God, conversion, fidelity to the Church. Only Francis spoke. But Giles, full of admiration for these words that had such a simple and spontaneous eloquence, used to conclude the discourse ingenuously, "What he is saying to you, good people, is the truth. Listen to him, and put his words into practice."

When they returned to the Portiuncula, there were three recruits waiting for them: Sabbatino, Morico, and John, nicknamed John of Cappella, since he wore a cap and insisted on continuing to wear it after his investiture. Francis deemed them worthy of being admitted into his community.

After the ceremony the young man, who was becoming the father of an entire clan, addressed this admonition to them: "My dearly beloved brothers, let us consider our vocation. God, in his mercy, has chosen us not only to bring about our salvation, but also to save many souls; let us go through the world and, by our example even more than by our words, let us exhort the people to do penance for their sins and to keep in mind the divine commandments. Do not be alarmed by the thought of your weakness and your ignorance, but preach repentance, fearlessly and simply. Have confidence in God, who has conquered the world: it is his Spirit that speaks in you and through you, to exhort all the sinners to convert and to keep his precepts. You will meet faithful, kind, and well-disposed people, who will welcome you with joy, and others—rebellious, proud blasphemers—who will resist you and respond to what you say with insults. Therefore engrave in your hearts the resolution to bear everything with patience and humility."

A discourse like this was nothing less than a preparation for mission work. And in fact, the next day, after Mass, he sent them two by two to preach the Kingdom of God; and these new missionaries, full of ardor, went off in three different directions, treasuring in their hearts the precious recommendations of their superior and yearning to conform themselves to them, regardless of the mockery and resistance.

Indeed, did these impromptu preachers, who had never studied theology, have the right to preach, in the sight of the Church? The biographers do not declare this explicitly, but they suggest it. *The Three Companions* report that Francis went regularly to consult with the bishop, who received him benevolently, counseled him, and gave him his protection.

It happened one day that this worthy prelate uttered a remark that, although not a reproach, contained at least a hint of a doubt: "Your life seems to me to be too austere. How can one live without possessing anything at all in this world?"

Francis immediately replied, "Your Excellency, if we had property, we would also have to have weapons with which to defend it. For it is wealth that engenders disputes and lawsuits; that is what creates so many obstacles to the love of God and love of neighbor. That is why we prefer to possess no temporal goods in this world."

And the bishop acquiesced. He was giving ecclesiastical approval —orally, of course, but effectively—to the brothers' way of life. So the six of them went out, two by two, after their superior had blessed them. And they spread out through the towns and villages of Umbria, inciting the people to be good-hearted and to repent. They astonished the inhabitants. The usual preachers had neither this garb nor this simplicity of speech. Instead, they gave the impression that they were "wooden men", as *The Three Companions* put it. A certain number of the listeners asked them, however, what religious order they belonged to. They replied, without further explanation, "We are penitents from Assisi."

There were mixed feelings about them. Some admired them, others showed interest or sympathy, while still others got the impression that they were dealing with fools or jokesters. A few even supposed that these loquacious beggars were hypocrites, and therefore dangerous individuals, since under that devout appearance they might be concealing unspeakable designs against other people's property. That is why it was difficult for them to find lodgings, even in a barn or a hovel: the owners feared that they would carry off by night whatever they could find in their dwelling. So then they would bed down beneath the portico of the church.

Two of them, who had made their way as far as Florence (180 kilometers distant from Assisi, by the shortest routes), were reluctantly taken in by a charitable woman and sent to some dank corner of the house, but were then thrown out by her husband when he returned. The next morning she found the two mendicants in church, absorbed in prayer. At that moment a benefactor, in charge of distributing alms, came up to them and put his hand into his purse to take out a few coins, but they protested vehemently, "No money!"

Since the man was astonished and demanded an explanation, Bernard (whom the record names at this point) said to him, "It is true that we are poor. But for us, poverty is not a curse. For God, whose counsels we wish to carry out, has made us voluntarily poor by his grace."

The good man was amazed and, upon gleaning some information about these virtuous preachers, learned that they had spent the night outdoors in the cold. He invited them to stay in his house, put them up there for several days, and was edified by their conversation. Not everyone acted this way, however, and the friars had to suffer a thousand inconveniences, which they accepted with humble equanimity.

Nevertheless, the amazement caused by the virtue of the mendicant preachers was not always merely a sentimental thing, for they returned to the sheepfold with four new recruits: Philip the Tall, John of San Costanzo, Barbaro, and Bernard of Vigilanzio. Francis himself had gone off, alone (he had to, since there was now an uneven number of friars in the community), this time heading south. He had gone as far as Rieti, a distance of 120 kilometers, via Foligno, Spoleto, and Terni. He had not made any disciples en route. But once he had arrived in Rieti, he came across a young knight named Angelo Tancredi and addressed him with that boldness that men of God sometimes have: "Young man, you have worn a belt, a sword, and spurs long enough. It is time for you to exchange henceforth your belt for a cord, your sword for a cross, and your spurs for the dust and mire of the roads. Follow me, and I will dub you a knight in the army of Christ."

Without any resistance, Angelo followed Francis. He would remain one of Francis' closest collaborators and become one of his biographers, along with two other companions.

This Brother Angelo has sometimes been confused with another by the same name, who was also from a noble family. His name, though, was not Tancredi, but Tarlati, which is not specified by the texts in which he is mentioned. Still, even though this friar did not belong to the earliest community, it is interesting, because of his namesake, to watch him in action in a famous anecdote related by the *Fioretti*.

Francis had appointed him Guardian (that is to say, the superior) of the little friary of Monte Casale near Borgo Sansepolcro, at the border between Umbria and Tuscany. At that time, three dreadful robbers were terrorizing the countryside. They showed up one fine day at the door of the friary and asked for something to eat. The porter, trembling with fright, called the Guardian, who did not allow himself to be intimidated.

"What's this?" he exclaimed. "You vile thieves, cruel assassins! You are not ashamed to steal the fruits of others' labors, and to make matters worse—brazen blackguards that you are—you now want to devour the alms received by the servants of God. You are unworthy of the ground that you walk on, for you have no respect for men or for God who created you. Go away, and don't let me ever see you again!"

Livid with rage, both at the refusal of their request and at the humiliating words that accompanied it, the three villains went off, hungry. Now it happened that Francis, who was staying then at this friary, returned happily, carrying over his shoulder a sack full of alms that he had begged. Angelo made sure to report the incident to him.

Francis was indignant. "You did wrong. That was cruel. Sinners are brought back to God, not with harsh rebukes, but with kindness. That is why our Lord Jesus Christ, whose Gospel we have promised to observe, says that sick people need a physician, not those who are well; and that he came to call sinners to repentance, and not those who are just. That is why he used to eat with them. And so, therefore, since you have acted against charity and against the holy Gospel of Christ, I order you, in the name of holy obedience, to take right now this sack containing the bread and wine that I have begged, and to go without delay over mountains and through valleys until you find those robbers. When you do, you are to offer them this bread and wine. Then you shall ask them, on my behalf, to stop doing evil and to fear God instead and to refrain in the future from offending their neighbors. If they act accordingly, I promise to provide for their needs and always to give them food and drink."

Brother Angelo, completely disconcerted, hoisted the sack over his shoulder and, as a perfect practitioner of holy obedience, set out on his journey, while Francis immersed himself in prayer to obtain from God the repentance of the villains. They were not far off, and Angelo quickly caught up with them. He then amiably offered them the contents of his sack and gave them the little sermon that went along with it, which was nothing like the hostile words that he had spoken to them minutes before. While they were devouring the provisions and listening to the commentary, the robbers felt their hearts melting.

"Woe to us," said one of them, "miserable wretches that we are! The pains of hell that await us must be very cruel, since we strike our neighbor, wound him, and even go so far as to kill him. And despite all the misdeeds and criminal acts that we commit, we have neither remorse nor fear of God. And here this holy friar has come to us and, on account of a few harsh words that he had said to us because of our wickedness, has humbly accused himself for his fault. Furthermore he has brought us some bread and wine and the generous promise of his saintly father."

One of the accomplices agreed: "You are quite right. What you say is true. But what should we do now?"

"It's simple: let us go find Brother Francis, and ask him to obtain from God mercy for our sins."

All three returned therefore to the friary, asked to speak to Francis, and said to him: "Father, we have committed so many and such abominable sins, that we do not believe that we can obtain the mercy of God. But if you have some hope that God will receive us in his mercy, we are ready to do whatever you command, and to do penance with you."

Then Francis launched into a heartfelt discourse praising the divine mercy, which is greater than all our iniquities. All at once, the *Fioretti* tell us, "the robbers renounced the devil and all his works; Saint Francis received them into the order, and they began to do great penance."

As for Angelo Tancredi, the original companion, he was one of the three friars whom Francis chose to accompany him during his retreat on Mount La Verna, where he received the stigmata.

At the moment, he was only a new trainee, full of good will and eager to carry out his duties as a knight of Jesus Christ. His arrival brought the number of Francis' disciples to eleven. Wouldn't there be a twelfth, corresponding to the twelve apostles of our Lord?

The twelfth one soon arrived, quite unexpectedly. It was a priest of Assisi named Sylvester, although we do not know in what sort of ministry he had been engaged. Once, when Francis was looking for stones to repair San Damiano, Sylvester had sold him some. He didn't give, but sold them. And at a price that seemed to him far too modest. When Bernard of Quintavalle was generously distributing gold and silver coins, Sylvester came up to Francis, who was accompanying Bernard, and insinuated, in a tone of voice that was both bitter and ironic, "I sold you some stones recently, and you were very stingy about paying me for them."

Francis, without batting an eyelid, put his hand in the sack of money that Bernard was carrying, took a handful of coins and let them fall into Sylvester's hands, with the disdainful comment, "And now, Sir Priest, do you have enough?"

The other man went off, more ashamed than content. He could not help comparing his keen love of money with the detachment that these two young men displayed. And upon returning home, he recalled the Gospel verse: "No man can serve two masters, God and mammon."

That night he slept poorly. And he had a wonderful dream: a monstrous dragon was invading the town of Assisi, spreading terror and threatening to destroy everything. But suddenly a radiant hermit appeared, who had the face of Francis. From his mouth came an immense golden cross, the top of which touched the sky, while the arms extended to the ends of the world. Confronted by this vision, the bloodthirsty dragon was seized with panic and fled, never to return.

Upon awakening, Sylvester murmured, "Yes, this Francis is truly a servant and a friend of God. The community that he is assembling now will grow by the grace of God and reach all the corners of the world."

He lost his taste for luxury and the good life and began to envy Bernard and Peter, who had given up everything and followed Francis down the path of renunciation. But he still remained for a time in the world, becoming more and more unhappy with it and envious of the friars at the Portiuncula whose virtues he heard being extolled. At last he could stand it no longer, and he went to see Francis, saying, "Admit me. I would like to be one of your followers."

He was an invaluable recruit, because now the friars had a priest among them, who was one of them. From now on they could count on having the Mass and the sacraments, without being dependent upon the good will of those outside the community.

Now they were thirteen. The rickety hut constructed nearby the Portiuncula had become uninhabitable, not only because of its flimsiness, but also because of its inadequacy. Two or three men can spend the night between walls of dried mud, and then go to the river for their ablutions, but a group consisting of a dozen men governed by a rule cannot tolerate that sort of casualness. Besides, the makeshift hut was in danger of being carried off by the first storm.

The community of poor friars moved two kilometers to the south, along the road to Bettona, to a place called Rivo Torto, because the stream that flows nearby makes a detour there. They received as a donation a building that was in ruins but easy to repair: Francis had a certain amount of experience now in that sort of labor. This worthless gift was given to them by an order of crusaders, the *Cruciati* of the Holy Savior, who had no use for the ruins. Jörgensen supposes that the deal was arranged by Morico, who had belonged to that institute before receiving the Franciscan habit; those good religious did not hold it against him. But space was still very limited, so much so that they had to divide the dormitory into as many places as there were friars; furthermore, to avoid disorder, Francis wrote upon the wall the name of each friar above the place reserved for him.

It seems very likely that this dormitory doubled as an oratory and a refectory. Anyway, weather permitting, the friars used to chant the psalms outdoors, in front of a wooden cross that their father had erected in the middle of their little property. They quickly came to know this office by heart, since they arose at midnight, like the monks, to recite Matins in semi-darkness.

During the day they devoted themselves to manual work. Francis mentions it briefly in his "Testament": "I worked with my hands, and I intend to continue doing so; and I also want all my brothers to work at an honorable job. Those who do not have a trade must learn one; not out of a desire for profit, but in order to give good example and not to remain idle." They continued to beg, besides, both out of humility and in order to feed themselves when the fruit of their labor did not suffice. This happened frequently, no doubt, because their rule did not allow them to receive payments in kind.

What sorts of items could the friars have manufactured that were decent enough to be offered to the public, but insufficiently profitable, so that they had to be supplemented by begging? Probably small, commonly used objects, such as the ascetics in the East used to make at the time of Saint Athanasius and Saint Macarius: wickerwork, wooden bowls, canvas bags. Perhaps flutes as well?

The most remarkable thing about their community life was their love for one another. Here again, we should leave the description to *The Three Companions*, since one of them was Angelo Tancredi, a witness to and a participant in that initial fraternity:

> The most ardent charity reigned among them, which made it evident that they were true disciples of Our Lord. They loved one another with a deep affection; they served and fed each other, as a mother feeds her dearly beloved, only son. They were inflamed with such charity that it seemed to them an easy thing to risk death, not only for the love of Christ, but also for the well-being of the soul or body of any one of the friars. And so, one day as two friars were walking together, they encountered a madman, who began throwing stones at them. One of them, seeing that they were going to hit his companion, immediately stood in front of him to receive the blows; he preferred to be injured rather than to see his brother struck. Their humility and their charity were so deeply rooted that each one had as much respect for the other as for a father and master. If it happened that one brother said to another a word that might offend him, pangs of conscience and remorse

prevented him from getting any rest until he had confessed his fault, humbly prostrating himself to the ground, and had asked his brother to place his foot on his mouth.

They practiced charity toward those who did not belong to their community, as well.

They delighted in giving, for the love of God, to anyone who asked them, and especially to the poor, the alms that they themselves had received. When they met along the way poor people who asked them for something for the love of God, if they had nothing to give, they let them have a piece of their habits, miserable as they were: sometimes their cowl, or hood, which they detached from their tunic, sometimes a sleeve, or some other piece that they ripped out of their garment.

Francis was not beyond marveling at the workings of grace in this handful of men, who yesterday were so mediocre and ordinary, yet suddenly had become saints. Spontaneously he had gone from being a model who attracted followers to being an educator who formed disciples. Celano remarks: "He employed all his vigilance and solicitude in forming his new sons by means of new lessons and taught them to walk sure-footedly along the path of holy poverty and blessed simplicity."

Driven by this task, which weighed upon him imperiously, he fulfilled his duties zealously, but at the same time he was troubled by the memory of his frivolous past, and he could only doubt the success of this fledgling community. So one day he withdrew to pray without any witnesses and knelt before God as a miserable wretch; he lamented the lost years of his youth, and repeated, in the bitterness of his soul, "Lord, have mercy on me, a sinner."

And suddenly an ineffable peace and a delicious sweetness rushed in upon his soul, to such a degree that he lost consciousness. When he returned to his senses, all the fears that he had experienced had vanished, and he was ruled by the certainty that he had been pardoned and that God was showering him with grace; at the same time, a blessed illumination made him understand the sort of religious institute that he had just formed under the influence of circumstances. Filled with new ardor, he returned to the tumbledown cottage in Rivo Torto and assembled his brothers. Then he communicated to them what the Lord had taught him.

Take courage and rejoice in the Lord. Be not saddened by the fact that you are few; let my simplicity and yours not be a cause of discouragement. For the Lord has shown me clearly that he will make us grow and multiply to the ends of the earth. For your profit, I find myself obliged to relate to you my vision, about which I should keep silence if charity did not make it my duty to speak:

I saw a great multitude of men who came to us to live in the habit of our holy religion and according to the rule of our blessed order. I still have in my ears the sound of the footsteps of those who were coming and going, guided by holy obedience. I saw the roads covered with the crowds who were converging on our country from almost every land. The French arrive, the Spaniards hurry, the Germans and the English come running, and immense multitudes speaking different languages hasten their steps.

To help you to thank God faithfully and devoutly for these blessings, and to teach you how you should behave toward your present and future brothers, listen to the truth about what will soon happen. In its beginnings, the order, will enjoy fruits of an exquisite sweetness. The second harvest will be less pleasant, and finally, we will gather fruits so bitter that they will be inedible, because despite their aroma and their delectable appearance, their tartness will be so great that no one will be able to taste them. In truth, God will make of us a great nation; but it will be with us like the fisherman who cast his nets into the sea and caught a great quantity of fish and put them in his boat. Finally, when the catch was too abundant for him to bring it all in, he stored up the biggest and most appetizing fish and threw the others overboard.

This certainty and this joy incited the founder to send his disciples "throughout the world" for a new mission. He assembled them first for a discourse on the gospel, in which he spoke to them at length about the Kingdom of God, disdain for the world, and the renunciation of self-will. Then, in keeping with the recommendation of the Gospel, he paired them two by two and assigned them to go off in different directions. The friars spontaneously threw themselves at his feet as a sign of obedience; he embraced them affectionately, and they dispersed.

How long did this time of preaching last? Too long for Francis, for one fine day he begged heaven to send his sons back to him. Then they all arrived at the same time and, with one accord, rejoiced over their twofold experience: the successes that they had had by their preaching, which were an occasion to praise the Lord, and the insults and humiliations that they had suffered, which were so many opportunities to admit their own misery.

2. Audience with the Pope

In his "Testament", after describing his devotion to lepers and his renunciation of the world, Francis relates: "After the Lord had given me brothers, no one showed me what I ought to do, but the Most High himself revealed to me that I should live according to the Holy Gospel." We should not infer that there was a supernatural revelation, but simply recall the Mass that he attended at San Damiano on the Feast of Saint Matthias, during which Francis heard the discourse of Christ sending his apostles on a mission. "Then," he adds, "I had a brief document drawn up, and my Lord the Pope confirmed it for me."

This brief document constituted the original rule of the Friars Minor, or Franciscans. It has since been lost. But we can easily imagine what it contained. First of all, since it directs the friars to live according to the Gospel, it repeats the language of the passage that Francis heard. Furthermore, he continues the statement in his "Testament" by giving a few details that plainly indicate the practice of several articles of the rule: "Those who came to share our way of life gave to the poor all that they owned; they were content to have one tunic that was patched inside and out, and also one cord and breeches." This one sentence mentions the condition for admittance to the order and the garb adopted by the friars. Then follow references to the obligation of clerics to recite the Divine Office, work, almsgiving, collective poverty, and obedience to the superior.

Some specialists, examining the question under the microscope, have attempted to reconstitute the primitive rule and are pretty much in agreement. We cite in particular the Swiss scholar, K. Müller and the British Capuchin, Dom Cuthbert. In all, the reconstructed text fills two pages, which can be summarized as follows:

> *Preamble.* Francis and his successors promise obedience to Innocent III and his successors. The friars will obey Francis and his successors.

The Rule. It obliges the friars to conform their lives completely to the Gospel.

Admission. The postulant can be admitted only if he has renounced all his property and distributed it to the poor.

Habit. Only one tunic, with a cowl (or hood) and tied around the waist with a cord; and breeches. [One wonders what the friars wore when they did their laundry.]

Precedence. None. The friars will have no authority one over another [which tends to contradict the obligation to obey Brother Francis].

Charity and humility. The friars will take care not to act or speak in a way that could injure the others. On the contrary, they should seek opportunities to be mutually obliging.

Work and poverty. The friars will do manual work. They are forbidden to hold worldly positions in which they would have to exercise authority or handle money. They will have recourse to begging whenever necessary. It is forbidden to own houses; they are to be lodged as guests.

Preaching. The friars will go about the world preaching the Gospel in very simple terms.

Orthodoxy. The friars will behave and speak like Catholics, subject to the see of the Holy Roman Church.

This was certainly the shortest rule of a religious community. The rule of Saint Benedict, used throughout the West, was made up of sixty-three chapters in as many pages. The rule of "The Master", which is contemporary with it, although it is not known for what monastery it was intended, fills 170 pages. The rule of Saint Columban, which preceded that of Saint Benedict in Gaul, reached a length of about fifty pages. As for the rule of Saint Basil, which legislates for the monks of the East, it is actually composed of three separate elements (the *Great Rules*, the *Shorter Rules*, and the *Monastic Constitutions*), which, combined, run to more than five hundred pages. The primitive rule of Saint Francis, which did not bear that name but was no doubt called the rule "of the Penitents of Assisi", posed hardly any problems of interpretation, since it was formulated in clear, simple language, nor canonical difficulties, except perhaps for the article on absolute poverty. Indeed, the rule was for the most part negative: the friars will own nothing, the friars will have no authority; the friars will demand nothing from the authorities, whether civil or ecclesiastical. Everything positive that it included was drawn from the Gospels.

There was no use, therefore, in submitting this document to the clerical authorities, which, *de jure* could find nothing rash or reprehensible in it. But Francis insisted that it be sanctioned at the very highest level of the Church hierarchy: by the Pope himself. This vigilant submission to the Supreme Pontiff would remain for him a rule of conduct for the rest of his life.

In the liturgy for the Feast of Saint Francis, one antiphon carefully underscores this concern of the founder:

> *Franciscus, vir catholicus*
> *Et totus apostolicus,*
> *Ecclesiae teneri*
>
> *Fidem Romanae docuit*
> *Presbyterosque monuit*
> *Prae cunctis revereri.*

Which means: "Francis, a Catholic and entirely apostolic man, taught fidelity to the faith of the Roman Church and admonished [his followers] to revere priests above all others." *Apostolic* here means devoted to the successors of the apostles. The first rule, dated 1221 (the first, that is, which has come down to us), would begin with a declaration of dependence of the new order with respect to the Supreme Pontiff. Another article would prescribe that "none of the friars will preach anything contrary to the customs and the institution of the Holy Roman Church." Chapter 17 would return to this subject: "All the friars should be Catholics. If one of them strays from the Catholic faith and way of life, in word or action, and does not amend his ways, he will be permanently expelled from our brotherhood."

The second rule, from the year 1223, would take up these themes again. The *Mirror of Perfection*, which is probably the work of Brother Leo, the confessor of Saint Francis, relates that the latter, as death was approaching, dictated to Brother Benedict of Prato several of his final requests, among which were the following: "May all of my brothers always prove loyal to the bishops and the priests of Holy Mother Church." Saint Bonaventure, for his part, informs us that in their preaching "the friars, without any affectation of style, taught what the Holy Roman Church believes and teaches."

And so, at the onset of Autumn in the year 1209 (some historians prefer the spring of 1210), Francis decided to set out for Rome with his disciples to have his rule approved by the Pope. With how many disciples? Celano and *The Three Companions* say "eleven". Bonaventure and the *Fioretti* say twelve. It is possible that the *Companions* are repeating what Celano says, and that the *Fioretti* follow Bonaventure. The discrepancy remains. How can we explain it? In the preceding chapter we counted correctly: by the end of 1209, twelve men had joined Francis, and the sources cite their names explicitly according to their functions in the community. Could Celano have miscounted, for example, by forgetting Sylvester, who entered the community late? Nevertheless this priest was a recruit who would be difficult to overlook. Let us not get bogged down by this difference in the details; having counted the friars again, let us admit that there were twelve of them in Francis' circle at the moment of their departure.

He addressed them in a brief discourse: "My brothers, I see that the Lord, in his mercy, wishes to make our community grow. Let us go, then, to visit our mother, the Holy Roman Church; let us make known to the Supreme Pontiff what the Lord has already accomplished by making use of us, so as to continue the work that he has begun, according to his will and his commands."

The amazing thing, at these important junctures, was that no one debated, no one brought up difficulties, no one posed embarrassing questions. The *Companions* report that "the father's idea pleased the brothers." That is all: since they had followed this prophet one fine day by abandoning everything and had chosen him as their model and their leader, they had only to follow him, in humility and obedience.

However, while he was in fact their leader, Francis renounced that office. He decided on the destination, but preferred to have someone else exercise authority during the journey. He left the friars free to select him. With one accord, they designated Bernard, the first among them after their father, Francis. And so they set out, joyful and unperturbed, abandoning their lot to Providence. And they were right, because during their journey of fifty leagues, they always received hospitality. This is remarkable. For to welcome a dusty, enthusiastic beggar is generosity; to welcome two is an act of charity; but to welcome thirteen is madness.

The bishop of Assisi, Guido, who had placed himself so earnestly at the service of the friars, was sojourning in Rome at that time; and it is likely that Francis, aware of the fact, chose this moment to go there, counting on that prelate, who was well-disposed toward them, to arrange for them an audience with the Pope. To be sure, they knew the address of the place where he was staying, so that they did not have to go house to house looking for him. Besides, medieval Rome was a little town, not at all on the scale of modern-day Rome or with the great cities of Lombardy at that time; it had no industries, and only a limited number of craftsmen and merchants, and thus its population was poor and unemployed, ripe for all sorts of unrest. Furthermore, that population was composed, to a great extent, of clergymen, whether resident or transient, and so it was possible to find a prelate there quickly enough.

When the bishop of Assisi saw the thirteen poor men gathered before him, an unpleasant thought occurred to him at first. These holy friars were, in his eyes, the ornament of his city, a compendium of exemplary evangelical virtues; and he suspected that they were coming to settle in Rome. What a loss for his diocese! But after Francis explained to him the purpose of their journey, he promised them that he would work in their favor. He himself was not important enough as a prelate to arrange an audience with the Pope for his protégés, but among his friends was one of the Pope's close collaborators, the cardinal Giovanni di San Paolo, bishop of Sabine, "a man truly full of divine grace". According to Celano, "while living among the princes and the great ones of the Roman Curia, he nevertheless despised earthly things and sought only the things of heaven." In other words, the sort of man who would understand Saint Francis very well. Indeed, he received him kindly and asked him all sorts of questions. Then, while waiting to obtain an interview with the Holy Father for the mendicants of God, he put them up in his own residence; out of charity, to be sure, but also in order to study their conduct, which ultimately enraptured him.

At the end of this time of probation, the cardinal again summoned the friars to appear before him, and he presented to them his conclusions: "My dear sons, I greatly admire your piety, your regularity in chanting the Divine Office, the evangelical character of your conversation, the firmness of your faith. God is certainly calling you to religious life. My advice, therefore, is simple: seek admission to a monastery, the most fervent one that you can find; or else request the status of hermits. It will be granted to you most willingly."

Brother Francis humbly rejected this suggestion: he and his brothers did not want to be monks or hermits, even though they did not disdain those forms of consecrated life. They desired to live according to a completely different rule, the one that they would present to the Pope so as to obtain his blessing. Giovanni di San Paolo understood, but was not convinced. He gladly consented to obtain an interview with the Supreme Pontiff, and even to recommend in advance this edifying little community, but he feared that his request would be refused.

In fact, the cardinal made an effort to win the heart of the Pope.

"I have just found", he told him, "a man of great virtue, who has gathered fervent disciples. He wants to lead, together with his brothers, a life in conformity with the gospel ideal, and to observe evangelical perfection in everything. It seems to me, indeed, that the Lord wants to make use of him in order to revive the faith of the Holy Church throughout the world."

Innocent was persuaded, and he asked Giovanni di San Paolo to bring these exceptional men to him the following day.

Far from being anxious or simply intimidated by the thought of appearing before the prestigious head of the Church, Francis rejoiced wholeheartedly. What a formidable figure, though, this Innocent III was. Besides his role as head of the Church, which conferred unlimited spiritual authority upon him, he had made a name for himself throughout Christendom as a domineering, intractable personage.

On January 8, 1198, the very day on which Celestine III expired, the cardinals elected as his successor Cardinal Lothar of Segni (i.e., from the family of the counts of Segni), who took the name of Innocent III. The new Pope was thirty-seven years old. He had studied law and theology at the universities of Paris and Bologna and had demonstrated diplomatic talents under the preceding pontiffs; as a young man he had written a brilliant work of spirituality on *Contempt for the World*. In keeping with the tradition of nepotism, his uncle, Clement III, had made him a cardinal while he was still quite young. But his elevation was not due solely to his family: in every situation he displayed an ardent zeal, a combative character, an indefatigable devotion to the

cause of the Church. After his accession to the See of Peter, he did not
hide his intention to fight for the triumph of the ecclesiastical ideal to
which his predecessors had dedicated themselves, especially Gregory
VII and Urban II, and he proclaimed with full voice the preeminence
of papal authority, which should extend not only to the bishops and
Church matters, but also to worldly princes. Some decades earlier,
Saint Bernard had expressed the famous doctrine of the two swords,
the spiritual and the temporal; Innocent replaced this, along the same
lines, with the doctrine of the two stars:

> Just as God has placed in the firmament two great stars to illuminate
> it, the sun that rules by day, and the moon that governs the night, so
> also He instituted two great dignitaries in the firmament of the Church:
> the papacy which reigns over souls, and the royalty which has dominion
> over bodies. But the first is quite superior to the second. As the moon
> receives her light from the sun, which surpasses her by far in the quality
> and quantity of its rays, so the royal power derives all of its splendor
> and prestige from the pontifical power.

A century later, Boniface VIII would publish the bull, *Clericis laïcos*,
which set forth the same theory, in almost the same terms, but was
addressed solely to Philip the Fair, [king of France], who would per-
ceive this as an act of aggression on the part of the Pope.

At the moment, as during the reign of Gregory VII, it was still
the German power that was opposed to the application of this principle. Emperor Henry VI, a tireless enemy of the Holy See, had died in
1197, of course, but his governors and his garrisons were still deployed
throughout Italy. Furthermore, they now controlled southern Italy,
which until recently had been in the hands of the Norman princes,
but which Henry VI had inherited by his marriage with Constance of
Sicily. The new Pope had to arbitrate between the two candidates for
the Germanic throne of the Holy Roman Empire, Philip of Swabia,
a brother of Henry VI, and Otto of Brunswick [von Braunschweig],
son of the duke of Bavaria, Henry the Black. He recognized the latter
and had to excommunicate him almost immediately for his treachery.
He placed the kingdom of France under interdict, since King Philip
Augustus had repudiated his legitimate wife, Ingeborg of Denmark,
in order to marry Agnes of Meran. Most importantly, he called on the
princes of the West to participate in the Fourth Crusade, which took

place from 1201 to 1204 and went awry in taking Constantinople and founding the Latin Empire of Constantinople.

All of this political activity, which Innocent deemed necessary because it appealed to his supreme authority, had not left him sufficient leisure, despite his formidable capacity for work, to begin putting into effect the ecclesiastical reforms that he had favored from the beginning of his pontificate. But he was working at it, and they would come to fruition five years later at the famous Lateran Council, which would witness the confirmation of the Franciscan order.

The Cardinal of Sabine, therefore, accompanied our thirteen mendicants to their audience with the Vicar of Christ. Francis, with great simplicity, presented the text of his rule and commented on it at length, which gladdened the Pope. The latter did not hesitate to express his approval for such a supernatural view of religious life, although he did not yet commit himself. But several cardinals in his entourage began to exhibit their disagreement. "This is a novelty", they protested, "as yet unheard of in the Church; what's more, it is an enterprise that exceeds human strength."

Giovanni di San Paolo leaped into the fray. "Completely on fire with the Spirit of God", as Bonaventure says, he exclaimed: "If we reject as a novelty or recklessness the plan of this poor man, which is to live in conformity with the Gospel, we risk doing harm to the Gospel of Christ. For to maintain that practicing evangelical perfection is a novelty, or madness, or recklessness, is to blaspheme against Christ, who is the author of the Gospel."

Certainly, in principle the cardinal was right, but he was mistaken as to the facts. For at the beginning of the thirteenth century there were many inspired men who were spontaneously practicing poverty and preaching the Gospel. But almost all of them, not content to call attention to themselves by unfortunate extravagances, larded their discourses with astounding heresies and refused to bow to the remonstrations of the Church. These movements had started during the twelfth century and had spread through all of western Europe. A monk who had fled his monastery in Brabant [in the Netherlands], Tanchelm or Tanquelin, passed himself off as a bishop consecrated by the Pope. He pretended to possess the fullness of the Holy Spirit, called himself "the Betrothed of the Virgin" and "the Son of God". He denied the

Church's hierarchy and the validity of the sacraments. He had acquired a certain popularity in the Rhineland. Eventually he was arrested and imprisoned by order of the Archbishop of Cologne. After escaping, thanks to the complicity of his disciples, he arrived in Bruges, where he was killed by a cleric whose way of life he had censured.

In Languedoc, a certain Pierre de Bruys went from town to village proclaiming the good news, denying the need for churches and images, infant baptism, and the Real Presence of Christ in the Eucharist. Soon he was at the head of a large sect. He died on Good Friday: on that day he lit a bonfire made of crucifixes and was roasting meat over it; the horrified crowd threw him into the furnace. Soon afterward a defrocked Cistercian monk, Henry of Lausanne, was raging through the same region, preaching against the clergy and secretly giving himself over to debauchery. Arrested on the order of the Archbishop of Arles, he recanted his errors and was set free again; he took advantage of his liberty to recommence his delirious sermons and was seized in Toulouse, where he died in the episcopal prison.

Amaury de Bène, a professor of theology at the University of Paris, was teaching that the time had come for God to be living within us, and therefore we were incapable of sinning and had no more need of sacraments or mortification. Deprived of his professorial chair, he went to visit Innocent III (two years before Saint Francis did), to justify himself, but the Pope demanded that he retract his errors.

In Flanders and in the Rhine Valley there were informal groups living together that called themselves brothers and sisters of the free Spirit, who rejected all hierarchy, all worship, and all moral law, and indulged their passions at will.

Closer to Assisi the Waldensians had spread, so called after their founder, Peter Waldo, a citizen of Lyons; after selling all his belongings, in keeping with the evangelical counsel, and giving the proceeds to the poor, he had recruited disciples and sent them two by two to preach the Kingdom of God. So he was a precursor of Saint Francis. But most of his preachers, ignorant of theology, devised strange commentaries on Sacred Scripture. To the point where, in 1179, the Archbishop of Lyons forbade them to preach, but they paid him no heed. Expelled from Lyons, they spread through northern Italy, where they were known as the Poor Men of Lombardy.

Finally, at the beginning of the thirteenth century, the sect of the

Cathari ["the Pure"] started to inundate Languedoc; to their way of thinking, only spirits (God and the human soul) were good, whereas matter was evil—hence their condemnation of property, of eating meat, and of marriage.

Innocent III was well aware of all these movements in which non-commissioned laymen were spreading errors and setting themselves up against the hierarchical Church. He also understood why the cardinals in his entourage would mistrust this handful of mendicants, most of whom scarcely knew the *Pater Noster*. Yet he felt himself drawn irresistibly by a strong confidence in the mission of Francis of Assisi. Nevertheless, hesitating between the two views expressed by his counselors, he preferred to remain reticent.

"My dear sons," he said to the suppliants, "your way of life seems to me very hard and very troublesome. I am quite certain that you have great fervor, and I do not doubt your sincerity. But will your successors have the same spiritual fortitude? I fear that your ways might appear too austere for them."

Francis' heart was pierced with pangs of sorrow. Despite his ringing defense, the Pope was still being circumspect and was not consenting to give his approval. He hazarded a final attempt, in which he put all his faith and love of Christ, and protested that neither he nor his brothers had the intention of abandoning this rule of life. The Pope, wishing to prove his magnanimity, blessed the little paupers in these words, "May the Lord be with you, my brothers. Pray that he will manifest his will. Once he has deigned to instruct us about it, then with joy I will accede to your request." Nothing was lost. And since the Pope commanded them to pray to know the will of heaven, the thirteen men, confident of a celestial response, immersed themselves in prayer. And behold, while Francis was praying with all his soul, Christ spoke to him: "Francis, here is what you are to say to the Pope. There was once, in the desert, a very poor but very beautiful woman. Captivated by her beauty, a king wanted to marry her, hoping that she would give him handsome children. The marriage took place, and from that union were born many sons. When they were grown and well educated, the mother said to them, 'My dear children, be not ashamed of your poverty, because you are all the sons of a great king. Go, then, to the court and ask him for what you need.' When they arrived in court, they presented themselves confidently to the king, whose features they reproduced. And the king, recognizing in them his own image, asked them, filled with astonishment, whose sons they were. They then stated that they were the sons of a poor woman who lived in the desert. The king, filled with gladness, embraced them, saying, 'You are my sons and heirs; fear not. I feed strangers at my table; all the more reason that I will take care of you, who are my own children.' At once the king sent a message to that woman, telling her to send to his court all the sons that she had had by him, so as to provide for their needs.''

When Christ had finished speaking, Francis was radiant with joy. ''Yes, I understand,'' he said. ''It is I, that poor woman.''

Immediately he asked for another audience with Innocent III. Was not this parable Christ's response to his questions? The Pope had him brought into his presence once again, and Francis related to him the words of Christ. He concluded with this commentary: ''Most Holy Father, I am that poor woman whom the Lord, in his love and mercy, made beautiful and by whom he wished to have children. The King of Kings promised me that he would feed all the children that he would give me; for if he treats strangers so well, he must treat his own children even better. If God gives temporal favors to pilgrims, how much more will he grant them to evangelical men who are really worthy of them.''

The Pope marveled at the parable and admitted that it was Christ speaking through this man. But, even though he felt profoundly well-disposed toward this handful of Christian disciples, he sent him away only with an assurance of his protection and encouragement to follow the path that he had chosen.

Francis did not despair: since Christ had given him this assurance, he would not fail to influence the Holy Father, in one way or another. Since he had a roof over his head, thanks to the generosity of the Cardinal of Sabine, he could stay for a few more days and continue waiting. During the following night, he had another premonition in a dream. He was walking on a road, alongside of which he suddenly spied a marvelous tree with a mighty trunk, an immense height, and abundant branches and foliage. And while he was admiring this giant, he felt that he himself was growing, until he reached the same height: he had become a tree, a tree of a prodigious height with many branches.

During this time Innocent III, too, was having a dream. A frightening dream. The Lateran Basilica, the cathedral of Rome and the mother of all the churches in Christendom, was shaking on its foundations. And suddenly it tilted as though it was about to collapse. But a little man, puny and emaciated, ran up and, putting his shoulder to the building, kept it from falling. Then the Pope recognized the little man who was preventing the fall of the Church: it was Francis of Assisi.

This time Christ's intervention was all too evident; he was urging his Vicar to acknowledge the divine mission of Francis. Was the Poverello still in Rome? The Pope summoned him and received him once more at his feet. The humble friar, who was expecting this course of events, brought along with him his sole treasure: his rule. The Pontiff approved it unreservedly and furthermore granted to the bearer of it the right to preach penance everywhere, declaring that he had permission to send out his brothers to preach, at his own discretion.

The Pope did not stop there. So as to deal with the matter within the parameters of the Church, he gathered the cardinals in a consistory and obtained from them the favors that he had just granted to the humble community, which by that very fact became a religious institute. And he entrusted the fulfillment of these plans to the Cardinal of Sabine, who had made himself the protector and advocate of the community. He gathered the friars for a solemn ceremony, during which Francis, on his knees, promised to obey and honor the Supreme Pontiff, and each of the friars promised to obey and honor Francis, who thus became the official superior of the new institute. And since they had a mission to preach, the cardinal had them all tonsured; thus they became clerics and were solely dependent upon ecclesiastical jurisdiction. Their fondest desire had been granted.

The new religious, free now of all care, set out on a pilgrimage to the great Roman basilicas, lingering with fervor at the tombs of the apostles, and ready at last, with the blessing of the Church, to go throughout the world preaching the Gospel.

This series of scenes from the life of Saint Francis, which marked a decisive turning point in it and constituted the founding of the Order of Friars Minor, has served as an inspiration to painters, especially the dream of Innocent III. Starting, obviously, with Giotto. The sixth fresco of the upper church in Assisi depicts the Pope lying down, completely clothed, with the tiara on his head, on an ostentatious bed, while in the other half of the picture the little poor man is supporting on his shoulder, with no apparent effort, and without even bending under the weight of the building, the glorious Lateran Basilica, which is not crumbling, like San Damiano of yore, but is just leaning, a little like the Tower of Pisa. The seventh fresco presents the very solemn image of Pope Innocent III approving the rule, which is being held out by the friars kneeling at his feet. The same scenes appear in the Church of San Francesco di Montefalco, but executed with more feeling by Benozzo Gozzoli. In the picture of Innocent's dream, Francis, who is facing the building and supporting it with his two shriveled hands, expends a heroic effort; in the scene of the approval of the rule, he stares intently at the Pope, his anxious face illuminated by his bright eyes.

3. A Flourishing Community of Friars

The new religious departed from Rome, transfigured with joy, and set out again on the road back to their country. Autumn, in the region of Latium, is usually a late summer; the heat there is often unbearable, and there is danger of malaria. Besides, they had no more need of the dignitaries of the Roman Curia: they were recognized members of a religious order, subject to an officially approved rule, crowned with the clerical halo—the tonsure—and endowed with the right to preach. What else could they possibly want from now on, these men who did not desire earthly things? One might ask, nevertheless, what sort of opinion was formed by the people who lived along the way traveled by these starving clerics clothed in rags, who marched to the chanting of Latin psalms or to the tune of cheerful songs in the vernacular.

They went out by the Porta Salaria, to the north of the city, so as to follow the Tiber valley. A simple itinerary: they had only to travel upstream beside the river, which has its source north of Assisi, between Perugia and Gubbio. Did they preach along the way? It seems that they did not. Celano relates only that they stopped "in a place near Orta", around fifty kilometers distant from Rome. Was it the countryside that they liked? The coolness of the shade after their long journey under the sun's rays? They settled down there as though in a favorite vacation spot. We must assume that their tonsures reassured the inhabitants of Orta, since, in order to feed his friars, Francis had only to send a few of them into town, and they would come back with their arms full of food.

This carefree life lasted for two weeks. But suddenly, as it sometimes happens, the superior of the band deemed that this stopover was not part of their plan. So they struck camp and made their way to the valley of Spoleto, perhaps so as to shorten their route somewhat. This forced them to veer off for a moment toward the east, probably

via Narni and Acquasparta. Soon they found themselves in the woods
of Rivo Torto, which no one had yet dreamed of inhabiting.

Their return caused a sensation. The citizens of Assisi had probably concluded, from this long absence, that that handful of miserable wretches had chosen to reside elsewhere, and no doubt many of
them were happy about it. But suddenly they reappeared, and the news
spread through town, soon to be confirmed by the bishop: Francis
had seen the Pope, Francis had received his blessing, Francis was now
the superior of a genuine religious order, and his brothers sported the
clerical tonsure. Their reputation was made; the clergy tempered their
disdain; the burghers felt obliged to show them a certain reverence.

There was nothing different, though, about the life of these vagabonds of God. They ate, they slept, they prayed outdoors, heedless of
inclement weather. They had chosen this place, however, Celano explains, because there was a large shed there that may or may not have
had an owner and that served to shelter them from storms. From that
moment on recruits came streaming in, and the friars could scarcely
house them all, but no one complained about the inconvenience. The
day came, however, when the shed which, in Francis' words, was a
better dwelling for their band than a palace, was snatched away from
them. Almost all of them were gathered under that roof, probably
because of bad weather, when a peasant arrived with his donkey and,
intending to cause trouble, pushed it into the midst of the friars,
shouting: "Move it! Go on! Get in there! It will do that shanty some
good!"

The occupants had to jostle each other to make room for the beast
and its master. What was Francis going to say? Would he ask the
troublemaker to let them pray in peace? They knew his talent for
persuasion. But Francis insisted on avoiding any sort of argument. It
was to his companions that he spoke, "My brothers, God did not
choose you to give hospitality to a donkey, or to have dealings with
the world, but rather to preach the way of salvation, to give salutary
advice to souls, and above all so that we might devote ourselves to
prayer and thanksgiving."

And so they all left the shed, to the great satisfaction of the peasant,
and they returned to the Portiuncula, which was not far away, since
there was an abandoned tumbledown cottage there, too. But this time
Francis wanted to occupy the place legitimately and to find a much

larger dwelling in which to house his growing order. He therefore turned to his community to obtain their approval: "My dear brothers and dear children, I know that the Lord wants to increase our number. And so it seems to me fitting and pious that we should ask our bishop, the canons of San Rufino, and the abbot of the Benedictine monastery for a poor little church where the friars can chant the office, and, nearby, a poor little house made of mud and branches, where the friars would take their rest. The place where we are living now is not suitable, and the house is becoming too small, since it has pleased the Lord to increase our number."

They all approved. And Francis' first step was to pay a visit to the bishop; out of respect, of course, for the bishop of the diocese, but also because in him he had a protector. But His Excellency was quite at a loss: he did not have the smallest piece of ground, the tiniest chapel or the meanest hut to give to his protégés. Francis went therefore to speak to the dean of the cathedral chapter; typically, the chapters owned lands and a certain number of churches from which they derived their income. But the dean apologized: he did not have the least bit of land or the smallest oratory to grant to these new religious.

Francis was not unaware that the land on which Santa Maria degli Angeli was built belonged to the Benedictine Abbey of Monte Subasio, which loomed over Assisi, two leagues to the east. Perhaps, God willing, the abbot might have some solitary place to offer generously to the importunate beggar? He went to visit him. The abbot, who had a little more charity than the one in Vallingegno, where Francis had worked as a dishwasher, was moved with pity, according to the *Legenda antiqua*. He immediately convened his council, and with their approval, made a gift of the Portiuncula itself to Francis and his order. Not only did the community of mendicants not have to move, but it was already at home there. The understanding abbot said to his visitor:

"My brother, we have granted your request. But we insist that, if the Lord increases your order, this convent should be your mother house."

Thus Saint Benedict became the foster father of the Franciscan order. Francis was astounded by this grace, which no doubt he was not expecting. Two important things seemed to him providential: the chapel was poor, and it was dedicated to the Mother of Christ.

There was one difficulty, however, for this lover of poverty: the abbot had made a gift of this church and the land surrounding it "without restriction, without payment, and without yearly rent". Francis insisted on not being the owner, but of playing the part of a tenant. Every year from then on he sent to the monks a basket of fish.

"We who have lived with Blessed Francis", say the authors of the *Legenda*, who were the three companions, Angelo, Leo, and Rufino, "testify that he said: 'Among all the churches of the world that the Blessed Virgin loves, she has the most love for this one.' That is why, throughout his life, he had a great reverence for this place and a great devotion to it."

When the number of the friars had increased, the inhabitants of Assisi (who now held them in esteem) decided to build for them a convent capable of housing them all. The communal council adopted a resolution to this effect and, dispensing with the authorization of Francis, who at that moment was traveling and preaching, they performed the work so quickly that when he arrived he found the little house standing. He was highly indignant when he learned that this new bourgeois residence was intended for his community. At once he summoned several of his brothers, who climbed onto the roof with him and began to throw down the tiles. Now several members of the communal council were there. They called to the demolition expert and pointed out to him that this house belonged to the commune of Assisi, and that he was obliged to respect their property. It was a weak argument, since the little house stood on the land granted by the Benedictine abbey and occupied by the friars. But Francis bowed to it, since he held the plot as a loan and not as a possession. And since the structure had been built with the money and sweat of the townsfolk of Assisi, he had no alternative but to respect what belonged to others. So he came down from the roof, protesting that he considered the house to be the property of the commune, and that he would refrain henceforth from putting a hand to it.

The inhabitants of Assisi cited the multiplication of Francis' disciples as their reason for building a convent made of stone. Indeed, every day since they returned to the Portiuncula, one or two postulants appeared, and they were usually recruits after Francis' heart, who had been amazed by the spectacle of the life led by the first friars, or captivated by the preaching of the superior. Most times the recruits were as pious and unusual as the original companions.

Furthermore, the latter continued to bring glory to the new order, and there is no end to the anecdotes that the early biographers tell about them. Bernard of Quintavalle was still the older brother of them all, a beloved son of the founder. He distinguished himself by his gift of prayer. The *Fioretti* relate that "he very often experienced divine raptures through his contemplation of heavenly things." One day, during Mass, he was so absorbed in God that he took leave of his senses. When the time came for the elevation of the Blessed Sacrament, he remained standing instead of prostrating himself like the others who were in attendance and failed to lower his cowl as they did. When the other Mass-goers left, he remained immobile and unconscious. At the dinner hour, as the friars said grace over their meager rations, Bernard was still deep in rapture. Finally, at three o'clock in the afternoon, as his brothers were gathering to recite the office of None, he came out of it. Beside himself, he walked by the rows of his companions, exclaiming, "Oh, brothers, brothers, brothers! There is no man in this land, however great and noble he may be, who would not willingly carry a sack of dung if someone promised him that it would earn him a palace full of gold."

After this wondrous vision, Bernard remained in a constant state of spiritual exaltation. For fifteen years he could be seen praying, with his face radiant and his eyes lifted up to heaven. At the same time, he acquired such an understanding of heavenly things that even the learned theologians came to him for an explanation of obscure passages from Scripture. Because of these marvelous graces, Francis liked to converse with his eldest son; and sometimes, during the night, while the others were sleeping, one could hear the whispering of their celestial dialogue.

Another amazing friar was Brother Giles. He was always on the road, traveling to ever more distant destinations, to Rome, Bari, Compostela, Jerusalem. Was it at Francis' orders, or did he have broad discretion in this regard? On the way to Compostela he met a poor man (he must have met more than one, but because of his wretched appearance few were inclined to look to him for charity) who held out his hand for an alms. But Giles had nothing but his habit. Now this habit was topped with a cowl; he ripped out the seam that attached the cowl, gave it to the poor man, and thus went about for the next twenty days with his head uncovered. On another occasion he planned to set out for the Holy Land and went as far as Brindisi, but then he had to obtain funds so as to pay for the voyage. He found a jug, then a spring, filled the jug at the source and then went selling water: enough for him to board a ship. In order to get a place on a boat for the return trip, he settled down for a time in Acre [Akko, north of Mount Carmel] as a basket-weaver.

One day a rather feeble landowner asked him to shake his nut trees so as to make the nuts fall. As payment, he could take half of the harvest. Now Giles was a big, muscular fellow. He shook so hard that he earned more than a bushel. How could he carry so much? He undressed, put the nuts in his habit, and, bare-chested, wearing nothing but breeches, returned to the conventual house with his precious load.

During a severe winter, Giles heard that the Pope and his Curia were staying in Rieti. He wanted to go pay him homage and joined up with a companion to make the journey, which was more in keeping with the custom then than traveling alone. Both friars were the guests of Cardinal Chiaramonte, who was extremely attentive to the penitents from Assisi, because of their virtue and the papal protection that they enjoyed. When the cardinal invited them to dine, they protested: it was Lent, and they were content to gather the scraps that kindly people left to them out of pity. The cardinal was alarmed and pointed out to the good friars that the temperature was rather inclement, and that they were in danger not only of failing to find benefactors, but also of freezing to death. The mendicants paid no heed to this warning and went off into the icy north wind. As they made their way, they came upon a chapel dedicated to Saint Lawrence. This was a stroke of good luck for the devout friars. They went in and immersed themselves in prayer; so absorbed were they that they did not notice that a heavy snowstorm let loose outdoors. When they tried to go out again, the door of the chapel was blocked by the snow.

"What is to become of us?" the companion asked, anxiously.

"Is that all that you're worried about?" Giles replied. "It is enough for us to call on our Lord, and he will see to it that we are rescued."

No doubt the eventual rescuer was not inclined to venture out of his house, because the two religious remained shut up in that icy prison for three days and three nights. But they prayed, despite the cold, their hunger, and weakness. They prayed, and Giles calmly reassured his companion, declaring to him that God would no longer delay in rescuing them. At last a man who was passing by, seeing the chapel standing not far off, snowed in, said to himself, as though by a heavenly inspiration, "Maybe there is someone inside that house of God who went in to pray and now can't get out."

He went up to the door, swept the snow away, and managed to enter. He found the two poor religious brothers, who seemed more dead than alive, and since he was transporting foodstuffs, he gave them food and drink.

Giles lived to a ripe old age, surviving his master by thirty-five years. During the final years of his life he often met with Saint Bonaventure, who was the general of the Franciscan order at that time. One day the old sage posed a question to the great doctor, "Father, God has showered you with all sorts of graces. But we, poor ignorant men, how can we attain salvation?"

Was the question simple or mischievous? The theologian answered in the way that the humble friar no doubt expected, "Even if God gave men only his love, that would be enough."

"What?! An ignorant man could love God as much as the most learned doctor?"

"Certainly, and even an old woman can love God as much, and even more, than a master of theology."

At once Giles ran off, exclaiming to the passersby: "Come, you simple, unlettered men; come, you poor, weak and ignorant women! Come and love Our Lord. Because you can love him as much as Friar Bonaventure can, and even more."

This simpleton, too, was a great contemplative. During his latter years he went into ecstasy several times a day, and these raptures continued for hours. One night Christ himself appeared to him in sensible form; this vision gladdened his heart so much that he could scarcely endure it; he felt his entire body failing, to the point that it seemed that he was going to depart for the next world. His neighbor noticed what was happening and became frightened; he cried out, "Brother

Giles is dying!" But the elderly friar, returning to his senses, reassured him that it was only a visit from God, and that he was not yet leaving this world.

The thought of heaven, in particular, sent Giles into ecstasy. The boys who played in the street knew this; if they saw him walking by, they would call out, "Paradiso!" Immediately the funny, mystical friar was plunged into a state of bliss. For the rascals it may have been a game, but it was also a wonderful lesson.

Rufino, who was also from Assisi, was a nobleman. He belonged to Offreduccios, a senatorial family, and may have been a relative, or else an ally, of Bernard; at any rate he was a first cousin of Saint Clare. He had rejoined the band of the first disciples upon his return from Rome and fit in well with them, as though in his natural element. He had become enamored of prayer and loved to go off alone for long periods of time. He reproached Francis for devising an overly busy life for the friars, and he sometimes considered running away so as to be in solitude.

This excessively spiritual poor man infuriated the devil by his candor and his devotion to prayer. The devil resolved to ruin him. He started by tormenting him with the idea of predestination and suggesting to him that he was damned. As a result, the unfortunate friar, hitherto so joyful, sank into a gloomy sadness. Nevertheless, by sheer acts of will, he continued his life of prayer and asceticism. That was not exactly what the evil spirit wanted. So he decided to try exterior temptations, instead—a subterfuge that demons usually employ only to conquer the most recalcitrant saints. Therefore he appeared to Rufino in the form of the Crucified Savior and said to him: "Brother Rufino, why are you tormenting yourself by penance and prayer, since you are not in that number of men who are predestined to eternal life? Believe me: I know whom I have elected and predestined. Above all, do not believe the son of Pietro di Bernardone if he tells you otherwise. Do not even ask him about this subject, because neither he nor any other man knows anything about it. Besides, Pietro's son, like his father, is among the damned. And anyone who follows him is his dupe."

From then on, Rufino's distress began to engulf him. He lost his great confidence in Francis and avoided speaking with him. Well, what Rufino was unwilling to tell his spiritual father, the Holy Spirit told him. And, not wishing to frighten the unfortunate man by broaching the subject himself, he sent Masseo, who encouraged him to speak to their master.

Rufino shrugged. "What business have I with Brother Francis?"

"O, Brother Rufino, don't you know that Brother Francis is like an angel of God? He has enlightened so many souls in the world, and through him we have received God's grace. And so, I absolutely insist that you go to see him, for I know that you have been deceived by the devil."

In order to comply with his companion, whom he respected, Rufino went off grumbling to find Francis, who called to him from afar, "Rufino, you wicked little brother, in whom have you placed your faith?"

And once his troubled companion was at his side again, he told him all about the suggestions, wiles, and sayings of the devil.

And [Francis] concluded, "It was the devil, and not Christ, who appeared to you. And so, the next time that he comes to tell you, 'You are damned', answer him, 'Open your mouth, so that I can poop in it.' And then you'll have proof that he is the devil, because he will take flight immediately."

He went on to draw a lesson. "Don't you know how to recognize the devil? He hardens the heart and draws it away from everything that is good. That is his job. But our blessed Savior never hardens the heart of a faithful man; he fills it with sweetness."

Then Rufino, having been instructed and consoled, threw himself upon the ground at the feet of Francis and wept copiously.

Hadn't the devil heard Francis' admonition? He resumed his attack while Rufino was behind the shrubbery that surrounded the hermitage of the Carceri family, pouring out his prayers and tears. This time the little friar did not allow himself to be intimidated, and hurled at the imposter's face the message that his master had taught him.

"All at once", the *Fioretti* relate, "the indignant demon left in such a storm that it shook the stones of Monte Subasio; for a long time the stones continued to fall, crashing so hard against each other that they sent terrible sparks of fire flying into the valley. Then Brother Rufino understood clearly that this was the work of the devil, who had deceived him. And returning to Saint Francis' side, he once more threw himself down at his feet."

As a result of fresh graces, Rufino, delivered from all sadness and melancholy, devoted himself from then on to contemplation; so lost in God was he that he became, as it were, speechless and unperceiving. Besides, he had no skill at speaking and was afraid to preach.

One day Francis ordered him, "Go to Assisi and preach to the people whatever God inspires you to say."

"My Father," the humble friar objected, "I beg you not to send me there, because, as you know, I do not have the grace of preaching."

Francis turned deathly pale: this was a religious, who had made a profession of obedience to his superior; how dared he refuse to carry out such an explicit command? He gave him another order, "Since you did not obey promptly, I order you, in the name of holy obedience, to go to Assisi naked, wearing only your breeches, to enter a church and to preach to the people in that state of undress."

Rufino did what he was told: with no other clothing than a pair of drawers, he went into a church where he saw a crowd gathering; he ascended the pulpit, and began to speak to the people. Obviously, he heard some laughter. Some were saying, "Those fellows fast so much that they lose their minds!"

Meanwhile, Francis had misgivings as soon as his indignation had passed: Wasn't the penance that he had given to that good friar somewhat excessive? Shouldn't a superior moderate the burdens that he requires others to carry?

"Well, then," he said to himself, "you will experience for yourself what you have imposed upon others."

There and then he took off his habit, which he draped over the arm of Brother Leo, and went into town himself, greeted along the way with jokes and snickers. When he arrived at the church where Rufino was preaching, he went in and heard an eloquent sermon: "O, my dearly beloved brethren, flee the world, renounce sin, give back the property of others which you are keeping unjustly."

But the people were giving his words a cool reception. Then Francis climbed the steps of the pulpit and began a ringing sermon: on voluntary poverty, on longing for the heavenly Kingdom, but especially on the nakedness of Jesus Christ, who had been the object of so many mockeries along his way of the cross. At that, those in attendance began sobbing, and all went home with a great devotion to the Savior's Passion in their hearts.

Masseo (a variant of the name Matteo, Matthew), whom we have seen advising Rufino in a time of trial, was from Marignano—not the Marignano that figured in the victory of François I over the Swiss, which is near Milan, but rather a village [now known as Meleg-nano] not far from Assisi. He was quite different from his master Francis: tall, broad-shouldered, handsome, charming, endowed with a sonorous voice and a captivating eloquence—qualities that were very useful during their mendicant hours. When he went as Francis' part-ner begging alms, they gathered unequal shares: whereas the little friar whom nature had not favored received a few crusts of stale bread, the big, strapping, majestic friar always had his arms full of food.

Nevertheless, apart from those moments when the people saw the friars only superficially, Francis was the one who, by a special grace, attracted the downtrodden and the sinners, a fact that continually as-tonished Masseo. It was not that he was jealous of his spiritual father, but this preference seemed somewhat strange to him.

One day, as Francis was walking toward him, he could no longer keep silence, and exclaimed, "Why you? Why you? Why you?"

Francis, intrigued, stared at him, "What do you mean?"

"Why does everyone run after you? Why do so many people want to see you, hear you, and obey you? After all, physically speaking, one really can't say that you are a handsome man."

Francis was not amused by this unsubtle answer. He paused for a moment first, with his eyes uplifted toward heaven, then knelt down in an intense meditation. Finally he got up and said: "Do you want to know: Why me? Why me? Why me? Well, then, listen: it is because the eyes of God, which watch over the good and the wicked, saw no one among the sinners who was more vile, more inadequate, and more sinful than I. And since he found on earth no creature more worthless than I to undertake the wonderful work that he wanted to accomplish, he chose me to confound the nobility, the grandeur, the beauty, the strength, and the knowledge of this world, so that every-one might know that all virtue and all good come from him and not from his creature, and that no one can boast in his presence."

Francis liked to team up with Masseo for his preaching tours. Masseo was, indeed, not only a stately man who impressed the crowds, but also a practical man who knew how to take advantage of any sit-uation. Whenever Francis withdrew to a corner to devote himself to prayer, Masseo, although he too was very spiritual, always refrained from imitating him; instead he played the watchdog and kept the crowd from coming near the man of God and disturbing his prayer.

One day, while the two men were traveling together in Tuscany, they arrived at a crossing of roads (perhaps at Poggibonsi) that led to Florence, Siena, and Arezzo. Masseo, who was walking in the lead, stopped, perplexed. "What road should we take now?"

"The one that God wills."

"But how can we know God's will?"

"In the name of holy obedience, I order you to spin around until I tell you to stop."

Obediently, the big fellow started to turn around and around. Masseo, becoming dizzy, stumbled and fell. He got up, spun around, and fell again. But Francis did not say a word. Staggering, Masseo continued rotating mindlessly. Finally his master exclaimed, "Enough! Stop moving."

Then, making sure that his disciple was immobile, he asked, "Toward what direction are you looking?"

"Toward Siena."

"Well, then, that is the road that God is pointing out to us."

Brother Leo, a native of Assisi, was the closest to Francis, serving simultaneously as his confessor, his secretary, and his confidant. Because of his simplicity and purity, Francis used to call him "God's little lamb": *pecorella di Dio*. He was one of the three friars chosen by Francis to accompany him to Mount La Verna, where they were witnesses to his stigmatization. Then, during the founder's final years, Leo remained his constant companion; and since he was literate, it was not difficult for him to record his memories in many written works. And so he is the inspiration, direct or indirect, of the biographies composed by Thomas of Celano, and also of *The Legend of the Three Companions*, the *Actus beati Francisci* by Anonymous of Perugia, *The Mirror of Perfection*, the *Fioretti*, and the compiler of *The Life of Blessed Giles*.

The most famous of the conversations between Francis and Leo is the one about perfect joy. It takes place along the road to Perugia, in the dead of winter. The two preachers are very cold. Francis begins relating his parable to Leo, who is marching two paces ahead of him, "Brother Leo! Even if the Friars Minor gave the finest example of sanctity and edifying behavior everywhere, write down and note carefully that that is not perfect joy."

The two walked on for a moment in silence, and Francis spoke again, "Brother Leo! Even if a Friar Minor restored sight to the blind, made the crooked straight, expelled demons, made the deaf hear, the lame walk, and the mute speak—and an even greater miracle, raised those who had been dead for four days—write down that that is not perfect joy."

Silence again. Then Francis said in a louder voice, "Brother Leo! Even if a Friar Minor knew all languages and all sciences and all the Scriptures, so as to prophesy and reveal not only future events, but also the secrets of consciences and of hearts, write down that that would not be perfect joy."

Another interval of silent walking. Then Francis spoke, "Brother Leo, little lamb of God! Even if a Friar Minor spoke in the tongue of the angels, knew the course of the stars and the properties of the herbs; even if all the treasures of the earth were revealed to him, even if he knew the virtues of the birds and the fish, of all the animals and of men, trees, and rocks, of the roots and the waters, write down that that is not perfect joy."

Again they proceeded down the road in silence. And Francis spoke yet again, "Brother Leo! Even if the Friar Minor knew how to preach so well that he converted all the infidels to the Christian faith, write down that that is not perfect joy."

The fragmentary monologue of Francis had gone on for a league already, without his having conveyed his thought. Finally, Leo, wanting to know more about it, turned around and said, "Father, I beg you, in the name of God, please tell me where perfect joy is to be found."

Then Francis, who perhaps was only waiting for this intervention, explained himself at last: "When we arrive at Santa Maria degli Angeli, drenched as we are by the rain and chilled by the cold, spattered with mud, tormented with hunger, if we knock at the door of the friary, and the porter comes to ask us angrily, 'Who are you?' and we answer, 'We are two of your brothers', and he replies, 'That's not true. You are two scoundrels who go about deceiving the world and stealing alms from the poor. Off with you!'; and if he does not open the door for us and makes us stay outside in the snow and the rain, cold and hungry, until midnight; and if we endure so many insults, cruelties, and rebuffs without being disturbed and without murmuring; and if we think, in humility and charity, that this porter truly knows us and that God is the one who made him speak against us, then, O Brother Leo, write down that that is where perfect joy is found. And if we continue to knock, and he comes out furious and chases us away like importunate good-for-nothings, with insults and blows, crying, 'Away from here, you villains, go to the inn, for you will find no food or lodgings here'; if we endure all that patiently and gladly, in a true spirit of charity, then, O Brother Leo, write down that that is perfect joy. And if the hunger, the cold, and the darkness force us to knock yet again, to call and groan and beg him, for the love of God, to open the door for us, and he says, in an even greater fury, 'Well, these certainly are importunate good-for-nothings! I will give them what they deserve'; and he comes after us with a knotty cudgel, grabs us by the cowl, throws us to the ground, rolls us in the snow, and strikes us with all the knots on his cudgel; and if we endure all that patiently and happily, thinking of the sufferings of our Blessed Savior and that we should put up with it for love of him, O Brother Leo, write that that is perfect joy.

Finally, listen to the conclusion, Brother Leo. Over and above all the graces and gifts of the Holy Spirit that Christ grants to his friends, there is the gift of conquering self, of enduring sufferings, insults, opprobrium, and inconveniences for the love of Christ; for we cannot boast about all the other gifts of God, since they do not come from us, but from God. But we can boast in the cross of tribulation and affliction, because that comes from us."

Another dialogue between Francis and Leo is even more moving. The author who records it in the *Fioretti* (who may have heard it from Leo himself), explains that the scene took place at night, in the early days of the Order.

Francis: "My dear brother, so as to use our time to praise God, I will speak, and you will answer me as I instruct you. Above all, beware of changing the words that I shall teach you. I will say, 'O Brother Francis, you committed so much evil and so many sins when you were in the world that you deserve hell.' And you, Leo, will reply: 'Indeed, it is true that you deserve the depths of hell.' "

Leo: "Very gladly, my Father. Let us begin."

Francis: "O Brother Francis, you did so much evil and committed so many sins in the world that you deserve hell."

Leo: "Francis, God will do so much good through you that you will go to paradise."

Francis: "Don't talk like that, Brother Leo! But when I say, 'O Brother Francis, you have committed so many injustices against God that you deserve to be cursed by God', you will reply, 'Truly, you deserve to be numbered among the accursed.' "

Leo: "Yes, Father, gladly."

Then Francis, shedding hot tears and striking his breast, said, "O my Lord, God of heaven and earth, I have committed so many injustices and so many sins that I thoroughly deserve to be cursed by you."

"O Brother Francis, God will make you so holy that you will be especially blessed among the Blessèd."

"Come, now, Brother Leo, why do you not answer me as I instruct you? I order you, in the name of holy obedience, to answer as I tell you. I will say, 'O wicked little Brother Francis, do you think that God will be merciful to you, when you have committed so many sins against the Father of mercies and against the God of all consolation, that you are unworthy to find mercy.' And you, Leo, little Lamb, will answer, 'In no way are you worthy to receive mercy.' "

When Francis had finished his ardent speech against himself, Leo, making an effort to repeat what had been taught him, spoke the words, "God the Father, whose mercy is infinite and greater than your sin, will have great mercy upon you, and in addition will grant you many graces."

This time, Francis was "slightly annoyed" and severely reprimanded his intractable religious, "Why, oh why, do you presume to speak contrary to obedience? Why did you answer so many times the opposite of what I ordered you to say?"

Then Leo answered, humbly and respectfully, "God is my witness: each time, I resolved in my heart to answer as you ordered me. But God made me speak as it pleases him, and not as it pleases me. I cannot speak otherwise, because it is God who speaks by my mouth."

Among the friars from the second group of recruits to arrive there was a Brother John; not Fra John of Cappella, who left the order because he lacked a spirit of obedience, but John the Simple, who was admired and liked by all. Francis made a disciple of him one day while he was going about preaching in the villages of Umbria. He had brought a broom with him that day, because he noticed that many churches, alas, were poorly maintained, soiled with dust and debris. After obtaining permission to enter one such church, in the hamlet of Nottiano, he went to work cleaning up. But Francis' arrival had been noted, and the news spread through the village. A peasant named John, who was tilling the ground at the time, left his oxen and plow and went to meet the preacher. Somewhat ashamed to see that this religious brother, who was renowned for his sanctity, considered it necessary to take upon himself a chore that should have been done by the parishioners, he asked for a broom and completed the task. Then the two men sat down side by side, and John spoke, "Brother, for a long time now I have had a desire to serve God, especially since I heard about you and your friars. But I did not know where to find you. Now that it has pleased God to bring us together, I am ready to obey you."

Francis, discerning the peasant's zeal, gave him the advice that is written in the rule and in the Gospel, "If it really is your intention to live as we do, you must divest yourself of all your belongings and give them to the poor."

The other man immediately returned to his field, unyoked one of the oxen and brought it to Francis. "Brother," he explained, "I have served my father and my whole family for quite a few years. And so I consider this ox as my share of the inheritance. Therefore this is what I will give to the poor."

At the news of this, John's parents and brothers raised a hue and cry. Not only was their son being taken away from them, but the preacher was making off with one of their oxen as well. The father pleaded his advanced age; the mother shed tears. What could be done in a situation like that? Francis found the solution quickly: the poor were these peasants who were losing an ox and their best worker at the same time; therefore the animal ought to be given to them. Celano makes a cruel remark about the incident, "They were much more desolate about losing an ox than their brother. The saint told them: Be at peace; I'm returning the ox and taking the brother."

Henceforth John took Francis as his model. The other friars had told him that the Father did all things well, and that by imitating him one could attain perfection. Therefore, if Francis knelt down to pray, he knelt down; if he raised his eyes to heaven, he raised his eyes to heaven; if he coughed, he also coughed; if he spat, he spat, too. Francis did not take offense—far from it; he marveled at it and called the new friar "holy John". As it happened, he died an early death, and his brethren honored him as one chosen by heaven.

Certainly the most fantastic, the most unexpected of the friars was Juniper (in Latin *Juniperus*, in Italian *Ginepro*); he entered the order in 1210, right after the journey to Rome, and died in 1258, thirty-two years after Saint Francis. He is alluded to in the principal sources, but an anonymous biography of him has been discovered, interpolated into the *Chronicle of the Twenty-four Generals*, a compilation from the fourteenth century. No doubt, if he had been admitted to some religious order two or three centuries later, Juniper would quickly have been dismissed from the novitiate. Yet the author of the short biography states at the very beginning that he was one of the most beloved companions of Saint Francis.

We see this naïve soul making every blunder imaginable or unimaginable, for virtuous or charitable reasons. With a knife he cut off silver rings that were hanging from an altar cloth to give them to a poor woman who was asking for an alms. In order to learn humility, he went walking through Viterbo naked, accepting taunts and stones without flinching. Put in charge of the kitchen, he threw whole chickens, complete with innards and feathers, into a pot along with some vegetables and eggs in their shells, then served the mess to his brothers while congratulating them on the penance that they were doing. But the narrator tells us that even a dog would not have wanted it.

The most famous of Brother Juniper's follies is the one involving the pig's foot. He liked to visit the sick and help them. One day, in the encampment of Santa Maria degli Angeli, he found a plaintive friar lying on his mat, and asked him, "What can I do for you?"

The other replied, "It would console me to eat a pig's foot."

Juniper did not try to find out whether that was a legitimate request, or an effective remedy; since it was to console his brother, he promised to obtain one for him. And he went off into the woods armed with a kitchen knife. Suddenly he came upon a herd of swine that were feeding there. He pounced on one of them and, after a brief struggle, pinned it down and managed to cut off one of its feet. Then he returned to the friary, washed the precious foot, and cooked it with salt and savory herbs. He served it to the sick man, who devoured it avidly, while his benefactor recounted for him in picturesque detail his battle with the beast.

Meanwhile the swineherd, who had been lounging idly some distance away, heard the strident cries of one of his piglets. Curious, he went to the scene and found it lying on its side, with one of its four legs cut short and bleeding. Obviously he guessed that this was the work of one of those hairy vagabonds who lived in the neighborhood, but he was afraid to intervene himself, and so he ran to the farmhouse to tell his master. The latter hurried to the friary, demanded to speak to Francis, and rebuked him caustically, refusing to accept any excuse or offer of reparation; then he left, cursing those miscreants.

Francis, ashamed and distraught, decided to conduct an inquiry. His suspicions led him at once to Juniper, who not only acknowledged his misdeed without hesitation, but congratulated himself on it, arguing that he had performed a praiseworthy act of charity for a sick brother. But his superior didn't see it that way; he ordered him to run after the offended landowner and to present his apologies to him with the utmost humility. Juniper, who had a vague sense of personal property, since he had given up everything, did not understand much of this sudden severity, but since he had professed humility and obedience, he ran off and caught up with the landowner. Listening only to his own heart, instead of prostrating himself on the ground as Francis had ordered him, he put his arms around the man's neck and kissed him, describing his poor sick brother and the joy that he had experienced in gulping down the savory pig's foot, and singing the praises of charity. The landowner, thoroughly mollified, congratulated that good friar, embraced him, and promised to return. Back at the farmhouse, he ordered his servants to take the pig, slaughter it, and roast it. Then, when the animal was well-done and the pleasant aroma was wafting through the house, he had it brought piping hot to Francis and his brothers.

Among so many other possible candidates, it would be unfair not to include Brother Pacificus in our list. In secular life he was called Guglielmo [William] Divini and was born in the Marches of Ancona.

He was a man of the world. He belonged to the nobility and was furthermore a court poet, receiving the nickname "the king of verse" after he was crowned by the German emperor, probably Henry VI. In his later years he would play an important role in extending the order: in 1217 Saint Francis sent him to France, where he founded the first friaries: La Cordelle in Vézelay and Saint-Denis. Saint Bonaventure assures us that he deserved to become the first provincial in France because he was "quite advanced in sanctity".

One day Francis went preaching in the Marches of Ancona and stopped to give a sermon in San Severino. William thought that it would be fitting to go and hear this renowned preacher, just as he considered it fitting that the audience at court should listen to him recite his poetry. But as soon as the saint began to speak, the poet witnessed an unheard-of prodigy. Francis was marked by the sign of the cross formed by two crossed swords; one went from his head to his feet, the other from his right hand to his left hand. God was pointing out to him his new master. As soon as the sermon was over, he went to see Francis and asked to be admitted into his order.

The best-known story concerning this choice recruit is a vision that he had during a preaching tour with his revered master. Taken up to the highest heaven, he saw there several thrones at God's feet. One of them, raised higher than the others, was resplendent and ornamented with precious stones. And he heard God say to him, "This throne belonged to Lucifer. It is reserved for Francis."

At the next Mass that he attended, a voice from on high gave a commentary on his nocturnal vision, "Just as Lucifer, by his pride, was driven from his throne, so too Francis, by his humility, will merit to be raised up to it."

So many anecdotes embellished the idyllic life at the Portiuncula, during this springtime of the order, that the early biographers report them in abundance, often without being able to identify the participants.

What was the name of the young friar from the early days of the order who practiced an immoderate form of asceticism, to the point where his nature rebelled? The author of the *Legenda antiqua* no longer recalls it, but he remembers the story so well that he puts it in the very first chapter of his account. In the middle of the night the friars were awakened by distressing cries of "I'm dying! I'm dying!"

The religious in charge of illumination lit a candle. Francis asked, "Who was shouting?"

"It was I", groaned the little friar.

"And why are you dying?"

"I'm dying of hunger."

The superior could have (some said, "should have") reprimanded him. But he called two of his sons and told them, "Prepare a meal for him."

Only after the famished friar had eaten his fill did he give the expected sermon: "Brothers, each one of you should observe his constitution, so that he can determine what his body needs. And now, all of you shall sit down to breakfast, so that this poor imprudent friar will not have the embarrassment of being the only one who has been fed. But I warn you that I will not do this again, because that would be neither fitting for a religious nor honest."

4. *Vita Nuova*

This community of religious, whose concise rule did not specify any of their daily obligations, lived without being cloistered, immersed in the world. They led a rigorous life of prayer and penance, but they combined poetry with piety and imagination with mortification.

A similar spirit of Christian humor prevailed among the monks of the Egyptian desert, who were scattered through dozens of hermitages and colonies of anchorites. In their lives we read a plethora of anecdotes, which contain marvels surpassing anything that one could find at the Portiuncula. Saint Serapion the Sindonite (d. 356) met a weeping widow who asked him for alms, because her children were dying of hunger. He owned nothing, but he immediately sold himself into slavery and gave the proceeds to the poor woman. Saint Moses the Ethiopian (d. 395) was a converted bandit; one night four famished robbers, perhaps from the band to which he had once belonged, slipped into the monastery; Moses heard them, followed them, overpowered, and bound all four of them; moved by his exhortation, they humbly asked to receive the penitential habit. Saint Macarius of Alexandria, while meditating in his cell, felt a mosquito biting his foot; with a thoughtless gesture he flattened the creature. To punish himself he removed his tunic, made his way into the nearby marsh and remained there for six months, exposed to mosquitoes that were noted for being especially bloodthirsty.

The virtues and the practices of Saint Francis and his companions were more community oriented, and as a result they checked and tempered one another; they complemented each other so as to form a composite example of perfection; so much so that Francis, who had observed this phenomenon, combined the best of them to fashion the ideal friar:

> The true Friar Minor would be a religious who combined within himself
> the merits of the holiest brothers: the faith of Bernard, which is as perfect

as his love of poverty; the simplicity and chastity of Leo, whose purity is very holy; the courtesy of Angelo, the first knight to enter the order; the discernment and common sense of Masseo, as well as his beautiful eloquence; the capacity for contemplation of Giles, who possesses it to perfection; the prayer of Rufino, who prays without ceasing, even while sleeping; the patience of Juniper, who is ever mindful of his own lowliness and has a great and constant desire to imitate the suffering Christ.

At that time there was only one friary, if one can use that term to designate the shed that the community occupied by turns in Rivo Torto and in the Portiuncula. Francis could wield his authority directly over his friars as a group. As Celano relates:

> They strove very diligently to put his teaching into practice. They did not limit themselves to listening to his fraternal counsels and carrying out his paternal orders; their zeal also prompted them to anticipate his thoughts and desires whenever the slightest indication had enabled them to discern them. The friars were so full of holy simplicity, the innocence of their life had formed them so well, they had such purity of heart that they were completely devoid of duplicity. Sharing the same faith, they had the same mind, the same will, the same charity, the same union of hearts, and were in fact one by the harmony of their ways, their practice of the virtues, the conformity of their aspirations, and the unity of their actions.

In keeping with this spirit, the principal virtue of the friars was charity. To cite an eyewitness account, once again we turn to *The Three Companions*: "They loved one another with a deep affection. They served and fed each other as a mother feeds her dearly beloved and only son. When they met again [after a mission], they experienced so much joy that they seemed no longer to remember what they had suffered on account of the wicked."

We would be remiss if we did not reprint here also an eloquent passage by Celano on the unity that prevailed among the friars and on the comments that their father made about it:

> His constant desire and vigilant concern was always to preserve among his sons the bond of unity, so that those who had been drawn by the same spirit and begotten by the same father might be raised in peace in the bosom of the same mother. He wanted the older children and the younger children to be united among themselves, and a fraternal

affection to draw together the learned and the simple, and the bond of love to reunite those whom distance had separated.

In support of this statement, the biographer relates for us a parable that Francis proposed to his brothers:

It so happened that all the religious were assembled in the general chapter. Since they included some who were lettered and some who were illiterate, some who were learned and some who were ignorant yet knew how to please God, they asked for a sermon to be given by one of the learned and one of the simple friars. The learned friar reflected, for he was wise, and said to himself, "This is not the time to parade my knowledge, because there are accomplished scholars present, nor to develop subtle arguments for their subtle minds so as to distinguish myself by my intellectual display. No doubt it will be more advantageous for me to speak simply." On the appointed day, all the holy religious gathered, eager to hear the sermon. The learned friar arrived, clothed in sackcloth, his head covered with ashes, and to the amazement of all, he preached in particular by his comportment, pronouncing these brief words: "We have received great promises, and even greater ones have been made to us; let us keep the first and yearn for the others. Pleasure is brief, punishment eternal; suffering is insignificant, glory is infinite. Many are called, few are chosen, all shall receive their reward."

The hearts of the listeners were moved with compunction; they all burst into tears and revered this truly learned man as a saint. Then the simple friar said to himself in his heart, "The learned friar has taken from me everything that I was going to say. What shall I say now? I know a few verses from the psalms. Well, then, I will behave as the learned do, since this friar has just acted in the manner of the simple." At the next assembly the simple friar stood up and read a psalm verse. Then, filled with the divine spirit, he began to speak with so much fervor, insight and sweetness, as God inspired him, that all, filled with astonishment, exclaimed: "God has dealings with the simple."

From this parable, Francis drew a lesson:

The great assembly is our order. In it, the learned derive instruction from their dealings with the simple. They see uneducated friars seeking heavenly things with a burning ardor, and those who have not been instructed by men attaining the knowledge of spiritual things through the Holy Spirit. For the simple souls, too, familiarity with the learned is productive, because they see illustrious men who could enjoy renown humbling themselves with them and like them.

Obviously, this charity was not reserved to the community circle, but spread all around it, especially to those who were most deprived of charity. We have observed the friars devoting a part of their time to the lepers, imitating their master, who had begun his life of renunciation with this particularly troublesome service. As he started the order, Francis made it an obligation for the brothers as a whole.

Another obligation, both evangelical and canonical, which the friars diligently fulfilled was prayer. According to Celano, "one might say that they never ceased praising God and praying to him." They gave thanks continually for so many blessings received, groaned and wept over their failings and infidelities, sang the canonical office like monks, rising at midnight for Matins; and eyewitnesses assure us that it was done with abundant tears and deep sighs. Along the roads, when they encountered a church or a chapel, they knelt down to recite the short prayer taught by their father: "*Adoramus te, sanctissime Domine Jesu Christe, hic et ad omnes ecclesias tuas quae sunt in toto mundo, et benedicimus tibi quia per sanctam crucem tuam redemisti mundum*" [We adore you, most holy Lord Jesus Christ, here and in all your churches throughout the world, and we bless you, because by your holy Cross you have redeemed the world.]

The friars also devoted themselves, every day and continually, to penance. After all, this was the name by which they were known at the beginning: the Penitents of Assisi, or the Brothers of Penance. Even though Francis sometimes had to moderate the ardor of overzealous ascetics, as we have seen in the case of the imprudent friar, as a group the friars devoted themselves to the traditional practices of mortification, such as were found in the Eastern deserts as well as in the Frankish monasteries of the Merovingian era [sixth to mid-eighth centuries]. Most of them wore a hair shirt, usually of animal hair, which constantly scratched the skin; others girded themselves with iron belts. If they felt too inclined to carnal pleasure, they would throw themselves into icy water or thornbushes. Their mortification in eating did not consist of abstaining from certain foods (e.g., meat, fat, sauces, spices), as in the other monastic rules then in use, but rather in the condition, the appearance, and the mixture of the infe-

rior foods that were given to them as alms, whether they were stationed at the friary or traveling on a mission.

Francis recognized, moreover, that prayer and penance not only pro-
mote the personal sanctification of those who practice them, but also
sanctify the souls of others. In a discourse addressed to his brothers, he
questions the merits of preachers who become puffed up with pride
when they have the slightest oratorical success. In fact, he declares,
"they think that they have edified or converted others to penance by
their sermons, whereas it is God who edifies or converts them, because of the prayers of holy friars who know nothing themselves."

The evangelical virtue on which Francis insisted the most with regard
to his friars, and which he stubbornly guarded with a fierce vigilance,
was poverty. Celano remarks that the friars "possessed nothing and
had no fear of losing anything, because they were not attached to anything". Even the prayer books and Gospel books were common to
all. Owning no furniture, no cupboard in which to store provisions,
they were compelled to go in search of food every day; when the
collection was meager, they would rejoice in their neediness; when
it was abundant, they sought out poor people with whom to share
it. Indeed, there were days when they did not even have a crust of
bread to chew on.

The friars slept on pallets consisting of a cloth sack stuffed with
straw, which they spread out on the ground. They never saw pillows.
Tables, either, since they used to eat sitting on the tamped earth. Nor
did they customarily have kitchen utensils, since they brought back
their pittance in a bowl. We saw how Brother Juniper cooked a pig's
foot; no doubt he had found a discarded pot on a garbage heap. In any
case, the friars certainly could not have roasted the piglet themselves;
the donor took care of that.

Since poverty is the sister of charity, these disciples of the Gospel
were not content to bring their extra food to the needy; often they
divested themselves as well in order to clothe them. Many times when
one of them came across a miserable wretch who was inadequately
clad, he repeated the gesture of Saint Martin of Tours and cut off a
part of his garment for him; thus some of the religious would appear
for evening prayers with only one sleeve on their tunic.

The first rule, for which we no longer have the text itself, but only copious citations, demanded that the friars perform manual labor. This was cultivated by all during the early years in the original community, but in an anarchic way, as with the food. Sometimes they helped the peasants to crop hay or bring in the harvest. Although the economic efficiency of these labors was mediocre at best, the moral efficacy was considered important, as it had been for the ascetics in the desert. Francis combined these two purposes in his discourses: "I want my brothers to labor and to busy themselves humbly with good works so as to be less of a burden on the people and to prevent their hearts or their tongues from straying in idleness."

These two intentions are already part of the rule of Saint Benedict (chapter 48): "Idleness is the enemy of the soul. Therefore at certain times the brothers must busy themselves working with their hands."

The biographers insist as well on the humility of this handful of poor men, "little people who were subject to all", as Celano calls them, "seeking constantly to humble themselves and to find employment that would earn them insults". Their reliance on alms, although it was a way of feeding themselves, was also an occasion to practice humility, both in the abasement of begging and in the acceptance of the response, whatever it might be. But Francis admonished them that they should not be ashamed of this practice, which was the direct result of their poverty.

Following the instructions of their father, the friars combined humility with chastity, since both of these virtues, like holy poverty, consist in keeping oneself at a certain distance from desire. The inner sanctum of the Portiuncula was off-limits to women—not because they were contemptible in themselves, but rather, as Celano puts it, because "they feared that for weak souls this would be an occasion for a swift fall, and a source of weakness even for the strong souls." To be sure, all of these humble friars practiced modesty and custody of the eyes, but in order to encourage them, their formation director liked to tell them this parable:

A God-fearing and mighty king sent two messengers to the queen. The first one returned, simply bringing his message without saying anything about the queen, because he had kept his glances to himself and had not directed them toward the queen at all. The other one returned and, after relating the few words of her reply, described the queen's beauty at great length. "In truth, Sire," he said, "I have seen the most beautiful of all women. Happy the man whose wife she is!" The king said to him, "You wicked servant, you have looked immodestly at my wife." Then he summoned the first messenger and asked him, "What do you think of the queen?" "She is as good as can be", the other answered, "because she patiently gave me a favorable hearing." The king then asked him, "Isn't she beautiful?" The messenger replied, "Sire, that is for you to see and to judge. As for me, I was only supposed to deliver a message." The king declared, "Your eyes are chaste. Enter into my chambers and share in the entertainment. As for that immodest messenger, let him depart from my house, so as not to sully my home."

Obviously, the friars of this exemplary community carefully cultivated the virtue of obedience, as described in *The Three Companions.* "They showed toward all the most perfect obedience and were ready to carry out the will of their superior, without seeking to determine whether the orders to be carried out were just or not. Since everything that they were commanded to do appeared to them to be the will of the Lord, it was easy and pleasant for them to perform all the tasks that they were ordered to do."

They took to heart this lesson that their father frequently taught them: genuine obedience must not be merely external, but also interior; it must not be merely accepted, but desired. Furthermore, each one of the friars, when he heard his superior calling him, made sure that he was mentally well-disposed to carry out the order that he was about to receive, without even trying to imagine what it would consist of. Here again there is a parallel in the rule of Saint Benedict (chapter 5): "If the disciple obeys reluctantly, if he murmurs, not just with his mouth but also in his heart, then even if he were to carry out the order that he received, his work would not be acceptable to God."

It was not an echo of Saint Benedict, but rather an anticipation of Saint Ignatius of Loyola when the friars asked their common father what sort of obedience was most perfect, and he answered them with this parable: Take a corpse. Put it wherever you want. You will see that it offers no resistance to your effort, it does not complain about the place where it has been put, it does not ask to be moved somewhere else. If you set it on one seat, it does not look higher, but looks down. If you dress it in purple, it only appears even more pale. Such is the truly obedient man: he does not ask why he is moved, he does not worry about the place where he is put, he does not seek to be sent elsewhere.

On another occasion, it was not as a response to a question that he defined this capital virtue for consecrated religious, but after a meditation that was probably a painful one: "It would be difficult to find anywhere in the world one single religious who obeys his superior perfectly."

And he went on to sing the praises of the eager friar who is always ready to obey and always happy to carry out orders, without judging as to their value. Clearly, strict and lasting obedience is due to the rule, of which the superior himself is the servant—all the more so because it was derived from the Gospel. And he required members of the religious community to know by heart all the articles of it. "The rule," he used to say, "is the book of salvation, the pledge of glory, the marrow [or heart] of the Gospel, the way of the Cross, the state of perfection, the key to paradise, the treaty of the eternal covenant."

After the first missions to the Saracens, Francis loved to recount the martyrdom of that very young friar who, before undergoing it, grasped the rule that he carried on his person and said to his companion, "Dearest Brother, in the sight of the Divine Majesty and in your presence, I accuse myself of all the infidelities that I have committed against this rule."

Those were his last words; no sooner had he pronounced them than the sword of the infidel cut off his head.

Actually, all of those holy religious did not spend their time praying and working at the Portiuncula; they preached; that was the mission that the Pope had assigned to them. That was also the goal that Francis had set for himself, in order to imitate the life of Christ; he didn't stay at Nazareth to pray and work, but ventured out onto the roads of Palestine to proclaim the Kingdom of God. Therefore when the father [i.e., Francis] saw that he was blessed with an abundance of preachers, he decided to send them to different dioceses in Italy to spread the Good News, confident that, although they had not studied theology, their holy way of life would inspire them with suitable and efficacious exhortations. It was not a question of giving a commentary on the articles of the faith, but of calling believers to conversion. For that, it was useless to give a catechetical course. These little poor men were imbued with the Gospel: not only did they know it by heart; above all, they put it into practice. Therefore he presented to these new preachers, who this time had a mandate from the supreme authority in the Church, a brief discourse: "In the name of the Lord! Travel the road two by two, with humility and reserve. Observe silence, especially from dawn to the third hour [9:00 A.M.], praying to the Lord in your hearts that you will not utter a single idle or useless word. Although you are traveling, let your comportment be as humble and respectable as if you were in a hermitage or a cell. For wherever we may be staying or traveling, our cell is within us; indeed, our brother the body is a little cell, and our soul is a hermit who dwells there so as to pray to the Lord and meditate on him."

In this department as in all the others, Francis remained a living model for his friars, as he is depicted in *The Three Companions*:

> Blessed Francis, traveling through the cities and towns, set about preaching everywhere; not with the persuasive words of human wisdom, but in keeping with the truth and the power of the Holy Spirit, he confidently announced the Kingdom of God. He was a genuine preacher of the Gospel, strengthened by apostolic authority; he used no flattering phrases and despised the charm of rhetorical devices. For before he tried to convince others by his sermons, he had started by convincing himself, by laboring to proclaim the divine truth with the greatest possible fidelity. The power and truth of his words, which he did not owe to any schoolmaster, elicited the admiration of everyone, even the educated and the learned. A great number of them hastened to see and hear him, as though he were a man from another time.

Obviously, the preaching tours began in Assisi. Since they were now mandated by the Holy See, the father and his sons were allowed to ascend the pulpit in the cathedral and the parish churches of the city. The rivalry between the nobility and the bourgeoisie, which had provoked armed conflicts from 1200 to 1202, was raging once more. Francis, in the pulpit of Saint Rufino, cut through the egotism and the hatred with his fiery words and called so forcefully for reconciliation that by the end of the year 1210 the social classes had decided to make peace definitively by means of a treaty drawn up in due form. This was the Magna Carta whereby the commune of Assisi was thereafter governed by the representatives of the *majores* and the *minores*, and which stipulated that "they shall have to come to an agreement about everything that will contribute to the honor, the well-being, and the progress of the city of Assisi."

In Umbria, the city that was most famous in later generations was surely Gubbio, located forty kilometers north of Assisi, because of the famous story of the wolf. During this initial period of the Franciscan order, a wolf that was unusually large and particularly ferocious ravaged the outskirts of the city; not only was it decimating the flocks, but it also attacked people, to the point where a large number of the inhabitants no longer dared to venture outside the walls, and those who still did took care to arm themselves. Collective fear set in.

Francis went to preach in Gubbio together with an unnamed companion, and he remained there for several days. He heard the gossip: there was talk of nothing but the terrible beast. Full of pity for this terrorized populace, he declared that he would preach a sermon to the predator. Although the crowd knew of his power to work miracles, they protested in amazement: But that would be imprudent! Madness! He, however, was content to make the sign of the cross and walk calmly out of the city, followed by his companion, who was probably confident as to the outcome of the adventure. No sooner had they gone a short distance than the wolf, scenting that he was in luck, came to meet them. Francis seemed unimpressed; he traced over the animal a large sign of the cross and spoke softly to him, "Come here, Brother Wolf. I order you, on behalf of Jesus Christ, to do no harm, neither to me nor to anyone else."

Vanquished, the predator came up to the preacher and, peaceful as a lamb, curled up at his feet. Then Francis spoke at length, "Brother Wolf! You do much damage in this place. You have been guilty of terrible crimes, wounding and killing the creatures of God. Not only have you killed and eaten livestock, but you have had the audacity to wound and kill men who are created in the image of God. That is why, thief and cruel assassin that you are, you deserve the pitchforks. A whole populace is grumbling about you; this entire city detests you. But I want to make peace between them and you, Brother Wolf. You will no longer do them any harm, and they will forget your past misdeeds. Then neither men nor dogs will pursue you any more."

From afar the spectators at this scene saw the animal nodding his head and wagging his tail during this entire speech, as though consenting to the holy man's proposals. Observing this, the one who converted him pronounced the terms of the agreement that bound them: "Brother Wolf, since you are pleased to make peace and to keep it, I promise that what you need will always be provided for you, for the rest of your life, by the inhabitants of this city. From now on you will no longer suffer from hunger. For I know well that it is hunger that has made you commit so many wicked deeds. I ask you, for your part, Brother Wolf, to promise me that you will never again harm any man or any animal. Do you agree to this?"

He held out his hand to the animal, which, sitting up on its hind legs, lifted one paw and familiarly placed it in his hand. Satisfied, Francis said one last thing to him: "Now I command you, in the name of Jesus Christ, to have no fear and to follow me, and we will establish this pact in the name of God."

The wild beast, now docile, followed him and entered the city with him, in the midst of a rejoicing populace that lined up along their way, forgetting their fears. Francis, though, took the occasion to address a sermon to the crowd this time: "My brothers and sisters, if the jaws of a dumb animal can terrorize a whole multitude, how much more should we fear the jaws of hell. This animal can kill only the body; how much more fearsome are the fires of hell, which will torment the damned eternally."

Yet he insisted on sealing the promised pact. The crowd, with one voice, vowed to feed Brother Wolf generously until he died; at Francis' invitation, the wolf knelt down and, by movements of his head, tail, and ears, manifested his consent. Then he held out his paw to his benefactor, who clasped it with emotion.

Brother Wolf lived another two years, making himself at home in the city, walking all through it and fearlessly entering the houses, where he was very well fed, and not once provoking the dogs to attack, by an ongoing miracle. He died of old age, lamented by all the inhabitants.

During those same early years Francis accomplished a rescue mission of the same sort in Greccio, a town located ninety kilometers south of Assisi, between Terni and Rieti. He had established a little friary there and used to come visit the friars who had chosen to live in it. He had reserved for himself there a little cell where he could pray at length without being disturbed.

In that particular year, two disasters struck the town at the same time: hail, which devastated the harvests, and wolves, which were attacking the inhabitants. Since the people were begging him to intercede with heaven on their behalf, Francis went up into the pulpit and addressed the faithful who were gathered: "Listen to what I proclaim to you for the honor and glory of God. If each one of you abandons his sins and is converted to God with all his heart, with repentance and the intention of persevering, Our Lord Jesus Christ, in his mercy, will deliver you from the scourge of wolves and the scourge of hail. He will increase and multiply spiritual and temporal benefits for you. But I warn you that, if you return to your sins, this plague and this scourge will return, with other evils that are even more serious."

As Francis went out of the church, everyone was waiting to see the effects of his promise. Now the wolves kept quiet, and the hail, when it fell, struck the farms in the surrounding areas, but not those of the town. This blessing lasted for several years; but as abundant crops resulted in wealth, rivalries left families desolate, and a certain number of men who were not as well-to-do as the others turned to stealing and pillaging. Then new catastrophes befell the town, which burned down one fine day with all the houses in it.

On another occasion, Francis had gone to preach in Perugia, a city which, though Umbrian, did not belong to the duchy of Spoleto, but to the Papal States. He was probably alone. He was soon welcomed by one of his friends who lived on the shore of Lake Trasimeno. Since Lent was about to begin, he was inspired to live in solitude, and he asked his host to bring him by boat to a little island that was said to be deserted. The only provisions that he brought with him were two small loaves. After making a tour of the island, he determined that there was not a single building on it; so he fashioned a shed for himself in a thicket. And he remained there in prayer during that entire Lenten season. On Holy Thursday, the friend disembarked on the little island and found the ascetic. Of the two loaves, only half of one was gone; the hermit had spent forty days without eating or drinking, but finally, fearing that he would be overcome with pride at having resembled Jesus Christ, he decided that it was better to take that small amount of food.

One day, in setting out on another preaching tour, Francis took with him two of his companions from the early days, Angelo and Masseo; they traveled this time along the little road leading from the south of Assisi to Montefalco. Upon arriving in Cannara, after walking only two leagues, he was surrounded by the fervent crowd of inhabitants who were expecting him. He then climbed up on an elevation so that he could be seen by all and called for silence. The crowd grew quiet and respectfully waited for the holy man to begin teaching them. They were not counting on the swallows, though, a large flock of which came to perch on the nearby trees and substituted their chirping for that gossiping of the women, who had had the decency to stop talking. Realizing that he could not be heard, the preacher addressed a short sermon to the chatterboxes: "My sisters, you swallows, it is my turn to speak now, for you have said enough. Listen to the word of God, keep silence, and do not move until I have finished speaking about the Lord."

At once the swallows stopped singing and allowed the holy man to speak until the conclusion of his sermon.

Continuing along their route, the three friars reached the place called Pian d'Arca, between Cannara and Bevagna. They came upon a field where an unprecedented multitude of birds of all kinds had gathered. Enchanted by the spectacle, Francis said to his companions, "Wait for me here; I'm going to preach to my brothers, the birds."

He walked into the field and the multitude of winged creatures, instead of flying away, remained on the ground, turned toward him, as though they were expecting him. Then, filled with joy, he spoke to them: "My brothers, you birds, you have good reason to thank God your Creator, and to praise him, always and everywhere; for he has given you the freedom to fly where you will; he has endowed you with a double and triple garment; he preserved your ancestors in Noah's ark, so that your species would not disappear from the face of the earth; furthermore you are indebted to him for the air in which you fly. Then, too, you neither sow nor reap, and yet God feeds you; he offers you rivers and fountains to drink from; he grants you mountains and valleys where you find refuge, and the tall trees in which to build your nests. You can neither spin nor sew, but God provides garments for both you and your little ones. Your Creator, therefore, loves you dearly, because he bestows so many benefits upon you. And so, my little brothers, guard yourselves carefully against the sin of ingratitude, and devote yourselves always to the praise of God."

During the entire time of this discourse, the birds nodded, opened their beaks without singing, fluttered their wings without flying, and tilted their heads gracefully. When the preacher was finished and had made the sign of the cross over them, they all took flight, while making the air resound with their harmonious songs, which charmed and enraptured the listeners. Then they divided into four groups, which flew off toward the four points of the compass, signifying that the preaching of Francis, a renewal of Christ's, was spreading to the four corners of the world.

The preaching of Saint Francis to the birds has inspired many artists, notably Giotto.

No doubt Francis and his friars, as they criss-crossed Umbria in all directions, sowed many other words, aroused many other feelings, prompted many other conversions, and worked many other miracles. But they did not restrict themselves to this region; they also evangelized all the surrounding areas.

They often entered the Marches of Ancona, which extend from Umbria to the Adriatic, beyond Gubbio. That was where, not long before, Francis had conquered the heart of the troubadour Guglielmo Divini, who became Brother Pacificus. It was there, too, that he met two young scholars, Pellegrino ["Pilgrim"] and Rinieri, who joined the order without any hesitation; this allowed the Franciscans to establish a friary in that province. Of Pellegrino, who would one day become the provincial of the Marches of Ancona, Brother Bernard used to say that he was one of the most perfect religious in the order.

It was at Ascoli, in the Marches, south of Ancona, that Francis seems to have had one of his most impressive success stories. The whole village went to meet him, then listened to him, with the press of the crowd so great that some people were being crushed. He then gave the habit to thirty of the villagers. People from all the surrounding localities came to hear him and to venerate him; they gave him loaves to bless, which they then preserved as treasures and gave to the sick to eat so that they might be cured. They cut off bits of his tunic as relics, to the point that one day he found himself left with no outer garment.

And, of course, Francis and his disciples traversed Tuscany, which extends broadly to the north and west of Umbria, with its many cities, which are famous for their churches and their palaces. In the year 1211, Francis took Sylvester with him to go to Cortona. There he recruited, among others, Elias Bonibarone, who would later become famous under the name of Elias of Cortona and would build at Assisi, after his master's death, the marvelous Basilica of Saint Francis and the imposing Sacro Convento.

Thirty-five kilometers north of Cortona we find the charming city of Arezzo, where the prestigious Church of Santa Maria della Pieve was already standing; and sixty-five kilometers north of Arezzo is the marvel of Tuscany: Florence, which at that time had fewer artistic masterpieces, to be sure, but housed at least the famous baptistry of the Ponte Vecchio, with a different appearance from the one that we know today. In the latter city he conquered John Parenti, a doctor of the new University of Bologna, who would become the minister general of the order. At that time he was serving as a magistrate.

He was ripe for conversion, because shortly before he had heard a sow squeal, as she urged her piglets along, "Go on, you swine! Go to your pigsty, just as judges go to hell!" Shaken by this message, which he perceived as threatening his salvation, he was just waiting for a chance to quit his position, when he heard the preaching of Francis of Assisi. He left everything and followed the man of God. At Pisa, the latter gained another remarkable disciple, Agnello, the future provincial of England. During that entire tour, Francis received a triumphal welcome from the crowds—a veritable public canonization during his own lifetime.

And so he was somewhat relieved on the return trip, at Terni, when the bishop, before yielding to him his place in the pulpit, warned the people, "It is very strange that such an ignorant, insignificant man as this Francis should have such great success with the crowds!"

He personally tried to discourage this popular enthusiasm by staging little scenes that appeared comical to some and edifying to others. One day when he had taken sick, he agreed, at the urging of one of his brothers, to eat a bit of chicken. He then had a suitable occasion to manifest his lack of mortification. After removing his own habit, he had a friar, in the name of obedience, lead him by a rope around his neck through the streets, crying, "Here is a glutton who eats meat when you're not watching!"

In 1213 Francis, accompanied by Leo, traveled through Romagna, northeast of Umbria. Upon arriving at Montefeltro, he noticed that they were having a great festival: a tournament and a reception for a new knight. He waited for the latter ceremony to end and then climbed up onto the esplanade of the castle, quieted those in attendance, and gave a sermon. "The knight who wants to win the love of a lady must first go through many difficult trials. But he accepts all of these labors and dangers joyfully, because it is for the sake of love and his lady's honor. During all that time he thinks of only one thing: that little white hand on which he will place his lips when he returns after having completed his exploits. Now there is a knighthood different from the one belonging to this world, one that is even nobler, to which all men are called—not only those who are members of a noble lineage. There is another sort of combat, the purpose of which is not to please an earthly beauty, but to obey the eternal commandment of the everlasting and supreme Beauty, who is God. Really, now, isn't God much more beautiful than the most beautiful ladies, who are all the works of his hands, formed from the slime of the earth? And so he deserves that we should carry out for his sake chivalrous exploits and that we should fight for his honor against his enemies, which are the world, the flesh, and the devil. The favors that he promises us are infinitely greater and more precious than those that the most beautiful woman can bestow upon us."

This sermon went straight to the heart of Count Orlando of Catanio, the lord of Chiusi. After the lamps had been extinguished, he asked Francis to speak with him.

"Father," he said to him, "I own in Tuscany a mountain suitable for contemplation, which is called La Verna. It is secluded, covered with trees, far from the crowds: a refuge for someone who wants to devote himself to penance or to lead the life of a hermit. If you want it, I will give it to you, to you and your companions, for the salvation of my soul."

Francis listened enthusiastically to this offer. Not only did he accept it joyfully, but he promised that, when he returned to the Portiuncula, he would send him several of his companions with orders to visit the site. Indeed, as soon as he reached the friary that served as his home base, he sent two brothers to Chiusi. Count Orlando welcomed them cordially and sent with them, on their visit to the mountain, a company of around fifty armed men, in case they should encounter wild beasts. It was doubtless by way of reassuring them, because it is incomprehensible how such a large army would have been necessary against a wolf or a boar. Escorted in this manner, the religious took stock of the premises, making sure that they were suitable for establishing a hermitage. They even made an effort, aided by their escorts, to erect a cabin made of branches, thus demonstrating that they were taking possession of the property. The scene was now set for one of the final milestones in the spiritual life of Saint Francis: his stigmatization.

Francis himself did not go to Bologna, but in the year 1211 he sent Brother Bernard there. As soon as the latter entered the city he was surrounded by mocking street urchins who hounded him with their ridicule and insults; he, on the other hand, imitating his spiritual father, endured these indignities with joyful patience.

> Moreover, in order to be scoffed at even more [the *Fioretti* relate], he took up a position on the town square and sat down there. A large number of children and men gathered around him then and not only started to make fun of him again, but also pulled on his cowl from behind and before, threw dust and pebbles at him, and shoved him. But Brother Bernard, in the same way, with the same patience and a joyful expression, did not complain and was not disturbed.
>
> A passerby, the jurist Nicolas de Peppoli, instead of being amused by this revolting spectacle, marveled; for in his judgment patience was an exalted virtue, and it was being practiced to perfection before his very eyes. Dispersing the rascals, he spoke to their victim, to their astonishment: "Who are you? What are you doing here?"
>
> Bernard said nothing but put his hand into his tunic and brought out the rule that had been approved two years earlier by the Pope. [This shows that the original rule, no copy of which has come down to us,

was widely circulated at that time, and that each friar carried the text
of it on his person.] Nicolas solemnly read it. Then, turning to the bystanders, he said, "We are in the presence here of a member of the most
sublime religious order that I have ever heard tell of. This man and his
companions are numbered among the holiest men in this world, and
anyone who harms him commits a serious sin, for one should show him
instead a lively respect, since he is an eminent friend of God."

Then, to Bernard, he said kindly and considerately, "Brother, if you
want to found a convent of your order here, in which you can pray to
God suitably, I will find you one immediately."

At last Bernard, delighted by this providential intervention, spoke up,
"*Messire* [My Lord], it is our Lord Jesus Christ who has inspired you. I
willingly accept your proposal for the love of Christ."

At once the benefactor brought the friar to a dilapidated building,
which he promised to restore in short order. So it happened that the
Penitents of Assisi came into possession of a convent in Bologna. Or
rather, they came to occupy it, because, according to Francis' explicit
intention, his order should not own anything under the sun; we can
suppose that this building, although acquired by the brothers for their
use, remained the property of *Messire* Nicolas, who continued in name
to be the owner.

Francis went to Rome, too. Perhaps it was during that journey that he
stopped at Cannara and silenced the swallows. At Rome he preached.
And, most importantly, he won the admiration, the friendship, and
the devotion of a young woman whom he would call "his brother
Jacoba" (*frater Jacoba*): Lady Jacoba of Settesoli, the wife of the nobleman Gratian Frangipani (it is uncertain whether he was a count
or a prince). He belonged to one of the oldest aristocratic families
in Rome, among the descendants of which were Saint Benedict and
Saint Gregory the Great. To the ancient name of this family, *Anicia*,
had been added at the beginning of the eighth century the surname
Frangipani "breaker of bread", because they had fed the people during a severe famine. As for Jacoba, her ancestry is unknown. It appears that she came from southern Italy, probably a descendant of the
Norman conquerors. Her name itself is problematic. Jörgensen recalls
that there is a street in Rome called *Via delle Sette Sale*, where she was
living at that time. The "Street of the Seven Dwellings"? Nothing

unusual about that, since she herself and her husband were both the proprietors of great estates; Gratian owned entire sectors of Rome, and it is possible that Jacoba had acquired a group of seven houses as an inheritance. The pronunciation was distorted, and people began to call her the owner of the "*Settesoli*": the Lady of the Seven Suns. She was still young, between twenty and twenty-five years of age, and the mother of a newborn infant. Her portraits show that she was beautiful, distinguished, and reserved. And since the supernatural beauty of her soul surpassed her visible beauty, her husband, who loved both God and his wife, was able to understand and accept the marvelous spiritual love that she had for Saint Francis and that united her to him for fourteen years.

Their first meeting was brief, even though for Jacoba it seemed to be decisive. Indeed, Francis did not wish to linger in Rome; for some time he had been planning another project altogether: that of converting the rulers of the Muslim world. The noblemen and the men of arms had carried out a crusade with the sword; he wanted to conduct one, as the very name suggested, with the cross, with no other resources than the preaching of the Gospel.

He had fixed his choice upon the most prestigious sovereign in the Orient, the Caliph of Baghdad. That entire region beyond Palestine was included by the Latins under the name of Syria. Francis decided therefore to set off for Syria. Together with a companion, he arrived at Ancona [on the Adriatic] in 1212 and managed to board a ship destined for the shores of the East. We can assume that he paid for the voyage with alms collected along the way. But a storm cast the ship up on the coast of Dalmatia, which was then called Esclavonia; it had sustained damage and was no longer seaworthy. Francis saw the finger of God in this and decided to return to Italy. He and his companion soon found a vessel that was getting under way for Ancona, but they were not allowed on board; they had no funds with which to pay the price of the voyage. Fortunately a sailor who had been won over by their holiness secretly stowed them away in the ship's hold. And they returned to Italy.

But Francis did not abandon his plan. If God was not allowing him to travel in the East, perhaps he expected him to take the road to Morocco. The sultan's name was Muhammad al Nasir; the Muslims called him Emir el-Mu'minin, "commander of the believers", a title that the Christians changed to Miramolin. In the year 1212 he had experienced a crushing defeat at the hands of the Spaniards at Las Navas de Tolosa and had retreated ignominiously across the Strait of Gibraltar. Thus it was in the sultan's own country that Francis, trusting in the Lord, hoped to catch up with him. And so in 1213 he crossed the Alps, traveled through Provence, then the Pyrenees, and was thinking of continuing his journey to Compostela so as to venerate there the relics of the Apostle James, when he was halted by a sudden illness. Celano writes, "God opposed his plan, and in order to prevent him from going any further, sent him a sickness that interrupted his journey." As soon as he had obtained a cure, the servant made an about-face.

A few years passed before Francis tried again to make a spiritual crusade. Indeed, he was waiting for an occasion to assume a more official place in the Church. His order was growing, and he was intent on having it become a recognized part of the ecclesiastical renewal announced by Innocent III. The opportunity presented itself in 1215, when the Pope convoked the bishops of Christendom to the Fourth Lateran Council. This was an unprecedented assembly: four hundred bishops, eight hundred abbots, and some representatives of the Catholic sovereigns. We know from a few details mentioned by some historians that Francis of Assisi went to Rome for the occasion, but his biographers do not tell us about this journey. Nevertheless the founder influenced the papal court, for it was decided, given the abundance of new religious institutes, that henceforth not one of them would be allowed to have a new rule approved; therefore only two remained in the West: the rules of Saint Benedict and of Saint Augustine. Still, the Pope made an exception for the order of Saint Francis, since its rule, he recalled, had been approved six years previously.

Saint Dominic, the founder of the Friars Preachers [or Order of Preachers], was also at Rome at the time, and had to resign himself to adopting the rule of Saint Augustine. And that was when he and Francis met. The fact is related by the Dominican Gérard de Trachet and the Franciscan Thomas of Celano. One night, while Dominic was deep in prayer, he had a vision: Christ was angry at the Church and at Christians, and his Mother was trying to appease him; in order

to obtain his mercy, she presented two men to him. Dominic immediately recognized himself as the first; the second, whom he did not
know, was a humble and radiant little religious, clothed in a shabby
monastic robe; his face was so expressive that it was unforgettable.
Now the following day Dominic, upon entering a church, spied that
face. Immediately he ran over to the little poor man and threw his
arms around him. "You are my companion", he said to him. "You
will walk with me; let us work together and no one will be able to
prevail against us."

Then he proposed merging the two orders. But Francis refused
vehemently: his was a poor society of unlettered men that had no
ambition whatsoever in the realm of scholarship; besides, it was already obeying an approved rule. Still, as a souvenir of that fraternal
encounter, Dominic asked Francis for the cord that gathered his tunic
at the waist. Francis, out of humility, refused at first, but Dominic
insisted so forcefully and with such devotion, that he managed to obtain it and wore it from then on beneath his white robe. Ever since
then the tradition of that original friendship has been perpetuated: on
the Feast of Saint Francis, the Dominican superiors go to officiate at
services in the Franciscan friaries; on the Feast of Saint Dominic, the
Franciscan superiors go to officiate in the Dominican friaries.

Saint Francis seized another unusual opportunity to pay a visit to
the Pope. It happened during the summer of 1216, when the papal
court was staying in Perugia. The great Pope Innocent III had just
died, and the papal electors had immediately replaced him with Cen-
cio Savelli, the cardinal-priest of the Church of Saints John and Paul,
who had taken the name of Honorius III. Francis went there with
several of his friars, it seems. He did not go to ask for a renewed
approval of his rule, since he had probably already decided to write
a new one, and he did not actually submit it until five years later.
Rather, according to the account of the meeting written by Brother
Benedict of Arezzo, who was one of those who accompanied the saint,
he intended to obtain from the new Pope a special favor, which he
finally wrested from him despite the opposition of the cardinals in
attendance: an indulgence for the Portiuncula.

The favor in question was a plenary indulgence, to be granted to all
pilgrims who would henceforth make a devout visit to Santa Maria

degli Angeli between the hour of vespers on August 1 and nightfall on August 2, the feast of the patron saint of the church. It was a difficult favor to obtain, because until then only one indulgence of this type had ever been granted: to the pilgrims and the crusaders who traveled to Jerusalem. It is easy to see how, to the minds of certain prelates, the new indulgence would have been detrimental to the first; it was enough to go and venerate the Blessed Virgin in Assisi instead of kneeling at the tomb of Christ in Jerusalem. The subsequent popes confirmed this concession and extended it to the other Franciscan shrines, so that on August 2 of each year any Catholic who, with genuine contrition, goes to a shrine of the Franciscan order to pray there devoutly, experiences a heavenly remission of the punishments incurred by his sins.

5. The Poor Ladies

Like other founders, when he first entered God's service Saint Francis was not counting on establishing a women's monastic order someday. A chance occurrence had convinced him to start the Order of the Friars Minor: the arrival of the first disciples. It was a similar chance occurrence that led him to inaugurate the Order of the Poor Ladies: meeting Saint Clare.

She belonged to the nobility in Assisi, where her father was a senator. For a long time he was believed to be one of the Scifi, a ducal family, and Jörgensen himself echoes that tradition. But A. Fortini has demonstrated, in a study published in 1926, that Clare's father, Faverone [or Favorino] de Cocorano, was descended from a family of knights, and that he was usually called "Favarone di Offreduccio", a reference to his own father's first name.

Her mother's name was Ortolana ("the Gardener"). She had given birth to five children: a son, Boson, and four daughters: Penenda, Clare, Agnes, and Beatrice. She was a very devout woman, who made it her custom to go on major pilgrimages. Thomas of Celano, who became Clare's biographer, mentions those to Rome, to the Church of Saint Michael on Mount Gargano in Puglia, and especially to Jerusalem, which demonstrates her great courage.

The same author relates that, while she was pregnant with her second daughter, she was praying one day before the crucifix for the child that she would soon bring into the world, when a voice (interior or audible?) announced to her, "Woman, have no fear. For without danger you will give birth to a light whose radiance will increase the light of day." And so, when the child was born, she decided to give it the name *Chiara*, which means "luminous, bright", but also, in Latin (*Clara*), "famous". The newborn baby girl was destined to become radiant and renowned.

She had a pious Christian upbringing as a child, like many little girls of her day, but in addition she wore a hair shirt and secretly decided to consecrate herself to Jesus Christ. And so, when she had reached marriageable age and her parents were eager to choose a husband for her, she resolutely refused. They did not insist.

She was twelve years younger than Francis, since she was born in 1194. Thus she was still a little child when she heard about the escapades of the king of the golden youth, who actually fought against her father at the Ponte San Giovanni, and she was fifteen years old when she heard of the founding of the little community at Santa Maria degli Angeli. The reputation of Francis and of his companions was spreading; she wanted to hear him and was overwhelmed by his preaching. Furthermore she found out information about that community through her cousin Rufino, who was one of the founder's first disciples. Through Rufino also, and perhaps from the local gossip, Francis knew about Clare's virtues and her vow. It was probably Rufino again who foresaw the meetings between these two lovers of Christ, yet he was not the one who accompanied his spiritual father, but rather Brother Philip the Tall, whereas Clare brought along her companion Bona di Guelfuccio. We can easily surmise the questions that Clare asked Francis: How does one separate oneself from the world and live for God alone? Where could she find an abbey to live in according to the Franciscan spirit, in evangelical destitution?

During Lent of 1212 (she was eighteen then), she heard the preaching of Francis in the Church of Saint George. He spoke with inspired eloquence about contempt for the world, about holy poverty, about being united to the sufferings of Christ crucified. Consequently she was all the more eager to make her own gift of self, and she confided her desire to Francis. He agreed with her on a rendezvous for the night between Palm Sunday and Monday of Holy Week.

That Sunday Clare put on her most beautiful finery and went to Solemn Mass at the Cathedral of Saint Rufino. At the moment when palm branches were distributed—a ceremony performed by Bishop Guido himself—the young lady remained in her pew, whether due to distraction or to a desire to be discreet. Then His Excellency, as a gesture of kindness and perhaps of encouragement, descended the steps of the altar and came to place a palm branch in her hands.

That evening she prepared her flight. When the moment came, she left the family mansion without awakening her relatives, accompanied by Pacifica di Guelfuccio, Bona's sister. She cleared an abandoned back door and slipped through it, so that the night watchmen would not see her, and made her way to Santa Maria degli Angeli, where the friars were waiting for her by torchlight. Francis had her climb the steps to the altar, where she took off her finery and her jewels, then put on a coarse gray robe resembling a sack, with a cord instead of a belt, and gave up her radiant tresses, replacing them with a veil. Pacifica, quite envious, then declared that she would share her friend's lot. Then the procession of friars got underway and accompanied the new brides of Christ to the monastery of the Benedictine nuns of San Paolo di Bastia, on the road to Perugia. The abbess kindly welcomed them, not as her daughters, since they did not wish to make profession in the Order of Saint Benedict, but as refugees whom she would shelter while they were determining their final destination.

The next morning, Clare's family searched in vain for the girl, turning the whole house upside down without finding a trace of her. They asked the neighbors on every side. Then the tongues began to wag. Some witnesses had watched the procession of Franciscans from a distance; there was hardly any doubt: Clare was at Bastia. Faverone, mad with rage, called for the help of relatives and neighbors; the knights leaped upon their mounts and arrived at the abbey, where the portresses could not prevent them from forcing their way in. They quickly found Clare's cell. She fled into the church and climbed the steps of the altar to show that she was in a sacred and inviolable place. Her father commanded her to follow him. She replied that she was no longer under his authority. He grabbed her and tried to drag her off, but she clung to the altar cloths with invincible strength.

Then, while the men retreated to catch their breath, she removed her veil and showed her sheared head: "You see, my lords; this sign shows you that I no longer belong to the world. I belong to God, to whom you owe reverence."

Was it not better to proceed by persuasion? Faverone remained with a few of his men for several days, begging his daughter, reasoning with her, insulting her. Her response was always the same: "I am God's. I will never return to the world."

Seeing that his efforts were in vain and resigning himself to the loss of his daughter, Faverone gave the order to depart. We can imagine that the parents and friends of Pacifica employed the same devices to regain their daughter. Although Celano says nothing about it, the reason is obvious: he wrote his *Life of Saint Clare* in the 1250s, just as she was being canonized (1253). Therefore the account is focused entirely on her.

The abbess of Saint Paul's, however, was very unhappy about sheltering under her roof two girls—not even her own nuns—who "were thus a source of cares and troubles for her monastery". She asked Francis to find another refuge for them. He made an agreement with the abbess of another Benedictine monastery, San Angelo di Panzo, this one to the east of Assisi, not far from the hermitage of the Carceri. It was there that he brought his protégées.

Faverone and his relatives, vexed and bitter, had given up trying to get Clare back. But Agnes, her sixteen-year-old sister, did not; she envied her older sister with all her heart. Her parents were not worried about her in this regard; she was engaged and they were preparing for her wedding. Nevertheless, sixteen days after Clare's flight, Agnes went to join her sister in Panzo. The news quickly reached the Offreduccio mansion, and again there was an angry outburst from the father. He requested the assistance of his brother Monaldo, who had taken part in the expedition against the Abbey of Saint Paul and now assembled twelve armed men. These fierce warriors confronted the abbess in Panzo and demanded that she hand Agnes over to them. How could anyone refuse to yield to paternal authority? Agnes was less of a nun than her sister: she was still wearing her worldly clothing and had not embraced the religious state in any ceremony. Most of all, the abbess feared that these armed men might enter her monastery by force, violate it, and pillage it. She handed over the girl.

Once they saw her in front of them, the men ordered her to follow them. She proudly replied, "I will not be separated from my sister."

One of them went up to her and threw her to the ground. "Are you going to come with us?"

"I am going to stay."

Her statement unleashed a storm of blows and kicks. She fell silent. One knight took her by the hair and dragged her along the ground. She screamed, "Clare! Clare! Help me, sister!"

Clare, who was unable to begin a fight against those brutes, fell to her knees and prayed to Christ to deliver her sister. At that moment, they were dragging Agnes along the footpath that descends from the abbey to the plain, tearing her robe and her skin on the brambles and the pebbles. And suddenly that slim body became so heavy that it remained as though pinned to the ground by an irresistible force, and not one of the strong men could move it. There were some peasants in the fields who witnessed the repulsive scene.

"Well, then, you rustics!" cried Monaldo, who seems to have been in charge of the operation. "Come help us instead of stupidly watching us!"

The peasants, ashamed, came running and tried to budge that immovable mass. But in vain. One of the torturers sneered, "She must have been eating lead all night."

The jokes that followed did not succeed in calming Monaldo, who was worn out and wanted to have done with the matter. He raised his iron gauntlet and lunged forward as if to smash his victim's face. But his arm remained frozen in the air, as though paralyzed; he was overcome with terrible pain. He could no longer move a muscle. They all looked at him, dumbfounded. Was not this an intervention of heaven itself in favor of their victim?

That was when Clare arrived, majestic in her robe of poverty, and railed at them, "Go away! And leave this child alone! Do you dare to challenge God, who has shown you his love for her?"

They did not dare to look that heavenly spokesperson in the face. Besides, what could they do? The girl was unmovable, and their leader was paralyzed. They turned back, ashamed and helpless. Monaldo regained the use of his arm, which was still wracked with pain. They all mounted their horses, spurred them on, and rode off. Clare bent over Agnes, who was now as light as a feather, and took her in her arms. She, happy despite the wounds and bruises all over her body, rejoiced: she now belonged to God forever.

But the abbess of San Angelo did not rejoice. Her community had been disturbed for two hours, the good name of her abbey had been injured, and there was a danger that any day now she would again see those brutes who had no fear of the Lord. They gave up this time. But in their embarrassment and their vexation, might they come back? In greater numbers? With a more ruthless display of force? When Francis arrived to visit his protégées, she was unrelenting: he could take them wherever he wanted; she would have nothing more to do with them.

Besides, those two girls were not at home there. They considered themselves to be disciples of Francis and wanted to belong to a women's religious institute affiliated with the one at the Portiuncula. This was evidently Francis' wish as well. But where could they put these newly-professed nuns? Only one place seemed to be a suitable answer to his question: San Damiano. The little church, the cradle of his conversion, had a little house right nearby that could house these fervent female recruits. All they had to do was to introduce strict cloister around that new convent. Together with a few companions, Francis went to find the three little lambs in their temporary sheepfold, and brought them to San Damiano. There, in a new ceremony, he cut Agnes' hair and clothed her bruised body in the penitential habit. No man from the Faverone clan dared to show his face again.

The story of these three happy, zealous virgins enthralled the young people of Assisi. There was no doubt that other girls from the city would join the little community. The first one was another member of their family, Amata. She was renowned for her beauty and elegance, always appeared in public dressed in sumptuous attire and enjoyed the adulation of high society. Like Agnes, she was betrothed, and the day for her wedding had been set. Before entering marriage she insisted on visiting her cousin Clare, of whom she had such fond memories. Clare, instead of congratulating her on her wedding and offering her best wishes for her cousin's new home and family, sang the praises of the consecrated life:

> She began to speak to her about the loving kindness of the heavenly Bridegroom, the joy of solitude, the transience of worldly pleasures, and the incomparable worth of eternal blessings. Amata shed tears of compassion; she began to taste and see the goodness of the Lord. She had nothing now but contempt for the brilliant frivolities that had captivated her until then; horrified, she rejected those troublesome superfluities that go by the mendacious name of necessities and conveniences. She exclaimed that she would never leave the convent. Her relatives all arrived at San Damiano and caused an uproar in the seclusion. They considered the girl's heroic decision madness; they threatened to carry her off by force from the sacred shrine. Nothing could shake her resolve. Her parents, confounded by such firmness, gave their consent to her generous sacrifice.[1]

---

[1] Mère Marie-Angèle du Sacré-Coeur, abbess of the monastery of Sainte-Claire de Lyon, *Histoire abrégée de l'ordre de sainte Claire d'Assise*, vol. 1, (Lyon-Paris, 1906), p. 77.

Following this new vocation, more new recruits arrived at San Damiano. Agnes of Spello was a relative of Francis. One day, when she was a child, her mother brought her to Saint Clare to receive her blessing. The little girl was so moved and so enchanted that she declared that she wanted to remain there. Her mother did not object, on the condition that the superior, to whom Francis had given the title of abbess, consented to it. The abbess discerned such promise in the child that she allowed her to receive the habit; and she became a great ascetic and a great mystic.

Christine had been a friend of Clare in the world. She was disconsolate about her departure; finally, she went to visit her at the convent and was amazed at the life that she was leading; she remained with her. Francesca, whose real name is unknown, had such a great devotion to Francis of Assisi that she adopted his first name; her sister Angeluccia soon came to join her. After she entered the convent, two young women with the same name followed: Benvenuta of Assisi and Benvenuta of Perugia. Finally, three members of Clare's family rounded out the community: Balbina, her niece; Ortolana, her mother, now widowed; and Beatrice, her youngest sister. Shortly thereafter, Clare admitted Benedicta, who would succeed her as abbess in 1253.

The most surprising recruiting effort, and the most spectacular, was the incorporation of entire communities into the new order. In 1215, while Francis was preaching at San Severino, the native country of Brother Pacificus, the Benedictine abbess asked him to speak to her nuns. By the end of his sermon, the nuns had been won over, and when they learned that the holy friar had also established an order for women at San Damiano, they wrote to the Holy See asking to be affiliated with it. Their request was granted.

This example was followed by the Camaldolese nuns of Spello, who were already obeying very strict constitutions; nevertheless they preferred to abide by the spirit and the rule that governed San Damiano. They asked the founder for a new abbess who would be capable of initiating them into this new form of life, and he sent them Balbina, Clare's niece.

In 1219, while Cardinal Hugolino was visiting the convent of San Damiano, of which he was also the protector, he had an audience with the Benedictine abbess of Monticelli in Florence, who told him that her community was asking to be affiliated with the order at San Damiano. It was an even more courageous step for her, in that this decision compelled her to renounce her position as abbess. Hugolino understood the worth of this request and consented to it. As the new abbess for these nuns he appointed Agnes, Clare's sister; she was twenty-three years old, but she had lived for seven years under her sister's authority—years of very fruitful experience. Mother Agnes governed Monticelli for thirty-four years and turned that Benedictine abbey into a genuine Franciscan abbey.

The community at San Damiano kept growing and was able to found new houses in Perugia, Cremona, Milan, Venice, Spoleto, Ascoli, Pisa, Siena, and Padua. Eventually the Benedictines of Panzo, who once had taken in the two foundresses of the order, asked Clare for the privilege of placing themselves under her rule.

In France an abbey of "Damianites" came into existence in the year 1220. Four years earlier, the archbishop of Rheims, Albéric de Humbert, had been summoned to the Lateran Council and had met prelates there who unceasingly praised this new community of women religious. He traveled to Assisi in order to obtain a group of them and had a meeting with Francis, who promised to grant his request. A few years later a little group of the daughters of Saint Clare, led by the Genoese woman Maria di Bra, went to take possession of a parcel of land donated by the canons regular of Saint-Denys in Rheims, and they built a convent there.

In order for the new religious institute founded by Francis and Clare to gain legal recognition, it had to have a name, approval by church authority, and a rule. The name was quickly discovered: the Order of the Poor Ladies. The approval was given by Innocent III in 1215. As for the rule, Francis had already given his daughters a rule that was quite similar to that of the Friars Minor, but it was not approved by Rome. Furthermore by 1215, beginning with the Fourth Lateran Council, Rome was no longer accepting any new religious rule. Since the Poor Ladies were nuns, the rule of Saint Benedict was assigned to them. Now, Francis made it known in high places that the Benedictine rule differed in certain fundamental points from the original statutes of the daughters of Clare, first and foremost with regard to absolute poverty. Innocent III signed a very special brief, called the *privilegium pauperitatis* (privilege of poverty), which authorized the order of Saint Clare to own nothing. Among other things the document stated:

Desiring to consecrate yourselves to God alone, you have renounced all desire for the goods of this world. That is why, after having sold everything and distributed it all to the poor, you have decided to renounce any and all property so as to follow in the footsteps of him who made himself poor for our sakes. . . . That is why, in response to your request, we confirm by an apostolic favor your intention to live in extreme poverty; and by the authority of this document, we grant to you the privilege not to be compelled by anyone to accept property.

Both Clare and Francis were very pleased with this privilege. However, because of the abrupt decision of the Lateran Council, the Poor Ladies were not really governed by an existing rule: the rule of Saint Benedict modified along the lines of the rule of Francis of Assisi was a makeshift arrangement at best. In 1218 Honorius III decreed that the Poor Ladies would follow the Benedictine rule, but without adding the privilege of poverty, which had not been a part of it originally; this meant that Clare and her daughters came under the jurisdiction of the Benedictines. However, given that the rule of Saint Francis was considered valid, since approval for it had been granted before 1215, could it not be applied also to the institute of the Poor Ladies, which was the women's version of the Friars Minor? It was then simply a matter of revising certain articles. Instead of having an adaptation of the rule of Saint Benedict, they would adapt Francis' rule. Rome could not refuse this concession. This was the struggle that brought Clare to the Holy See after Francis' death; and she won. In 1253, some days after the death of the foundress, Pope Innocent IV signed the bull that governed the Order of the Poor Ladies.

What is commonly called the rule of Saint Clare, since she was mainly responsible for putting it into writing, begins with a touching reference to the co-founder: "The way of life instituted by Saint Francis for the Order of the Poor Ladies consists of observing the Holy Gospel by living in obedience, without owning anything, and in chastity."

Thus the three classical vows of religion are set forth: obedience, poverty, and chastity. But special mention is given to poverty: "without owning anything", which means that the nuns, like their Franciscan brothers, renounced all property. Another important note is the mention of the Gospel, which is ultimately the real rule and obliges the friars and the sisters to conform to the counsels formulated by Christ himself, even though they do not figure explicitly in the rule.

One half of chapter VI of this rule is taken up by copies of two letters written by the father to his daughters, spelling out his intentions. Thus, even though the founder was no longer in this world, he lived again in the rule of life that he formulated during his lifetime.

PART THREE

The Bitter Path of Fidelity

1217–1224

1. The Extension of the Franciscan Order

After the twofold foundation whereby he settled his disciples in two official religious institutes, one for men at Santa Maria degli Angeli, the other for women at San Damiano, Francis of Assisi felt useless. Too much so. He had managed a double kick-off: he had succeeded in starting two new religious orders that lived under strict rules. What was he good for now, even if he was treated as a father by all those men and all those women? Did he have a presentiment about the crisis that would soon shake the men's institute and feel powerless to resolve it? He suddenly wondered whether he had the wisdom to govern a community, and he had doubts about his mission as a preacher. The immense desire that gripped his soul was to withdraw to the silence of a hermitage, far from everyone, and to devote himself there to intense prayer for this double order which did not seem to need his oversight.

For a long time he pleaded with God to make known his will for him. But how was God going to answer? Through the mouth of his most faithful servants. It would be enough to question two of them, and if their answers were the same, God would have spoken through them. He called Masseo and spoke to him as follows: "Brother, go find our sister, Clare, and ask her for me: 'What is best for Brother Francis: to dedicate himself to preaching or to prayer alone?' When you have her answer, go and find Brother Sylvester, and ask him the same question. Then come back and tell me their answers."

Why Sylvester? The *Fioretti* explain: "He had such piety and such sanctity that he obtained all that he asked of God."

So Masseo left for San Damiano, where Clare asked him to come by again later for her answer. Then he went to Sylvester, who was staying at the hermitage of Carceri, one league east of Assisi. Sylvester immersed himself in prayer and then almost immediately gave the response: "Here is what God says: God did not call Brother Francis to

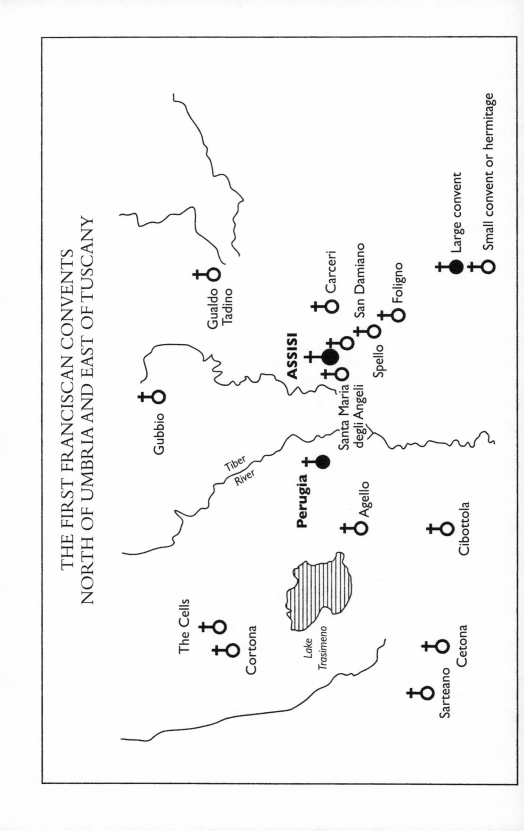

THE FIRST FRANCISCAN CONVENTS
NORTH OF UMBRIA AND EAST OF TUSCANY

Gualdo Tadino

Carceri

San Damiano

Foligno

Large convent

Small convent or hermitage

Gubbio

ASSISI

Spello

Tiber River

Santa Maria degli Angeli

Perugia

Agello

Cibottola

The Cells

Cortona

Lake Trasimeno

Sarteano

Cetona

this state of life for his own sake alone, but so that he might bring in a great harvest of souls and many men might be saved by means of him."

Masseo returned to San Damiano, and Clare said the same thing to him.

When the messenger had returned to the Portiuncula, Francis took him into the woods, knelt down, and, with his arms crossed over his chest, asked, "What does my Lord Jesus Christ order me to do?"

"His will", Masseo reported, "is for you to go preach in behalf of the world; for he did not choose you for your sake alone, but also for the salvation of others."

Francis accepted this answer as coming from God, and, although he stayed from time to time in hermitages, he stopped doubting his vocation to be a preacher; by the same token, he no longer called into question his task as the superior.

It was around that same time that Francis found the definitive name for his order. Celano gives a very brief explanation: "He had written in his rule: 'They should be little (*minores*).' Now, one day as he listened to a reading of this passage, he declared, 'I want this fraternity to be called the Order of the Friars Minor.' "

The Mirror of Perfection explains at greater length:

> One day Saint Francis said, "The order and the life of the Friars Minor are like a little flock that the Son of God requested of his Heavenly Father in these latter times, saying, 'Father, I would like you to form and to give to me, in these latter times, a new and humble people, different from all those that have gone before it because of its humility and poverty, a people that will be content to possess me alone.'
>
> "And the Father said to His dearly beloved Son, 'My Son, what you have asked of me has been accomplished.' "
>
> By that, Saint Francis meant to say that the Lord had willed that they should be called the Friars Minor and had revealed it to him.

Given the abundance of new recruits, as of the year 1211, this order could not continue to remain cooped up within the limits of the little estate of the Portiuncula. A swarm had to fly off in search of a new hive. Furthermore, the cramped quarters in the convents and the number of friars living in them demanded that this be done at a brisk tempo. Many of the new residences were only hermitages, staffed by

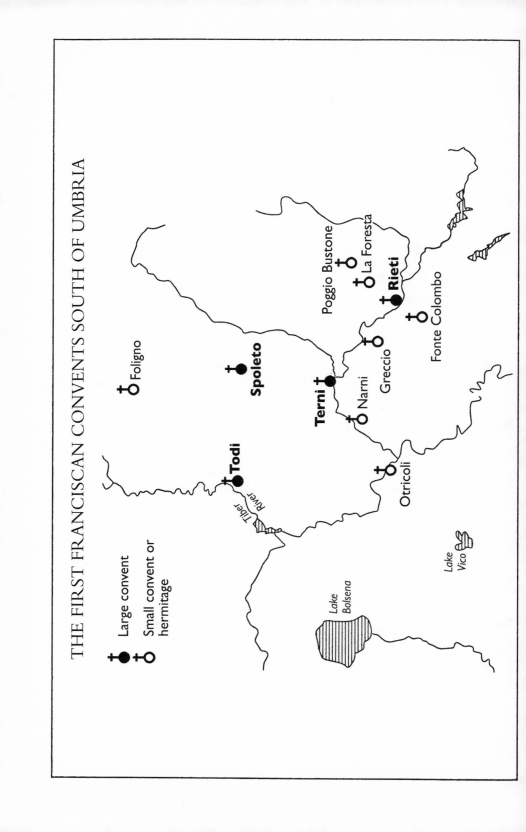

THE FIRST FRANCISCAN CONVENTS SOUTH OF UMBRIA

Large convent

Small convent or hermitage

Foligno

Todi

Spoleto

Terni

Narni

Otricoli

Greccio

Poggio Bustone

La Foresta

Rieti

Fonte Colombo

Tiber River

Lake Bolsena

Lake Vico

three or four religious, with a *guardian* as their superior—those great convents with twenty to thirty religious were never founded until the end of the century. Now, since the newly professed were arriving almost daily, it was necessary to find new houses for them.

We have little information about the number of convents founded during Saint Francis' lifetime. The first biographers, who focused their attention on the spiritual side of events, made no attempt to keep a record of the residences or to draw up a map of them. We have to look through a multitude of stories for their names. Then there are some that are not named; the chronicler describes a friar as being in "a convent", without specifying which one, since the important thing is the virtue or the eccentricity of the friar. His situation in time or space is a secondary matter—in time, because most often the account gives us no chronological cue, either. Therefore it is up to the historian to try to date the anecdote.

We have watched Bernard of Quintavalle founding a convent in Bologna; this was certainly the first one after the Portiuncula, the work of the first of the disciples. Again it was not Francis who took the initiative, but rather a benefactor who was filled with admiration for the preacher. This new convent seems to have admitted a considerable number of religious, because after a while the guardian (perhaps it was still Bernard) called the masons to build a real house. Francis, while returning one day from preaching in Verona, decided to visit his brothers in Bologna. Now, when he asked the way, they spoke to him about "the friars' house". This was an affront to his concern for poverty. Not only did he refuse to enter that convent owned by his confreres in religion, but he arrived unexpectedly and angrily ordered them to vacate the premises. Even the sick friars were ousted. Since there were several of them, we must assume that the total number was rather high. This is understandable, though, if we recall that not only Francis but also his first twelve friars had the authority to admit new postulants to profession; now Bernard was one of them, and his sanctity and his eloquence did not fail to attract recruits.

Where did those poor friars sleep once they had been thrown out by their superior general? Celano, who relates the anecdote for us, does not say. What he does tell us, on the other hand, shows how astute the friars were; without any acrimony against their superior, no doubt, they complained of their lot to Hugolino, the cardinal-bishop

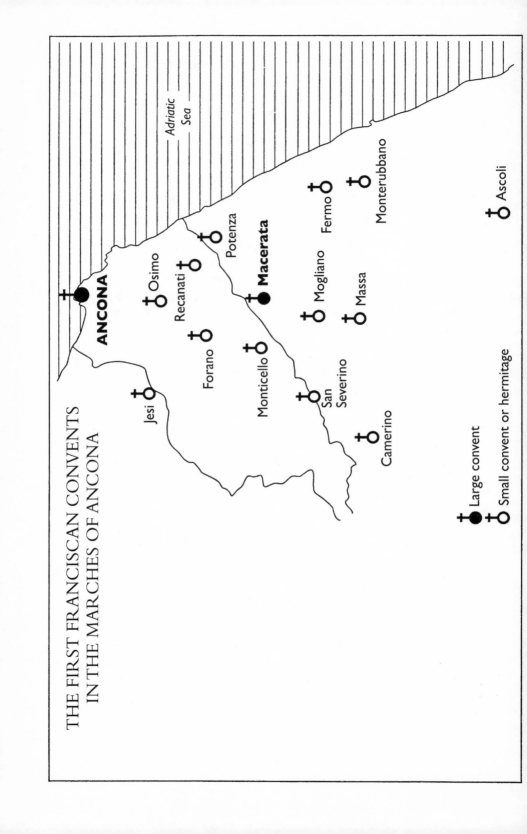

THE FIRST FRANCISCAN CONVENTS
IN THE MARCHES OF ANCONA

Adriatic
Sea

ANCONA

Osimo

Recanati

Potenza

Macerata

Mogliano
Fermo

Monterubbano

Massa

Forano

Ascoli

Monticello

Jesi

San
Severino

Camerino

Large convent

Small convent or hermitage

of Ostia, who had interceded for the approval of the rule and who would one day become the official "cardinal-protector" of the Order of Friars Minor. The cardinal, who at that time was serving as papal legate in Lombardy, found an elegant solution: he declared himself to be the proprietor of the convent. Therefore the friars could resume their occupation of it.

One of the very first convents was set up near Cortona, a city in Tuscany that would soon win renown because of Saint Margaret, the famous penitent of the seraphic order [the Franciscans]. It owed its existence to a young man from that city, Guido, who, although a layman, lived an austere life consecrated to prayer and penance. He invited Francis of Assisi, who had come to preach in that place, to stay at his house. From the moment that he set eyes on him, Francis understood that his host was made of extraordinary stuff; he accepted. In fact, after the meal, the young man threw himself at Francis' feet and begged to be admitted to his order. He was admitted, on the condition that he would sell all his belongings. He was rich, but even so he managed to transfer his inheritance quickly and to distribute the proceeds from it to the poor. Once that was done, Francis clothed him in the penitential robe in the presence of a great gathering of people. Guido asked for permission to live as a hermit and withdrew a half a league from the city, to a place that is still called *Les Celles di Cortona*, the Cells of Cortona. Others soon followed his example; new friars joined him, and a convent was established.

Whenever he was in that region, Francis loved to go to the Cells of Cortona and stay there. Once he was wearing over his shoulders a new coat (once does not mean customarily), which his brothers at the Portiuncula had taken great pains to make for him. No doubt he had left the previous one in the hands of a poor woman. But scarcely had he entered the convent when a destitute man appeared at the door, saying, "Good brothers, have pity on my misery! I am a widower, and I have a large family to feed."

True or false? At that time, no doubt, shams were more common than they are today. And if the beggar had been on the lookout, he would have found Francis' coat quite promising; the garment in question had no sleeves but was an enormous cape that covered the entire body.

Witnessing the scene, Francis immediately removed the cloak and put it over the beggar's arm. "There, I give it to you for the love of God. But you must sell it and get a good price for it."

Convinced that their father was letting himself be deceived, and with no respect whatsoever for this charitable gesture, the friars pounced on the coat and snatched it from the hands of the poor man (whether real or feigned). But Francis intervened on his behalf. Finally, the religious themselves sold it and gave him the proceeds.

There was also a Franciscan convent, probably contemporaneous to the Cells, midway between Perugia and Cortona, in the market town of Preggio. While walking in the vicinity, Francis heard behind him the footsteps of someone who was trying to catch up with him. He turned around: it was a woman, who asked him to pray for her. Indeed, her husband was an unjust and violent man, and she begged the saint to pray for his conversion. "Go", he told her. "Go back to your husband and tell him for me to save his soul."

She returned to her dwelling and found her husband.

"And where have you been?" he asked in a threatening tone.

"I have just seen Blessed Francis. He gave me a blessing and told me to save our souls."

A spiritual dew then fell on the soul of the wicked husband, who tenderly declared, "My dear wife, from now on we will serve the Lord, and we will save our souls."

Emboldened by this attitude, she went further, "And to do that, would not it be good for us to live in continence? That is a virtue which is very pleasing to God."

The husband acquiesced. "As you wish."

The *Legenda antiqua* adds: "Many persons, not only among the laity, but also among the religious, were quite astonished to see the holiness of that man, who had been so worldly and became spiritual so quickly. The husband and the wife persevered to the end in performing good works. They died a few days apart. They were much lamented."

In the year 1212 a convent in Rome was bestowed upon Francis, which was later called San Francesco a Ripa, where one of the oldest portraits of him is preserved, the one attributed to Margaritone d'Arezzo. The famous Brother Giles lived there for some time. In order to comply with the rule, he did manual labor. He began by walking to a forest situated at about fifteen kilometers from the city; there he collected bundles of sticks, which he then sold in order to buy food for the convent. In the autumn he hired himself out to gather in the grapes. He planned free time in the midst of his work, however, so as to pray and recite the Divine Office.

Giles then stayed for a time, under orders from Francis, at the convent in Fabriano, then at the one in Agello, south of Perugia, where he had to battle against demons. Then he took refuge in the hermitage of Cetona, not far from or perhaps right on the estates of Orlando of Chiusi, who had donated La Verna. Then he was admitted to the convent in Cibottola, south of Perugia again.

It was at that time also that the convent in Spoleto was established. Francis made at least one protracted stay there. At that time a violent, blasphemous individual was on the rampage in that town, who never missed an opportunity to insult and curse the friars as they went begging. The friars, who had not yet attained perfect joy, complained to their father. He called them together and had them kneel down, ordering them to pray for the conversion of that hardened sinner. Scarcely had they stood up when the man knocked on the door, tearfully asking forgiveness, which he readily obtained.

In 1213 the convent of Monte Casale was built, at the dead-end of a road that begins at Borgo Sansepolcro. Francis was on his way there when he was accosted by a young knight from the family of the counts of Tarlati, very refined in his appearance and speech, who said to him, "Father, I would like to be admitted to your community of friars."

"My son," the saint replied, "you are young and delicate. Will you be able to endure our poverty and our strict observance?"

"Are you not men like me?" the knight retorted proudly. "If you can endure it, why shouldn't I?"

Saint Francis liked him and admitted him in a clothing ceremony under the name of Brother Angelo. He made such progress toward perfection that a short time later he was appointed guardian of the convent of Monte Casale. He was the one who chased after and then admitted the bandits who became friars.

That locality, like Cortona, is in the eastern part of Tuscany, near the Marches of Ancona. The region was well traveled in all directions by the sons of Saint Francis, who easily found precipitous places where they could set up hermitages. Yet they pressed on even farther in making foundations in that province: in Florence, Prato, Pisa, San Gimignano, and Siena.

Obviously, the little Franciscan residences sprang up around Assisi, tentatively at first, as adjuncts to the Portiuncula. There was a convent in Foligno, in the city where Francis had sold his piece of cloth to pay for the repairs to San Damiano and which was made illustrious at the close of the century by the great mystic, Angela. It seems that around that area there were several hermitages where Brother Juniper stayed: in Spello and in Satriano. Is it possible that Francis stayed in the latter occasionally? In Celano's biography, we find the name "Sarteano", which is actually a place situated to the east of Tuscany, not far from Lake Trasimeno. But in this case the geographical terminology is confused.

The Rieti valley, at the border between Latium (the Papal States) and Umbria, was also criss-crossed by Francis and his disciples. In Rieti itself a convent loomed where Francis stayed at the end of his life, at the order of Cardinal Hugolino, for treatment of the eye disease from which he suffered. Immediately to the south of the city arose the hermitage of Fonte Colombo, where Francis had to stay in 1223 to write his definitive rule; that was also where the doctors from Rieti came to treat him. To the north, in Poggio Bustone, we see Francis celebrating Christmas and trying to persuade the pious people not to honor him, because he had eaten food prepared with lard.

Many, too, were the convents founded in that part of the Marches of Ancona, a region that borders on Umbria to the north and that had first heard the preaching of Brother Philip the Tall, one of the first twelve companions. We find three of them southwest of Macerata: Soffiano, Roquebrune, and Brunforte (later San Liberato). The *Fioretti* describe an anonymous religious from Soffiano who duplicated the miracles of the early days:

> There was a Friar Minor endowed with such great holiness and grace that he seemed entirely divine, and he was frequently enraptured in God. Sometimes, when he was absorbed and exalted in God, birds of different kinds came to him and perched familiarly on his shoulders, his head, his arms, his hands, and sang wondrously. This brother loved solitude, and spoke but rarely; when he was questioned on a subject, however, he answered so graciously that he seemed to be an angel rather than a man.

It is likely that Brother Philip resided at the convent that he had founded in Recanati, between Ancona and Macerata. While there he happened to receive into the order a young adolescent, John of Penna. The latter had had a dream: a beautiful child, adorned with divine graces, appeared to him and said, "Go to San Stefano. There you will find a large crowd listening to a preacher. That is Philip, one of my brothers, and I am the one who sent him. Listen to him, and act on his words."

The youth ran to San Stefano, listened to Philip's preaching and afterward went to speak to him, "Father, I want to do penance and serve Jesus Christ. Give me the habit of your order."

Philip did not make a face upon seeing how young his interlocutor was; he did not express doubts as to his ability to withstand the rigors of Franciscan life. He immediately perceived his purity of heart and generosity and admitted him without delay. After a time, Brother John asked to be sent to Provence, where he remained for twenty-five years, edifying the religious and the common people by his sanctity. When news of this reached the friars in the Marches, they demanded that he return. And he returned. He believed that his earthly pilgrimage was completed, but he lived for another thirty years.

The *Fioretti* also mention, in the vicinity of Fermo, the convents of Massa, Mogliano, Monterubbiano, Penne San Giovanni; and further to the north, between Macerata and Ancona, the convents of Forano, Monticello, Potenza Picena, and Sirolo.

From afar, to an imagination tinged with romanticism, life in a hermitage seems to possess a wonderful charm and to lend itself to contemplation by all souls that are in love with God. Now, as we have seen in Rivo Torto and at the Portiuncula, the first-generation Franciscans were, in many instances, imaginative and otherworldly individuals; despite their fervor, they tended too often to sacrifice discipline to the inspiration of the moment and to uncontrolled enthusiasm. The fewer brothers there were in a hermitage, the less coherence the community had. As a result, as Francis complained, many friars lived as they pleased, with no concern for their neighbors, disregarding the daily schedule and the preaching itinerary. Since there was no system for assigning personnel, there were many also who used to go from one hermitage to another as it suited them or when they became bored.

Francis was not unaware of these disorders. Every time that he had an opportunity, he preached adherence to the rule and consideration for others. But he could not be everywhere. Eventually, probably in the year 1218, he got around to composing a rule for the hermitages. It is a very curious document, scarcely one page long, in which charity wins out over austerity:

> Those who want to reside as religious in a hermitage should stay there in groups of three or four at the most. Two of them will be the mothers, and two (at least) will be the children. The former will lead the life of Martha, the two others—the life of Mary. . . . Those who lead the life of Mary will be subject to cloister; each one will have his own cell, so that they will neither dwell nor sleep together. . . . They will observe silence, recite the hours [of the Divine Office], and will rise [during the night] for Matins. . . . They will not allow anyone to enter their cloister. . . . The children will then take the part of the mothers, at intervals that they will have agreed on.

This rule, however—besides the fact that it was imposed only on the tiny convents with two or three friars and not on the large houses that were founded in the cities, which numbered anywhere from ten to twenty religious—was not enough to maintain discipline. The order had grown too fast, and Francis was unable to exercise his authority over so many convents. He required trusted intermediaries to oversee and govern in his place. These were the ministers: the word *minister* in Latin means servant; indeed, Francis was determined that none of his brothers should hold a title that would place him above the others.

Each minister, designated by the superior general (who could also revoke the appointment) had authority over a province, that is, a group of convents that were clustered geographically, if possible around an important town that itself had a convent, often with a larger number of personnel. As early as 1217, Francis set up eleven provinces, which shows how much the convents had proliferated.

The most curious thing is that Umbria, which had more than twenty houses, was not erected as a province: it was included in the province of Tuscany, along with the territory of Rome. The Marches of Ancona, where we have observed around fifteen houses, formed a province, at the head of which Francis placed Benedict of Arezzo. The whole northern part of Italy, that is, Lombardy, Piedmont, Emilia, Liguria, Venice, and Romagna, made up the province of Bologna; it was governed by Peter Stacia. The province of Terra di Lavoro included the region of Campania around Naples; its minister was Brother Augustine of Assisi, who died on the same day as Saint Francis. The province of Puglia extended throughout that duchy along the Adriatic coast. Finally, there was Calabria, which encompassed Sicily, covered the other half of the southern extreme of Italy, and had as its minister Brother Peter of San Andrea.

In addition to these six provinces there were five abroad. The province of France comprised the entire country to the north of the Loire River. But its foundation was more a project for the future than the organization of an existing reality. Francis, who dearly loved that land and had never stopped singing its poetry, resolved to go himself to establish his order there. In 1217, together with Masseo, he set off without further ado in a northerly direction. After his arrival in Florence, he went to see Cardinal Hugolino, who asked him where he was going in such a carefree manner. Upon hearing the news that this superior general of a rapidly expanding order that was threatened with disorder was leaving his command and observation post, his tone became severe: "You must not cross the Alps! Do you not know that in the Curia there are some prelates who are opposed to your order? You must remain in Italy to see to the defense of your rule and of your brothers."

Although Francis understood the legitimacy of this prohibition, he nevertheless presented an objection to it: Was it not unworthy of a superior to send his sons on a mission, to suffer weariness and run risks, while he remained safe and sound?

Hugolino swept the objection aside and ordered Francis to return to Assisi. He obeyed and appointed Brother Pacificus to plant the order in France. Pacificus departed with thirty friars and the title of provincial minister to go to a country where he was not the superior of any convent—a country with which he was furthermore unacquainted. But he had promised holy obedience. His destination, obviously, was Paris. But he was no doubt frightened by that imposing city with its high ramparts; he decided to skirt them with his friars and arrived instead at the Abbey of Saint-Denis. The abbot, upon seeing that troop of miserable wretches in rags who called themselves the poor of Jesus Christ, allowed them to take up temporary residence in an outbuilding of the monastery. But when they tried to preach, it was another matter altogether: they were mistaken for Cathari [members of a heretical sect]. They were summoned to Paris by Bishop Pierre de Nemours, who received them in an audience while flanked

by doctors from the Sorbonne. The only answer that Pacificus made
was to bring out from his pocket the text of the rule and to present it
to the bishop. The latter judged that there was nothing in it contrary
to the Catholic faith, and that he had no reason to bother the Friars
Minor. But the rector of the Sorbonne thought that that was insufficient, and he sent his theologians to Rome to inquire. They returned
with a letter personally written by Honorius III, stating that the sons
of Brother Francis were excellent Christians and that they should be
treated accordingly. This was in June of 1219; the friars had lost two
years.

But when they traveled to the areas surrounding Paris, to Meaux,
Senlis, and Soissons, to speak and perhaps to set up convents, the
bishops refused to grant them permission to preach. This time it was
the Franciscans who had recourse to Rome. The Pope manifested his
protection and support with great solemnity: he published on May
29, 1220, a bull that eulogized the Friars Minor. All of France was
now put on notice.

In 1223 Pacificus was relieved of his duties and returned to Italy. It
was probably understood that the order would make more progress
in France under the direction of a religious who had more experience in organization. Francis sent Gregory of Naples, who had served
as vicar general of the order while he himself had been in the Holy
Land: thus an administrator succeeded a poet. Gregory was convinced
that, in order to preach in Paris and also to organize missions in the
Île-de-France, Champagne, and Touraine, it was necessary to set up
headquarters in the capital. He obtained the grant of an estate located
at the present site of the Luxembourg Gardens, then called Vauvert
(= *le Val Vert*, the green valley). There, foreseeing an influx of recruits, he had an enormous convent of stone built. When news of it
reached Francis, he sent orders to demolish the structure. But he had
reached the end of his life and was sick and secluded, losing more and
more of his authority. Gregory, who was thinking first of the future,
refrained from obeying, and instead ordered the construction work
to proceed. Finally, in 1221, the project was completed. But the vicar
did not have a chance to consecrate the beautiful convent: it collapsed
from top to bottom. Both the friars and the crowd saw therein the
work of the devil, for different reasons, to be sure. The friars considered themselves punished for having opposed the will of their father;
the crowd blamed the devil for stopping the work of these men of

God. The place was called *"le diable Vauvert"* ["Vauvert the devil"], an expression which, by contraction, became *"le diable vert"*.

Gregory made haste to have a new convent built. Thanks to Saint Louis, king of France, and Blanche of Castile, who had great admiration for the new religious, he obtained for this purpose a tract of land near the Benedictine Abbey of Saint-Germain des Prés. Contrary to the intention of Saint Francis, he planned to make this house a center for higher studies and set up there a *studium*, a place where the Franciscan students who were taking courses at the university could find a library and some professors from their own order. The building project was carried out on an unexpectedly large scale. The structure ultimately reached 110 meters in length and 30 meters in width, with 140 cells, most of which were reserved for religious scholastics. During this time the influx of vocations allowed him to found a genuine convent in Saint-Denis and around thirty others in northern France.

Since this multiplication of houses belonging to the order had taken place in Italy, too, Francis organized them according to a new hierarchy: each province was subdivided into custodies, each one under the authority of a *custos* or guardian, who reported to a provincial minister. In 1219 Francis sent Brother Agnello of Pisa to hold that office in a future custody in Paris; his chief task was to oversee the construction of the great convent before occupying it. In 1224, when Francis gave the order to proceed to make foundations in England, Gregory appointed Agnello of Pisa for this mission, who landed at Dover in December together with eight companions. He immediately founded two convents: one at Cornhull near London, the other at Oxford, where he stationed himself and became a collaborator in founding the famous university. The success of the order was so dazzling that, within a few years, the province numbered seven custodies: London, Oxford, Cambridge, York, Worcester, Newcastle, and Bristol. Brother Agnello died in 1232, at the age of thirty-eight, and from that moment on received the veneration reserved to saints. When his body was exhumed seven or eight years later, it was incorrupt and gave off a sweet fragrance. He was beatified by Leo XIII.

While a legion of young men were taking the Franciscan habit in England, Gregory of Naples was recruiting an elite corps for the order in France. In 1224 he admitted the Englishman Aymon of Faversham, the future minister-general, with three of his learned countrymen. Then there was Julian of Speyer, precentor [or choirmaster] of

Saint Louis and future author of a biography of Saint Francis; then a professor at the University of Paris, the Englishman Alexander of Hales, who did not give up his teaching career and thus gave the Friars Minor a reserved chair on the faculty. The French province would grow to the point of subdividing into nine custodies, comprising fifty-three convents. The rule of Saint Francis had conquered France during the reign of Saint Louis.

The order of Saint Dominic enjoyed almost the same degree of success. So much so that the atmosphere of the Latin Quarter in Paris was transformed by it. During the first quarter-century of the University of Paris, the scholars, let loose at a very young age in a bustling district without supervision or guidance, soon developed a way of life that was hardly recommendable. Houses of prostitution cropped up everywhere, and they had a large clientele. The creation of the *colleges*—that is to say, boarding houses that offered the students room and board, tutors, and manuscripts—had started to impose a certain discipline on these youths, since they ran on strict schedules, with a curfew immediately after the evening meal. But these houses sheltered only a fraction of the university population. The ascendancy of the mendicant orders worked a veritable transformation within it.

"The Dominicans and the Franciscans", wrote Eudes de Châteauroux, chancellor of the university, "have completely reformed the students' morals. A very large number of the young men have entered these religious orders, and the others, although remaining in the world, have embraced a decent way of life."

In a parallel development, the sons of Francis in Oxford had a great intellectual and spiritual influence. At the university they procured an abundance of students, then their best teachers. Thomas of Eccleston dedicated a volume to this edifying foundation. He describes for us in great detail this new youth movement that filled the Franciscan *studium* [house of studies], how they went joyfully to their lectures, then returned immediately to chant the Divine Office in choir—an Office that was sung to perfection, because the Franciscans in Oxford would prove to be the most zealous teachers and interpreters of Gregorian chant in England. These young men, furthermore, were very high spirited, and it took rigorous efforts on the part of their superiors to prevent them from bursting out laughing in the middle of the Office at the slightest provocation. One novice, who failed to correct this fault quickly enough, had to take the discipline as many as eleven times in the same day.

The Friars Minor in Cambridge were less intellectual. They settled in a district inhabited by the common people, and their first convent, as at Santa Maria degli Angeli, consisted at first of a group of sheds side by side. They endeared themselves to the populace, which marveled at them as they walked barefoot in the snow.

The success that they experienced in France and England was not repeated in Germany; the arrival and establishment of the Friars Minor there have been narrated by one of them, Jordan of Giano, in a picturesque chronicle. Saint Francis had formed an idealized notion of the inhabitants of that country, when he watched the pilgrims visiting the tombs of the apostles: recollected, staff in hand, a gourd of water at their belt, they seemed to be a specimen of the devotion practiced by their compatriots.

In 1217 Francis, still lacking foresight, and counting on the protection of Providence, placed Brother John of Penna at the head of sixty religious and ordered him to preach and found convents in Germany. Neither he nor any of his companions spoke German. We cannot say that they did not know a single word of it, because they were acquainted with precisely one, without knowing what it meant, however. The word was *ja*. At the first stop that they made, in a hospitable town, the people asked them whether they were hungry; they did not understand, but answered *ja*, and were fed heartily. It was a good formula.

The next day, in contrast, they came to a market town where they immediately aroused suspicion. They were mistaken for heretics. Someone asked them, "Are you Waldensians?"

They promptly answered, "*Ja!*"

To their surprise, they were bullied and beaten. They were reported to the police. They were imprisoned, scourged, and finally driven away. They did an about-face and returned to Italy, insisting that they had no business in that dreadful country, unless someone wanted to gain the palm of martyrdom.

Francis did not lay down his arms. In 1223, at the conclusion of the general chapter at which the friars were gathered, he asked for volunteers for the foreign missions to sit down a slight distance away.

Ninety responded to the appeal. Jordan was among them. Brother Elias, who at that time was serving as Francis' vicar general, appointed Brother Caesarius of Speyer provincial for Germany—he was probably the only German present. The latter decided to choose on the spot those who would accompany him.

When he came to Jordan, Caesarius laconically said, "You!"

"Me what?"

"For Germany."

"Now," Jordan relates, "at that time I feared only two things, which I asked God in my prayers to spare me: falling into heresy and dying a victim of the fierce Teutons."

The good friar regretted having gone aside. "Not at all!" he exclaimed. "I do not want to go off to Germany. The country is too cold, very bad for my health."

Astonished by this lack of both mortification and obedience, the provincial minister did not dare to compel the reluctant friar and brought him to the vicar instead. After all, he had the authority.

Elias cut to the quick, "Brother, I order you, in the name of holy obedience, to make a decision. Do you want to go to Germany or not?"

Jordan was perplexed. Since it was in the name of obedience, he had to answer right away and without equivocating. Yet, on the one hand, he was afraid of being tortured by the Teutons and of renouncing his faith; on the other hand, it seemed cowardly to him to back out of this mission. Since his will remained in suspense, he consulted a brother who gave good advice, "What should I do, in your opinion?"

"The most religious thing to do is to go back and see Brother Vicar and tell him, 'Father, I have no preference. I will do what you consider good for me to do.' "

He followed the advice. Elias replied, "I order you to follow Brother Caesarius to Germany."

He resigned himself to his fate. Since it was under obedience, God was certainly happy with him. He counted the friars who were preparing to depart: twenty-seven in all, twelve clerics and fifteen lay brothers. Among them, Thomas of Celano, the future biographer of Saint Francis, and Giovanni di Piante de Carpine, who would one day be the ambassador of Innocent IV to the great Khan of the Mongols.

They crossed the Alps by the Brenner Pass and arrived in Tyrol in small groups, so as to avoid giving the impression that they were plotting an invasion. At any rate, no doubt thanks to the explanations offered by Brother Caesarius, they were received with open arms; they preached and received houses and lands on which to build. It was in the Rhine Valley, however, that they founded their first convents, perhaps because of Brother Caesarius' relatives: in Strasbourg, Speyer, Worms, Mainz, and Cologne; then, as they made their way eastward, in Würzburg, Regensburg, Salzburg, and Erfurt. Then, thanks to an abundance of recruits, the foundations multiplied. To the point where, in 1230, they had to divide the Teutonic province in half: Rhineland and Saxony.

In Hungary the welcome was not as warm as the one first received by the friars in Germany. Francis, more practical this time, insisted that his missionaries be accompanied by a man capable of speaking the language, which none of his own men knew. He found a Hungarian bishop who was returning to his diocese after a visit to Rome: an excellent introduction to that suspicious people. But the bishop, in his haste to get back to his palace, abandoned those straggling Friars Minor along the way, and they no longer had any defense against the antipathy and mistrust that they met with. As soon as they entered a town, the militia confronted them to throw them out; they took refuge in the villages, but then the peasants would set the dogs on them. Finally they returned to Italy. Not until Francis' successors headed the order was a new mission to Hungary planned.

2. Chapters and Far-Off Missions

The sheer number of convents and friars caused problems in governing them, and Francis resolved them by instituting provinces and custodies; but then the ministers and the guardians had to be determined to exercise their authority according to the mind and the will of the founder. Such a great number also posed a problem of unity: the dispersion of the religious throughout the world kept them outside the sphere of influence of Francis and his first disciples; the recruits in France, England, and Germany, having never gone to Assisi, were unacquainted with the spirit of the Portiuncula, and they never saw any other religious except those of their own province or custody. Furthermore, they solved their problems on the spot, without referring them to the superiors or confreres who had already solved them, along the lines of the initial spirit of the founder. In the long term, this dispersion threatened to break up the order: a physical break-up because the communities were leading almost separate lives, a breakdown in spirit because the rule was being interpreted freely in the different convents. To cope with this serious danger, but also to allow the distant friars to make the same decisions as the others, Francis created the chapter. The term was not new, since it was used by canons regular as a name for their clerical community, and also by the monks to designate their assembly around their abbot. Francis of Assisi would give the term an extended meaning proper to his order. Besides, the Cistercian abbots used to gather each year at a general chapter in Cîteaux. It is easy to see that the reunion of Franciscans on the meadows of the Portiuncula had nothing in common with that of the Cistercians in the capitular meeting-hall in Cîteaux.

The Franciscan chapters were held from the earliest years of the order, but they were smaller in size and less solemn. At that time their purpose was to reunite the friars (who at first were housed exclusively at the Portiuncula, and later in a few nearby hermitages) in a plenary assembly. Since the preaching tours of some lasted longer than those of others, there were always some friars absent when preachers returned to the mother house. Francis decided that twice a year, for the Feasts of the Portiuncula and of Saint Michael, all the friars had to be back home. As *The Three Companions* relate it:

> They discussed the best ways of observing the rule and appointed friars to go through the various provinces preaching to the people and founding new communities. Blessed Francis declared to them the admonitions, the rebukes, and the orders that seemed to him in keeping with God's designs. But he strove with all his heart to demonstrate in his own life everything that he recommended to them in these discussions.

With the passage of years, the most important chapter became the one held at Pentecost, which gathered not only the friars in Italy, but also those from far-off lands. Not all of them, obviously, for they numbered in the thousands; but of necessity the ministers, and if possible the guardians, along with a significant number of representatives for the other religious. In order to avoid too much disorganization in the convents, since the superior had to be absent for a time so as to attend these reunions, the chapters took place only once a year, starting in 1217, at Pentecost; then, from 1223 on, once every three years.

It was the chapter in 1217 which decided, in view of the great increase in the number of friars, on the division of the order into provinces and the commissioning of founders to work in foreign lands. However, once all of these friars had either returned to their usual convents or else had sallied forth to conquer new peoples, Francis suddenly felt unbearably alone. To be sure, he was still surrounded by his companions from the very beginnings, but the Portiuncula was now no more than a tiny island in the midst of an unknown sea. All of those new friars, admittedly full of faith, Gospel virtues and fervent dedication to the Kingdom of God, had only very little in common with the vagabonds who had created the order with him. They seemed to be much more refined and much more deliberate. No doubt, among the earliest friars had been Peter the jurist and Sylvester the priest; but neither the learning of the one nor the sacerdotal authority of the other had prevented them from blending in with the original group of inspired mendicants. But now he no longer felt that he was in communication with the large number of these newcomers, who nevertheless were Friars Minor through and through. But can a large order be compared with a little community?

One night he had a dream. He saw a little black hen, surrounded by a multitude of chicks, but, despite her efforts, she could not gather them under her wings. Besides, they scarcely even sought their mother's protection: they were coming and going freely, unconcerned about her distress.

Upon awakening, Francis understood the meaning of the dream: "The hen represents me. I am little and dark-skinned. But the Lord, in his mercy, has given me and shall give me many children, who cannot be protected by my strength alone. I must entrust them to the Church, so that she may guard them in the shadow of her wings, protect and govern them."

What did he mean, the Church? The Supreme Pontiff, of course, who had already approved the rule under which all these friars were living; and the cardinals of the Roman Curia, his counselors, among whom was his friend Hugolino, who had already done so much for the establishment and development of the order. He set out for Rome, and so great was the cardinal's affection for him that he received him at once in an audience. Francis confided to his friend the difficulties that he was encountering now in governing his order, which had members scattered everywhere and seemed likely to extend much farther still.

"The Pope", Francis said to him, "has enough business to attend to throughout the Church without counseling me and protecting my order as well. Couldn't he delegate to you his supervision of the order so that you could be its official protector?"

Hugolino thought that that was quite an extraordinary request and that it had little chance of being granted. The Pope's co-workers had other things to do than assisting the general of a religious order in the government of his subjects. Yet he suspected that if the little poor man of Assisi spoke openly to Honorius as he had done before, with his impetuosity and ingenuity, he would probably gain a hearing.

"Tomorrow", he said, "I will arrange a papal audience for you, to which I will summon all the cardinals now present in Rome. And you will preach for them."

Francis was alarmed. "But I am a poor, unlettered friar! I am quite willing to speak to peasants or soldiers, but not to the princes of the Church. I have neither the learning nor the talent for that."

Hugolino signaled that he should be silent. "It is not for you to protest. I command you, in the name of obedience, to come tomorrow to the Lateran Palace, where you will be brought to the papal apartments. There, you will speak as the Holy Spirit inspires you."

We should not be surprised that this prelate could arrange the Pope's schedule so easily: the Bishop of Ostia was the first among the cardinals, and he exercised a great deal of authority over the Curia and over the Pontiff himself. Incidentally, at the death of Honorius III, Hugolino would be elected by the Sacred College as his successor.

Francis gave in. The following day, escorted into the Pope's "chamber", that is, into the hall where he gave audiences, he discovered that he was expected. He spoke impromptu, without any preconceived order, without any striving for rhetorical effect; he spoke from the heart, out of his love for Christ, with his passion for the Gospel. When he was done, he noticed that his listeners were captivated. Hugolino nodded with a knowing smile, as though to assure him of his success. Then, without waiting for his intermediary to make his request, Francis himself turned to the Pope and said: "Holy Father, I am moved with compassion by the thought of the cares that beset you and the hardships that you endure constantly for the good of the Church. But what astounds me even more is that you should show so much concern and solicitude for us poor little brothers. Whereas the faithful who are of noble birth or rich and many religious cannot themselves gain admission to see you, we ought to be filled with fear and consternation—we, the poorest and most miserable of religious —at the thought that we are entering into your presence, that we cross the threshold of your palace and dare to knock at your door. And so with humility and reverence, I beg Your Holiness to deign to give us as a father the Lord Bishop of Ostia who is present here, so that the friars can have recourse to him in difficult times, while safeguarding, of course, the rights of your supreme authority."

The request was cause for astonishment, and the cardinals looked at one another, wondering how the Pope was going to react. But the Pope had been won over by the two speeches of Francis: the sermon and the request. And he had at his side the most imposing figure among his collaborators, who approved of the strange petition of the little poor man. He said yes and publicly declared the Cardinal-Bishop of Ostia to be the protector of the Order of Friars Minor.

At this point *The Three Companions* add a touching detail:

> Blessed Francis, admiring the fidelity and devotion of the Bishop of Ostia for the friars, had the deepest and most tender affection for him in return. Since he knew by a revelation from God that this cardinal would become the pope, he proclaimed it to him in all the letters that he sent him, and used to call him the Father of the whole world. He began the letters in this way: "To the venerable Father of the whole world in Christ".

Hugolino, taking his role as protector seriously, went to Assisi in 1218 to preside at the Pentecost chapter. Francis and the chief ministers went to meet him. At the sight of them, the cardinal dismounted and took off his cardinal's robes, revealing the plain Franciscan robe that he was wearing underneath. He took off his shoes and walked barefoot, followed by the friars who sang canticles, as far as Santa Maria degli Angeli, where he celebrated Solemn High Mass. Francis served as deacon. Indeed, we can tell from a number of allusions to it in the biographies that he had received that sacred order some years before, although there is no precise information as to the date and place of this ordination. Then, after the Mass, the protector asked to wash the feet of several friars, as we see Jesus doing in the Gospel of Saint John.

The most famous chapter in this period of the Franciscan order was the "Chapter of the Mats", so called because most of the participants had made themselves a litter of rushes or of woven straw so as to spend the night under the stars. The year in which it took place is debated; some give 1221 as the date. (However, Alexandre Masseron remarks that one of the most important personages in that assembly was Cardinal Hugolino, who was unable to travel in 1221 and therefore had sent Cardinal Rainier, bishop of Viterbo, as his delegate. The most probable date, therefore, is 1219.)

The order had become so well established everywhere that the number of participants was estimated at five thousand. When he arrived on the scene, the protector was amazed. Here is the description in the *Fioretti*:

> In such a vast multitude, no one could be heard telling stories or jokes; but in every place where a group of friars was gathered, they were praying, or reciting the Divine Office, or else lamenting their sins and those of their benefactors, or perhaps conversing about the salvation of souls. . . . So great was their renown that, from the court of the Pope, who was stationed at that time in Perugia, a number of counts, barons, and knights came to visit them, but also many of the common people, as well as cardinals, bishops and abbots, and other clerics. They came to marvel at this gathering, which was so holy, so large, so humble that the world had never seen so many saintly men in one place. They came, above all, to see the very holy head and father of this nation, that man who had seized such impressive booty from the world and gathered such a fine, pious flock to follow in the footsteps of the true shepherd, Jesus Christ.

This swarming but edifying chapter lasted eight days. No one had brought anything to eat, because, trusting in Divine Providence, not one of them had even suspected that he could die of hunger. And indeed, Providence took care of the provisions: every day supply lines were sent out from the nearby cities and towns. The Friars Minor had endeared themselves to the hearts of the people.

As for the cardinal-protector, he brought something even more precious than food for the body: a gift that he had probably begged for, a papal bull, addressed to all the archbishops, bishops, abbots, deacons, and prelates of every sort, explicitly recommending the Friars Minor, whom he declared to be "good Catholics who, like the apostles, sow the seed of the divine word, and whose way of life has been approved by the Supreme Pontiff".

With the cardinal's permission, Francis opened the assembly with a sermon: "My brothers, we have promised great things, but much greater are those things that God has promised us. Let us carry out, therefore, the things that we have promised, and let us await with complete assurance the things that have been promised us. The pleasure of the world is short, and the punishment that follows it is eternal. The suffering of this life is slight, but the glory of the life to come is infinite."

Then he exhorted his brethren to practice obedience to Holy Mother Church and to show reverence toward her ministers; to cultivate fraternal charity, prayer, and patience in adversities; to preserve purity, to be at peace with God and with men; and to keep the rule of holy poverty. He concluded on this theme, which was so dear to him, "By virtue of holy obedience, I order all you who are gathered here to have no care or concern for what you will eat or drink, nor about things that are necessary for the body, but rather that you should devote yourselves solely to prayer and the praise of God. You shall leave the care of your body to him, because he looks after you in a special way."

Saint Dominic had been invited, and he had come. When Francis was finished speaking, he had some doubt as to the validity of this exhortation to poverty: Was it not tempting God to abandon such a great multitude to his Providence? He was still lost in thought when a procession of donkeys, horses, barrows, and carts loaded with foodstuffs emerged onto the plain of the Portiuncula; and besides the food, they brought plates, jugs, goblets, and even napkins. Truly, God was taking care of the little poor men.

Once the provisions had been shared fraternally, Francis spoke up again. He declared that many of the friars, without permission, were resorting to mortifications that endangered their health, and that they all had to exercise great discernment and discretion in this area. Then he ordered all who were wearing penitential instruments to remove them and put them down in front of him. It was a long procession, resulting in a pile of more than five hundred hair shirts and countless bands made of rough bristles, meant to be worn as belts or around an arm or a leg.

When those days of merrymaking, prayer, and instruction were over, Francis gave the penitential habit to many postulants. Then he gave out the obediences. Brother Pacificus, who was representing his province, was appointed minister of France; Brother Benedict of Arezzo was sent to Greece.

But Francis was intent on evangelizing Muslim lands as well. He had made two fruitless attempts and was eager to depart again on a voyage. However, since the cardinal-protector ordered him to stay put so as to govern and oversee his order, he was waiting for the propitious time. For now, he called for missionaries to North Africa. Several volunteered.

He appointed two friars—Giles, whom we know well, and a brother named Electus, "the Chosen"—to go to Tunis in charge of a small but highly motivated group. In principle, the project ought to have been facilitated by the fact that the principality of Tunis, a dependency of the Moroccan Almohads, traded extensively with the Christians of Sicily and Calabria. There were even Italian merchants on site, who maintained commercial relationships both with their compatriots back home and with the Arab traders who did business in the immediate vicinity. All the missionaries had to do was to place themselves under the protection of these Italians, who could initiate them into the local customs. But the Italian merchants wanted nothing to do with sheltering missionaries; they were unwilling to mix business and religion, which would have ruined their economic interests. Surely, a group of friars brandishing the cross would have compromised them irremediably in the eyes of the Muslims. When Giles and his brothers landed and naïvely confided their plans and hopes to their compatriots, they were seized and thrown onto the first skiff to come along, which brought them back to the Italian shore.

But young Brother Electus, who had ardently set foot on African soil in pursuit of martyrdom, did not allow the intrusion of the merchants to interfere with his plan. When they showed up, he hid himself. Once the ship that was carrying off his brothers had departed, he came out of his hiding place to accomplish the mission ordered by his superior and to meet the death that he longed for. The financiers who had underestimated him had not misled him: no sooner had he uttered a few fine phrases (in Latin, no doubt) about converting to Christ, than he was arrested and condemned to death. A relatively painless death, all things considered: he was beheaded.

When his sentence was read to him (probably in Italian), he brought the text of the rule out of his breast pocket, knelt down piously, and, holding in his hands the rule that governed his life, extended his neck for the executioner.

At the end of that same chapter, Francis assigned the brothers who volunteered for the mission in Morocco. There were six of them. We know their names, because five of them have been canonized. They were Vitalis, their superior (who would become minister of Morocco if Providence decreed that the preachers should escape death), and his companions: Berard, Peter, Accursius, Adjutor, and Otto. Guessing what their fate would be, the father made sure of their willingness one last time. They declared that they were ready. Then Francis gave them a final instruction:

> My dear, dear brothers, so that you might conform yourselves better to the will of God, see to it that peace, unity, and unfailing love remain in your midst. Be patient in trials, humble in success. Imitate Christ in poverty, obedience, and chastity. For our Lord was born poor, lived as a poor man, taught poverty, and died poor. And to show us how much he loved chastity, he willed to be born of a virgin and remained virginal himself. He was obedient from his birth until his death on the Cross. Carry with you the rule and your breviary and never omit the recitation of the Hours. O my sons, I rejoice in your good intention, but my heart bleeds at the thought of being separated from you. I beg you to keep in mind always the Lord's sufferings so that this vision might strengthen and encourage you to suffer for him.

The poor friars were certain that they would suffer, but what saddened them was the fact that they knew not a single word of Arabic and therefore wondered how they were going to preach Jesus Christ to a people from a different culture. They simply asked their father, after bowing in submission, to pray for the success of their mission. Then all six knelt down and asked for his blessing.

And so the six preachers of Jesus Christ set out, with nothing but their rule and their breviaries, on a 3,000-kilometer voyage. They did not know how long it would last. They left, as demanded by the Gospel (the reading for the Feast of Saint Matthias, which precipitated Francis' conversion) without shoes, purse, walking staff, or money. Providence went before them to mark out their path and was at their side to arrange for their daily food. Thus they made their way through Tuscany and Liguria, thus they crossed the Alps, thus they traversed the southern part of France—the "Midi" which was so dear to Francis—thus they passed the Pyrenees and arrived in the kingdom of Aragon, which had been liberated from Muslim occupation. There Vitalis fell sick. Very sick, to the point of being unable to continue the journey. But waiting for him was out of the question, for their mission was urgent. Vitalis, unhappy to let his brothers keep traveling without him, unhappy that he was not going to win the palm of martyrdom, remained in the care of charitable people. The others chose Berard as their superior and continued their journey from one town to the next, acquiring as they went a few phrases of conversational Arabic.

And so they arrived in Seville, in the middle of Muslim territory. Their task was beginning, therefore. The city was the capital of the little kingdom of the Abbadids, an ephemeral dynasty ruling over a prosperous populace, where the Christian name was publicly dishonored. What did that matter to our missionaries? Their sole concern was to proclaim Jesus Christ. They had spied the minaret of a mosque: an especially promising place for a sermon. They entered the courtyard. The hour for prayer was approaching, no doubt, because a crowd of men was gathering. This was the moment. Berard started by shouting words to this effect, "My friends, Muhammad is an imposter, and the Qur'an is a tissue of lies."

No need to wait for a reaction: the five heralds of Jesus Christ were surrounded, jostled, beaten, thrown to the ground, and dragged outside. Anything serious? No. Just superficial wounds: some bruises. Well, why not speak to the king himself? Our stalwart preachers did not hesitate at all. They obtained directions to the royal palace and walked in as though they were right at home. And since they asked to see the king, they were brought into his presence. He was intrigued at the sight of these five ragged men covered with dust. Out of curiosity, he asked them, "Why have you come to my city?"

"To proclaim to you our faith in Jesus Christ, so that you might renounce Muhammad, that wretched slave of the devil, and thereby obtain eternal life."

The king gasped in horror and asked them nothing further. He immediately ordered that the blasphemers should be beheaded, but when he saw how joyful they were, he preferred not to make himself the cause of their martyrdom. He decided to expel them; cunningly, though, he had them conducted, not to Christian lands, but to Morocco, where a more powerful monarch than he was reigning: Abû Ya'qûb. His emissaries found it convenient to hand the prisoners over to Don Pedro of Portugal, who had become the leader of the armies and the chief of police for the Muslim sovereign. That Christian prince, like the merchants in Tunis, was afraid that the preaching of these religious or their mere presence might provoke a hostile reaction against the Christians who had entered the service of the Saracen king. And so he took our five dusty heroes into his house with instructions to keep quiet. But as soon as he turned his back, the missionaries went out and gathered the people on the squares. Berard, who had learned better than the others how to recite sentences entirely in Arabic, then spoke up with conviction. The crowd listened, but, being ignorant of the ABCs of Christianity, could they understand the theological presentation, however rudimentary? At least they could grasp the fact that their prophet was being ill-treated.

Now it happened that Abû Ya'qûb walked by the friars and personally heard a few snippets of what they were saying. He was not amused. However, since he hoped for collaboration with the Christians, he preferred not to resort to cruel measures. The best punishment for this untimely zeal was expulsion; at least the people would not hear their blasphemies. He summoned Don Pedro and ordered him to rid Morocco of those troublemakers. Pedro, who valued his honorable and lucrative post more than religious devotion, hastened to provide safe conduct for the missionaries to Ceuta, specifying that they had to board the first ship departing for Italy. But the friars escaped from the guards, returned to the capital, and started preaching again. Upon being informed of this, Don Pedro, full of zeal for his earthly master, instructed his policemen to spy on the preachers and to arrest them as soon as they made a move to speak in public.

This time, too, the five companions slipped through the holes in the net that was stretched out to ensnare them. Now it was a Friday, the day for prayer at the mosque. They knew this. And they took up a position in front of the building.

Someone warned them, "Be careful! The king will come in person!"

This was supposed to make them tremble. On the contrary, it was an unexpected encouragement. As soon as Abû Ya'qûb had dismounted from his horse, Berard, who had climbed up on a cart, began to address him. He was immediately arrested and brought with his companions before the sovereign.

"What business brings you to my city?" he asked severely.

Otto, who was a priest, took it upon himself to reply: "Proclaiming the truth."

"What is truth?"

"It is believing that the Father, the Son, and the Holy Spirit are three Persons in one God."

And in this way the friar presented the entire Nicene Creed. He was beginning to comment on these articles of faith, when the king flew into a rage. "It is the devil", he said, "talking through your mouth."

And he handed the five religious over to the executioners. This time our brave preachers could be sure of martyrdom, and no doubt it would be cruel. But their faith was ready for everything. First they were scourged until the flesh was torn from their bodies; meanwhile they chanted psalms. Then, with their entrails visible and their limbs in tatters, they were rolled over shards of broken pottery; meanwhile they sang canticles. Finally, in exasperation, Abû Ya'qûb (who was present at the torture) took out his scimitar and cut off their heads with his own hand. The date was January 16, 1220.

Don Pedro, who had done nothing to prevent these atrocious deaths, and who certainly was not upset that those troublemakers had been silenced, ordered that the bodies be brought to Portugal, where they could receive the funeral ceremonies that they deserved. The queen, Urraca, his sister-in-law, had already been notified. She was waiting with a large entourage on the wharf where the vessel was to land. All of the eminent clergymen in Portugal accompanied the five coffins with great pomp to Holy Cross Basilica in Coimbra, where they lay in state for the veneration of the faithful.

Upon hearing of this glorious martyrdom, Francis exclaimed, "Now I can say that I truly have five Friars Minor."

He did not yet know the rest of the story. In Coimbra, in the monastery of Santa Cruz near the basilica, lived a pious Canon Regular of Saint Augustine, twenty-five years of age, who was zealously applying himself to his university studies. His name was Ferdinand. He had entered the community of Canons in Lisbon at the age of fifteen and was later transferred to the chapter in Coimbra where, because of his superior intellectual gifts, he was admitted to the clerical course of studies and eventually to the priesthood. The news that

the bodies of the five martyrs had arrived filled him with enthusiasm for the order of Saint Francis: he, too, would go to Morocco
to bear witness, even to the shedding of blood! But to do that, he
would have to be clothed in the gray robe and the rope cincture.
He knew that the Friars Minor had recently established a convent in
Coimbra. His Augustinian superiors reluctantly gave him permission
to leave their institute, and he applied for admission to the Franciscans. He was accepted, took the name of Brother Anthony, and with
the guardian's blessing sailed for Morocco. There he fell sick and had
to board the first ship that departed for Italy. A storm cast him up on
the coast of Sicily. Preparations were being made there for the general
chapter of 1221; being a priest and theologian, he was sent to attend
it; then, since he was not affiliated with any particular convent, he
was recruited by the provincial of Romagna, who assigned him to the
convent of Montepaolo. Later on he ended his days in the convent
in Padua, and so he came to be called Friar Anthony of Padua.

At the moment it was Friar Francis who was envying the martyrs
and making ready to follow in their footsteps. One month after sending his brethren to the land of the Saracens, he learned that an army
of crusaders had just landed in Egypt. That was the place where he
would have to undertake his own mission. There was just one ob-
stacle: it would mean abandoning his post as minister general. He
recalled how, the last time he had started out to make such a voyage,
Cardinal Hugolino had solemnly warned him that his absence could
give free rein to all the starry-eyed idealists, contentious challengers,
and innovators in the order. And then his life's work would be ruined.
But had Christ not promised him that his order would survive him
and last forever? Therefore he would just have to place his confidence
in Christ, the heavenly protector of the Order of Friars Minor, and
entrust the government of it, during his absence, not to one friar (who
might usurp the position of general minister), but to two friars, who
would exercise their authority conjointly. And they would receive the
title of vicar. One of them, Matthew of Narni, would remain at the
Portiuncula to welcome the visiting ministers and to confer the habit
on new friars; the other, Gregory of Naples, having returned from
France, would visit the convents in Italy.

And so it was. Francis teamed up with Peter of Catanio, and on
June 24, having joined a troop of crusaders that was embarking at

Ancona, the two religious were allowed to board one of their ships. Upon landing at Acre, north of Mount Carmel, they were welcomed by the friars of the so-called Province of Syria. Immediately they recruited several of them to travel to Damietta, in the Nile Delta, which at that time was being besieged by the crusaders, under the command of Duke Leopold of Austria.

When he arrived at the Christian camp, he realized that his preaching would have to begin there. The euphoria that he had experienced until then, which had made it easier to bear with all the inconveniences, now gave way to consternation: the bitter smell of death mingled with regret for past sins. Francis' preaching resulted in a movement of repentance, and also in numerous vocations. Within a few days, many men asked to be admitted to his brotherhood, among them Rainier, the prior of the abbey of Saint Michael of Acre.

But eventually he could wait no longer to meet the sultan, the famous Malek-el-Kamel. For a visit like that he took with him only one friar, Illuminatus. While crossing the distance that separated the two camps, the companions chanted a psalm; although Francis sang fearlessly at the top of his lungs, his acolyte trembled a bit. And behold, in a meadow appeared two sheep that were trying to browse on the sparse grass.

Francis said to Illuminatus, "You see, brother, this is a sign from the Lord. For he told us, 'I am sending you like sheep in the midst of wolves.' "

It would take more than that to reassure him; indeed, they were approaching the enemy outposts, and already fierce warriors were striding toward them. Seeing what sort of men they were dealing with, they pounced on them and beat them. Then, not knowing what to do, they brought them to the sultan himself.

He, suspecting that these unarmed vagabonds were spies, unceremoniously asked them, "What are you doing here? Who sent you?"

Francis replied with admirable confidence: "We come from across the sea. And we have been sent to you, not by a man, but by God himself, so as to reveal to you and to your people the way of salvation."

Then he explained, like a theology manual, the dogmas of the Trinity, the Incarnation, and the Redemption. To his surprise he noticed that the sultan was listening to him attentively, and even with interest.

Finally Malek, to the displeasure of his courtiers, exclaimed, "Stay with me! You will be my guests, and you can stay as long as you like."

Francis preferred to go straight to the point, "If you want to be converted to Christ, along with your people, I will very gladly stay among you. But if you hesitate to renounce the law of Muhammad in exchange for faith in Christ, then order your men to light a big fire. I will walk into it with your priests, and then you will know which of the two religions is more certain and holier, and therefore which one you ought to prefer."

The sultan began to laugh. "I doubt very much that one of my priests would be willing, for the sake of his faith, to walk into a fire or to suffer any other torment."

Francis then proposed another deal: he would walk into the flames alone, and, if he came back out unharmed, the sultan would convert to the Christian faith. The other man saw fit to refuse; he was certainly not ready to make that step, which would have transformed his life and precipitated a revolt in the palace. But he offered Francis a reward: sumptuous gifts, which the man of God disdained and refused. "The sultan [Bonaventure writes] only felt more admiration for him, seeing that the saint professed such a profound contempt for worldly goods. Nevertheless, in order to be more certain of salvation, he asked the servant of God to take all those gifts with him and to distribute them among the poor Christians and the churches. But the saint, who dreaded carrying money, absolutely refused."

And so Francis did not manage to carry out either of the two plans that he had made several years before: martyrdom and the conversion of the Saracens. He was still pondering what course of action he should take now, when a messenger arrived in the Christian camp who had crossed the Mediterranean to find him. It was Brother Stephen, who of his own accord came to inform him about serious developments that were troubling the order: the two vicars appointed by the founder were modifying the rule and introducing laxity in the convents. It was time to intervene.

3. The Crisis

Brother Stephen's report was not that surprising. For several years Francis had sensed that a crisis was brewing in his order and would soon boil over. Recall the initial symptoms: the father's indignation at the handsome convent in Bologna where the friars had taken up residence as owners; the dream of the black hen; the increasing numbers of religious and convents, which confirmed the dream; and the annual chapters, in the midst of which Francis felt strange and lost. And then entrusting authority over the entire order in his absence to two religious in whom he did not have complete confidence. But to whom else could he hand over his powers? One friar, later on, asked him whom he could count on to hold the position of general minister; *The Mirror of Perfection* records that he gave the following answer, "My son, I see no one capable of being the leader of such a large and variegated army, the shepherd of such a numerous and extensive flock."

Therefore he had appointed two friars, not as ministers, but as vicars—his personal vicars, while he remained the head of the whole order and did not allow anyone to serve as representatives unless they were authentic Friars Minor, who shared his spirit. And perhaps he guessed that these vicars were not capable of replacing him. But why had he gone away, then? Was it not because, the first time he had decided to go to the lands of the infidels, wise Hugolino had stopped him and sent him back to govern his order? This time he had departed in haste and had not asked the cardinal-protector for his opinion. And the threat hanging over the order had fallen down on him.

What did little Brother Stephen, that zealous servant of the rule, actually report? That many friars (most of the newcomers, no doubt) considered that article of the rule to be senseless that claimed to impose absolute poverty upon them—beginning with the practice of living in makeshift houses with narrow cells. Every time that someone

179

built a solid and spacious convent to last, was the superior going to remove its occupants, as it had happened in Bologna? To be sure, when he left Italy he already knew that his will in this regard was no longer being respected. But how could he temper this opposition, which was hardening and spreading? The author of the *Legenda antiqua* depicts Francis in the final years of his life, resigned to this irrepressible development of his order:

> We, who were with him when he composed the rule and almost all his other writings, testify that he included in them some regulations which the friars—especially the superiors—opposed. During his life they merited him contradictions from his brothers; now that he is dead, they would be very useful to the entire order. But since he feared scandal, he reluctantly condescended to the will of the friars.
>
> However, he often said, "Woe to the friars who are opposed to what I know to be the will of God, for the greater good of the order, even if I bend to their will in spite of myself!"
>
> And he repeatedly told his companions, "What causes me sorrow and distress is to see how certain friars oppose the instructions that I receive from the Divine Mercy by prayer and meditation. They concern the present and future unity of the whole order, and I am confident that they are in conformity with the divine will. But certain friars, on their own authority and solely by the light of their own knowledge, are set against me."

What did Francis learn in Damietta from Brother Stephen's own lips? That there was now a rush of activity by friars who formerly had been close-mouthed about their accommodations. With the approval of the vicar, Gregory of Naples, Peter Stacia, the provincial of Bologna, had erected in that city—despite the previous intervention of the founder—a grand house of studies, in the style of the Order of Preachers, so that the Friars Minor could have the opportunity to take degrees at the university. A grand house! Studies so as to become learned! Both had been expressly forbidden by Francis.

He learned that Philip the Tall, the chaplain of the Poor Clares, had obtained from the Roman Curia a bull of excommunication against anyone who dared to trouble the nuns at San Damiano. A favor from the Roman Curia! This is what Francis had explicitly rejected.

Worse still: when the faithful friars remarked to Gregory that all of these liberties were contrary to the founder's will, the vicar had them imprisoned or whipped.

The opponents always gave the same old excuse: the order of Saint Francis had become impossible to govern because, due to a lack of precision in the rule (which was content simply to list Gospel texts), anarchy had made inroads into this immense army that had neither standing orders nor guidelines. Why had the founder not composed precise regulations, as in the rules of Saint Benedict and Saint Augustine? And so the recalcitrant friars ended up aspiring to the same practices as the Benedictines and the canons regular, as far as buildings, furniture, and food were concerned. Honorius III was prudent: he knew the express will of the founder but at the same time was aware of the weaknesses of the rule. In 1220 he published a bull which imposed a novitiate on the Friars Minor: every postulant to receive the habit had to undergo a year of probation, during which he could be thrown out of the order if he did not acquire its spirit. This was the epitome of wisdom. Yet, as the founder viewed it, this was introducing regrettable novelties into the legislation of the order.

Brother Stephen reported to his minister general another fact even more flabbergasting than the others: the incredible Brother John of Cappella (so called because he refused to comply with orders that he had received and continued to wear very secular headgear instead of a cowl) had just established a new religious institute for himself. Since he had been caring for the lepers (obeying this once the instructions of his spiritual father), he formed a community of lepers, with members of both sexes, and was at that very moment in Rome trying to obtain approval from the Pope.

Upon hearing the news, Francis felt crushed by profound discouragement. He had had a premonition of this crisis, and he had done nothing to avert it. And now?

He had sat down with Peter of Catanio, with a bowl on his knees. It was time for the midday meal. They did not have to prepare it; the crusaders, out of reverence for these men of God, let them share in their company mess. A soldier came along and placed a substantial piece of meat in each one of the bowls.

Brother Stephen smiled mischievously. "Do you know that you are about to violate the new constitutions?"

Francis looked up, astonished (although by then he should not have been surprised). "How do you mean?"

"Brother Gregory and his companions deemed your rule inadequate, and so they told everyone that you had been martyred in the Holy Land, and they composed an appendix modeled on the rule of the Benedictine abbeys nearby Assisi. Several articles specify days of fast and abstinence. Look here: I have those new constitutions with me. All the friars are obliged to comply with them."

Stephen pulled from his pocket a bundle of papers covered with fine handwriting. Francis read them, then looked at the bowl, where the meat was growing cold. "So today is a day of abstinence?" he murmured.

"Exactly."

Francis, shaken by scruples, turned to his companion, "Master Peter, what are we to do?"

Peter was of two minds also. But, when it came right down to it, was not the new rule contrary to the founder's intentions?

"Father," he replied, "we will do what pleases you. For ultimately it is your responsibility to give commands."

Francis reflected a moment. Had he not heard, at San Damiano, one year on the Feast of Saint Matthias, a reading from the Gospel in which Jesus sends his disciples to proclaim the Kingdom of God? And what did Jesus say to his disciples? "Whenever you enter a town and they receive you, eat what is set before you." Now, had not Francis and his brothers vowed to keep the precepts of the Gospel?

"We'll eat the meat," he declared, "since the Holy Gospel gives us the freedom to do so."

When the meal was over, he gave the order to depart. Two other companions of his had joined up with him again: Caesarius of Speyer and Elias Bonibarone, who had served as minister of Syria. All five of them easily boarded a ship that was setting sail, and they disembarked in Venice. There Francis had to seek medical attention: the blazing sun in the East had ruined his eyes. Then he insisted on traveling via Bologna so as to confirm the betrayal that had been reported to him.

As his traveling companion he chose a friar who had recently entered the order, Leonard, who was of noble birth. Francis, exhausted by sicknesses and voyages, was riding a donkey. And Leonard was thinking to himself, "This is certainly a curious situation! My parents ranked so high in society that they would not have had anything to do with the family of Pietro di Bernardone. And now I'm walking on my own two feet while his son is strutting along on a mount."

But Francis read his thoughts. He ordered the animal to stop, got off, and said to Leonard affectionately, "You are quite right, brother. You should ride, since you are a nobleman, and I should go on foot, since I am only a commoner."

Leonard, thunderstruck and ashamed, fell to his knees and asked the father's pardon.

Once they arrived in Bologna, Francis did not have to ask directions to the house of studies of the Friars Minor: the whole city was talking about that fine residence that was built to house religious scholars. He did not go in, but had someone bring the minister to him.

"Do you want to destroy my order?" he shouted. "Have you forgotten my intention, which is that the friars should prefer prayer to study?"

And then the scene was repeated: he ordered all the religious to vacate the premises, censured Peter of Stacia and left. But he knew very well that all that was a useless protest; that the friars who had been thrown out would return to their cells and their studies, and that Peter would remain the provincial minister. The order that he had founded no longer needed him.

The earthshaking news of his arrival reached Umbria. Whereas the disloyal ministers holed up at the Portiuncula, all of the friars who had fled, banished and destitute, emerged from their hiding places and went out joyfully to meet him. No, by the grace of God, he was not dead, their beloved father; he was reappearing in their midst; he would continue to serve as their example, tutor, and protector.

The first thing that Francis did was to dismiss the two vicars general. Of course, now that he was back, it was possible for him to take the order in hand again, but he felt too weak for such a task. He did want to continue being the father, the inspiration, the conscience of this unstable, undecided group of men who made up this order, which was still in its adolescence—but not its administrator. He needed at his side someone to rule the friars, a leader to govern who was animated by the same spirit: a vicar of the minister general. He chose Peter of Catanio; he, at least, would not deceive him.

But Peter died shortly thereafter, on March 10, 1221. His reputation was such that the pilgrims flocked to his tomb, where miracles multiplied; and the more the miracles multiplied, the greater the droves of pilgrims. It was an intolerable disturbance for the community at the Portiuncula.

Then Francis positioned himself beside the tomb and uttered these solemn words, "Brother Peter, you obeyed me perfectly while you were alive. Obey me again now that these crowds of lay people are invading our convent. I order you, in the name of obedience, to stop working miracles."

And the miracles ceased.

But he had to replace Peter. Francis did not choose a saint; he did not call on one of his first disciples, who were thoroughly imbued with his spirit. They were unpredictable vagabonds, contemplatives. He decided instead on a man of action who had proved his mettle as minister. He appointed Elias Bonibarone.

He was a strange character, on whom historians have spent much ink. An individual who was far from exemplifying the Franciscan spirit, and yet Francis put his trust in him. He was originally from Assisi, and, despite his talents, he was not an educated man. He had worked, however, as a schoolmaster, and then as a notary. Finally, won over by Saint Francis, he had asked to wear the habit of the order, which he immediately received. He had remained a lay brother, no doubt because his superior preferred that he not be involved in priestly ministry. This did not prevent him from distinguishing himself by his eloquence and his practical skills, so that, when it became necessary to find a replacement for the delicate job of provincial minister for "Syria" (actually for the entire Orient), Francis without hesitation sent him to the Holy Land to carry out those duties. Once he became the vicar, then the general of the Friars Minor, he won the esteem and favor of the Pope and the German emperor. He was the one who then constructed the basilica of Assisi to house the tomb of Saint Francis—a marvelous building flanked by the imposing Sacro Convento, which all of the original friars decried as an offense against Holy Poverty.

For the moment, though, in the year 1221, the founder entrusted to Elias the task of bringing some order into the chaos that had overtaken his order. It appeared to be a superhuman task, but the new vicar performed it with a rare skill, lavishing upon his father Francis every possible expression of deference and devotion, while at the same time making sure to keep in office those ministers and guardians (superiors of convents) who were least earnest about observing the rule. Because he would die (in the year 1253!) at "The Cells" of Cortona, the place of his retirement, history has called him Elias of Cortona.

Meanwhile, in an effort to strengthen the unity of his order, Francis did not neglect to convoke the general chapter at Pentecost in the year 1221. And of course he invited his friend and protector, Cardinal Hugolino. The convents had multiplied so rapidly throughout the world that more than five thousand religious came. The founder did not know them, and he no longer tried to get acquainted with them: the cordial community of friars had turned into an anonymous crowd. In the presence of that crowd, Hugolino recalled the new decision of the Holy See: the obligation to complete a year of probation before making the profession that affiliated the candidate to the order, a prohibition against leaving the order subsequently without a papal dispensation, the arrest and punishment of "gyrovagues", who had become rather numerous in some regions (these were friars who did not belong to any particular convent and practiced no obedience), and finally the confirmation of Brother Elias as vicar general of the order, who would exercise authority in administrative matters.

At the end of the octave, when the official meetings, sermons, and festivities were over, all the friars returned to the convents where they were stationed. One of them was left, standing aside, who seemed to be awaiting an assignment. Gratian, the minister of Romagna, whom Francis had appointed in place of Peter of Stacia after the latter was dismissed, came up to him and asked, "What is your name, Brother?"

"Anthony."

"Where do you come from?"

"From Coimbra in Portugal."

"Are you a priest?"

"Yes."

"I just happen to need a priest to say Mass and administer the sacraments at the little convent in Montepaolo, near Forlì. The community there consists of lay brothers only, and they will surely have need of you."

Brother Anthony followed the minister and was affiliated to the convent of Montepaolo. There he occupied a little cell carved into the rock, and in this mountainous seclusion he lived on bread, water, and contemplation. Nobody, in Romagna or in the rest of Italy, had heard of this little friar, holy priest, and learned theologian when, on the occasion of priestly ordinations at Forlì, his superiors ordered him to attend the ceremony. At the conclusion of it, the bishop, as was then the custom, looked for a preacher, and noticing in a corner this humble friar, dressed in rags, whom many mistook for a cook, he asked him to speak, convinced that that would edify all present. The little friar chose as his Scripture text: "Christ humbled himself and became obedient unto death." And, borne aloft by his eloquence, he gave a commentary on it that was rich in doctrine and overwhelming in its heartfelt sentiment, so that everyone was under his spell, and the diocesan clergy and the Friars Preachers [Dominicans], who earlier had looked down on this little friar with a smile of compassion, declared him to be a theologian. This success was brought to Francis' attention, and he sent orders that Anthony should devote himself to the preaching ministry.

Meanwhile Francis, although he had entrusted the administration of the order to one of his brothers, was not content to pray for its success. He visited the convents to strengthen the religious in the practice of the virtues and also, whenever the opportunity arose, to give lessons and salutary warnings.

Celano relates an anecdote on this subject that gives a typical example of the saint's ways. The incident took place in Greccio. They were celebrating Easter; Francis had decided to participate in the liturgical services there, no doubt assuming the role of deacon, an order which he had received some time before, at the hands of Hugolino or perhaps of the Pope himself. The friars decided to give their late-morning meal a festive air, considering both the solemn feast day and the presence among them of their father and founder. Therefore they decorated the table with tablecloths and placed fine dishes and beautiful goblets on it; they prepared succulent dishes.

Francis came down from his cell and, at the threshold of the refectory, noticed these preparations. He left and met a beggar (who expected to benefit from this stroke of good luck). He borrowed his hat and staff and waited until all the religious had sat down around the table. Then he knocked at the door, crying out in a quavering voice, "Good brothers, for the love of God, have pity on a poor, sick pilgrim!"

At once they asked the pilgrim to come in. And the friars, to their amazement, recognized Francis. But he, refusing the place of honor, sat in a corner, asked for a bowl, and declared, "Now I am set, as a true Friar Minor."

Then, addressing the community, he said, "The examples of poverty that the Son of God has given to us oblige us, poor friars, more than all the others."

But neither the administration of Brother Elias nor the impromptu visits of Brother Francis put an end to the disorder, and the murmuring of the older members against the laxity of the newer ones grew louder. We find repeated indications of this revolt in the earliest biographies, especially in *The Mirror of Perfection*. One day a friar who was faithful to the rule came up to Francis and asked him, at once, "Why, father, have you given up the direction of the religious and handed them over to the care of others?"

Francis did not quite know how to answer.

"My brother," he said at last, "I love our brothers as much as it is possible to love them. . . . But I would love them much more if they followed in my footsteps; and in that case I would not be a stranger to them."

One day, according to the same book, the Lord Jesus Christ appeared to the holy friar, Leo, and declared to him, "Brother Leo, the friars grieve me."

"But why, Lord?"

"For three reasons. *Primo*, because they do not recognize my benefits, which I nevertheless shower on them abundantly. *Secundo*, because they spend the entire day murmuring and remain idle. Finally, because they provoke one another to anger and afterward are not eager to forgive."

In another chapter of the book, Christ appears to Francis himself, while he is praying. "O, you simple, foolish little man! Why do you experience so much distress when a friar leaves the order, or when the brothers do not follow the path that I have shown you? After all, who founded this order? And who gives the courage to persevere in it? Is it not I? Although I have chosen you to be at the head of my family, it is not because you are learned and eloquent, since I do not want the true observers of the rule to walk in the way of knowledge and eloquence. Therefore do not fret, just because certain ones become disappointed in my order and leave it; for even if only three friars remained, it would still be my order, and I would never abandon it."

4. The New Rules

Francis kept a vigilant watch over his rule, for, as he used to say, it was not his, but Christ's, since it was made up of passages from the Gospel. However, despite the approbation of Innocent III, it had become incapable of governing an order of such vast dimensions. The great Pope had confirmed it for a community of twelve friars who were leading a carefree life on a meadow, without any attempt to determine how that community would increase and spread one day. And now his successor, at the well-reasoned request of several wise religious, who were lacking in neither experience nor piety, decided that this makeshift rule had to be replaced. Or rather, modified; for, in compliance with the law of the last Lateran Council, composing a *new* rule was out of the question; rather, the rule should be reworked, in a way that made much-needed clarifications.

But Honorius, who respected in Saint Francis the character of founder of the order, thought it better to ask him to write the new rule himself. Or rather, he instructed Cardinal Hugolino to convey the request to him. It was certainly not with a cheerful heart that Francis agreed to do so; he had told his friars so often that this Gospel rule could not be retouched; but since he sang the praises of obedience so forcefully, it was up to him first to set an example. And so that the new text would not be rejected by Rome, he decided to join forces with a brother who was both educated and loyal in order to bring this task to completion. He chose Caesarius of Speyer. Indeed, since this friar had great reverence for the original rule but was at the same time aware of its weaknesses and had been notified of the Pope's demands, he was in a position to make revisions that would be satisfactory both to his superior and to the Roman authorities.

In order to leave no doubt as to the essential conformity of the new rule to the original one, it begins with a preface that may seem to be introducing it as the primitive text: "In the name of the Father and of the Son and of the Holy Spirit. Amen. Here is the type of life that Brother Francis asked His Lordship Pope Innocent to grant and approve. And the Pope granted it to him and approved it for his present and future friars."

And so this document does contain, with clarifications and elaboration, of course, the original rule, the text of which was approved and blessed by Innocent III. Then comes an article in which Francis wisely places himself under obedience to the Pope as a way of demonstrating that his order belongs to the Church and that any eccentrics found in it put themselves outside the Church: "Brother Francis, and every one of those who will head this order, promise obedience and reverence to His Lordship Pope Innocent and to his successors. And the other friars are bound to obey Brother Francis and his successors."

The next paragraph spells out (in a more canonical form than in the original rule, which is vague on this point) the vows that the novice pledges to keep when he makes his profession: to live a life of obedience, chastity, and poverty. To express the last-mentioned virtue, the text says: "without owning anything (*sine proprio*)". The commentaries drawn from the Gospel dwell particularly on this vow. "If you would be perfect, go, sell what you possess. . . ."; "If any man would come after me, let him deny himself", etc.

The section that follows, dealing with the admission of postulants to the order, is certainly a new composition, in which the reader senses both the Pontiff's demand and the founder's insistence. It is the responsibility of the minister, that is to say, the provincial superior, to welcome the postulant and to explain to him of what the spirit and life of the Friars Minor consist. If the postulant perseveres in his intention to enter the order, he must sell all his goods without exception and give the proceeds thereof to the poor. The minister then clothes him in the habit of a novice, which is made up of two tunics without a cowl. If he continues to persevere when the year of the novitiate is over, he is admitted to the profession of vows and can no longer leave the institute in which he promises obedience.

The third section, too, is certainly a new composition: it deals with the Divine Office and with fasting. Until then the friars who were clerics had few breviaries, out of a concern for poverty, and the early Franciscan writers record various scenes in which they have to dispense themselves from reciting the office, or even substitute for it some prayer not specified in the canonical regulations. But now, all clerical friars are bound to recite the office, which means that for them it is not a sin against poverty to keep a permanent copy of this obligatory book. Before this new rule, we find the surprising spectacle of Brother Francis refusing to allow his priests to own a breviary; now, though, it is no longer a concession, it is an obligation. However (no doubt as the result of an intervention by Francis himself), it specifies that the Divine Office books shall be the only ones that the clerics will have permission to keep. The lay brothers who know how to read are permitted to "have" a Psalter; no such grant is made to the illiterate.

The lay brothers are not left in uncertainty or subject to the whim of a minister: they are obliged to pray a real office, which is recited by heart, and divided into parts corresponding to those of the office in choir:

For Matins: the *Credo*, twenty-four *Pater Nosters*, with a *Gloria Patri*.
For Lauds: five *Pater Nosters*, with a *Gloria Patri*.
For the hour of Prime: the *Credo*, seven *Pater Nosters*, with a *Gloria Patri*.
For each of the little hours (Terce, Sext, None): seven *Pater Nosters*.
For Vespers: twelve *Pater Nosters*.
For Compline: the *Credo* and seven *Pater Nosters*.

And in addition, every day, for the faithful departed: seven *Pater Nosters* with the antiphon, *Requiem aeternam*. . . .
As a penance for failings and neglects: three *Pater Nosters*.

With regard to fasting, Francis had been instructed to institute at least one penitential practice, comparable to those called for in the constitutions of the other religious orders. He introduced two fasts: the usual fast that precedes Easter, and another extending from the Feast of All Saints until Christmas. But he adds that, for the rest of the year, the friars are bound only to fast on Friday, since that is the Church's custom.

Section 4 deals, in a manner that is markedly spiritual rather than canonical, with the relations between ministers and their subordinates; section 5 concerns sanctions against friars who have committed infractions, and it was much needed, because these obligations figured in the other rules. They did not amount to much, compared with those found in the older rules; the *Penitential* of Saint Columban, which was then no longer in use, contained all the punishments to be inflicted on delinquent religious and was itself thicker than the rest of the rule. Section 5 of the rule of 1221 is quite short and rather terse. All the provisions for punishments are contained in one small paragraph: if a friar sins, "his companions shall warn him, reprove him with humility and concern. If, after the third admonition, he refuses to amend his ways, he shall be sent to the minister, who shall do what he deems fit in God's sight." Thus, nothing is specified in advance, none of those painful or humiliating punishments that were in use in the other religious orders, such as flagellation or lying face-down with arms extended in the form of a cross during the midday meal.

[Section 6 is on the role and title of the minister.]

Sections 7 through 9 restate the regulations of the original rule. They concern manual work, albeit formulated conditionally ("the friars who know how will practice a trade"), begging (which here is called "alms"), and most importantly the explicit and absolute prohibition against accepting money: "In any manner whatsoever, neither to buy clothing or books, nor as wages for work, nor under any other pretext." The prohibition goes so far as to apply to a friar who might happen to accompany someone who is collecting money for benefit of some other charity than the order.

Section 10 deals with the sick, and the reader senses that Francis put his whole heart into it. Every sick member of the community should have at his disposal a friar who tends him—several, if necessary. Sections 11 through 13 concern morality: they forbid slander, keeping company with women and fornication; the friar guilty of the last-mentioned sin will be expelled forever from the order.

Sections 14 through 17 develop the regulations of the original rule that pertain to preaching. They quote first the passage from the Gospel of Saint Luke on the sending of the apostles on a mission: "Take nothing for your journey, no staff, nor bag, nor bread, nor money. . . . Remain in the same house, eating and drinking what they provide." On the other hand, it is forbidden to ride a horse, unless for a serious reason, such as infirmity. Section 18 gives the chapters legal status: they are to be held every year on the Feast of Saint Michael for the provincial chapters, every three years at Pentecost for general chapters.

[Section 19 states that all the brothers must be Catholics, practice their Faith and respect clerics and religious.]

Section 20 is certainly new: it deals with the sacraments of penance and Holy Eucharist. In order to dispel all doubt as to the minister of penance, it is expressly stated that the friars must have recourse to priests in order to obtain sacramental absolution; and they are encouraged to receive the Body and Blood of the Lord "with a great deal of humility and reverence".

The last two sections, 22 and 23, can hardly be attributed to Hugolino or to Caesarius: they could have been inspired and written only by Saint Francis. The section numbered 22 is an "Admonition to the Friars", which, after the canonical considerations that are listed of necessity, recovers the Gospel emphasis that the author of the rule constantly used. The term *admonition*, furthermore, is dear to Francis: it applies to those little sermons addressed to religious so as to supplement the rule. Here, it refers to a series of considerations designed to imbue the Friars Minor with the Gospel message and to inspire in them a love for the rule. Of these fifty verses, thirty-eight are drawn from the Gospels.

Section 23, on the other hand, entitled, "Prayer, praise, and thanksgiving", is a long, resounding prayer composed to conclude the new rule, which neither Hugolino nor Caesarius was able to delete. Although we cannot reprint these four enthusiastic pages in their entirety, it is possible nonetheless to quote the first of them:

Almighty, Most High, Most Holy, and Sovereign God, holy and just Father, Lord, King of heaven and earth, we give you thanks for your own sake, for by your holy will and through your only-begotten Son, you have created in the Holy Spirit all things, spiritual and corporeal; you made us in your image and likeness, you placed us in your paradise, and we, by our sin, have fallen.

We give you thanks also because, just as you created us through your Son, so too, by the true and holy love with which you have loved us, you caused your son to be born, true God and true man, of the glorious, ever-virgin and Most Blessed Saint Mary; and by his Cross, his blood, and his death, you have deigned to redeem us from our captivity.

And we give you thanks because this same Son will come again in the glory of his majesty, to cast into the eternal fire those wretched men who have not done penance and who have not known you, and to say to all those who have known and adored you, and served you by a life of penance: "Come, O blessed of my Father, inherit the Kingdom prepared for you from the foundation of the world."

And because we, miserable sinners one and all, are not worthy to call upon your name, we pray and beg you that our Lord Jesus Christ, your Dearly Beloved Son, in whom you are well pleased, who always does all things well in your sight and through whom you have done so much for us, might give you thanks for everything with the Holy Spirit, the Paraclete, as it pleases you and as it pleases them.

This rule from the year 1221 is usually called "The First Rule", and many biographers note that, although it was the first to be published, it was in reality the second one written, approved, and presented to the friars for their obedience. However, as we have seen, this second rule and the original rule are actually one and the same, and furthermore the later version assumes this identity when it declares right at once that it was approved by Pope Innocent III, who had been dead for five years when it was composed.

It was presented to the friars on the occasion of the great Pentecost chapter that same year and was obviously approved by them. It was not greeted enthusiastically by the innovators, precisely because it did nothing but adopt the original regulations. Although a few passages might satisfy those who were calling for a resemblance to the rule of Saint Benedict, such as the sections on the novitiate and the regimentation of the Divine Office, it appeared that the rules of poverty had not been changed, with regard either to clothing or to the handling of money; moreover it is true that no regulation had been made as to the construction of convents, which the partisans of great stone houses must have considered as progress.

Nevertheless, this new rule, which was thoroughly imbued with the founder's spirit, was received with reservations and murmuring, despite the approval. The innovators clamored for another, objecting to the long spiritual considerations that encumbered the canonical terms of the text. In their view, a rule was a regimen, a set of practical regulations, and not a catechism or a devotional manual. Since the vicar general, Elias, agreed with them, and Cardinal Hugolino lent them a respectful ear, Honorius III, after two years of wavering and murmuring, demanded that Francis produce a new text that was more practical and, as far as possible, acceptable to all. But what sort of text for a rule could be equally welcome to the older friars, who loved holy poverty, and the modern ones, who loved ease and convenience?

It was with a heavy heart that Francis, out of respect for holy obedience, set about rewriting his rule. This time, however, as a sign of his stubbornness, he invited not only a learned religious to collaborate, but also one of his most conservative confreres who staunchly opposed the innovators. So it was that he went off to the hermitage of Fonte Colombo with two friars, Bonizo of Bologna and Leo of Assisi. The process of composition went rapidly; hadn't he distilled and preserved in his heart the essential elements of this rule? After returning to the Portiuncula, he entrusted the manuscript to Elias, out of consideration for his position as vicar general. Besides, Elias would probably conduct the meetings of the ministers responsible for approving (and probably discussing) the contents. For Francis, who anticipated that this new text would not easily satisfy the innovators, planned to confer a certain collegial authority upon it by presenting it together with the chief ministers of Italy. But when they arrived, and the hour came to review the articles, Elias confessed that he had lost the precious pages. The ploy was believable neither to the complicit ministers, who congratulated themselves on it, nor to Francis, who began to think that his vicar, in whom he had innocently placed his trust, was making a fool of him.

Well, then, he took up the gauntlet: he would compose yet again this rule that they were expecting, and Elias' maneuver would prove to be nothing but a pitiable prank. Bitter and sorrowful, he climbed once more to the promontory of Fonte Colombo with his two counselors and again sat down to write, in tears. Here again we ought to let the authors of *The Mirror of Perfection* continue the story, since they forcefully defended the Gospel ideal, during Francis' lifetime and after his death, against the objections of the innovators. The scene that they describe is so important that they placed the account of it at the very beginning of their work, as a sort of denunciatory prologue.

Several ministers met with Brother Elias, who was the vicar of Saint Francis, and said to him, "We have learned that this Brother Francis is writing a new rule; we fear that it is so strict that we cannot observe it. Therefore we want you to go see him and tell him that we do not want to be subject to that rule."

Brother Elias replied that he refused to go, since he feared the rebuke of Saint Francis. The ministers insisted, and he told them that he would not go without them. Therefore they all went together. When Brother Elias arrived at the place where Saint Francis was staying, he called him. Saint Francis came out, saw the ministers and asked, "Who are these men?"

Brother Elias replied, "There are ministers who have learned that you were writing a new rule. They fear that you are making it too strict, and they protest that they refuse to be subject to it."

Then Francis turned his face toward Heaven and said to Christ, "Lord, did I not tell you that they would not believe me?"

Then they heard the voice of Christ in the air, answering, "Francis, there is nothing of you in this rule; all that can be found there is of me. I want this rule to be observed to the letter and without comment."

And so the ministers returned to the Portiuncula empty-handed, together with Elias, who was childishly playing a double game that was all too transparent. Francis, who was dictating to Leo, hurried to put the rule into writing; and when the text was ready, he decided not to bring it to Elias or to present it to the ministers for their approval, since they would debate every sentence, perhaps every word of it. The simplest thing was to entrust this task of approving the rule, and if necessary correcting it, to the Pope himself. After that, who would dare to dispute it? And for his own peace of mind, the surest judgment was that of the Church: when she had spoken, he would know that the rule of the Friars Minor was not his rule, but that of the Church who proclaimed it to all the friars.

Pentecost of the year 1223, however, was near. Francis was still the minister general, and he intended to preside at the chapter. But we find scarcely any traces of his participation in it; it seems that he made sure to attend but hardly ever spoke up. He kept his new rule a secret; submitting it to so many friars would have caused an uproar. It was time for the Pope to speak now, not the challengers.

He left for Rome, therefore, where he visited Cardinal Hugolino, who was always favorably disposed, but still a useful critic of the text of the new rule. Now his very delicate job as protector of the order was to set aside the claims of the challengers and to obtain the approval of the Holy Father, all the while strictly respecting the will of Francis, who wanted his new rule to resemble the first version as one sister resembles another.

So it was that the new text, purged of all that was not canonical, came into the hands of Honorius III, together with the cordial recommendation of the cardinal-protector. One must admit that, despite the supplications of Francis, to which were joined the pleas of Brother Leo, who was supposed to represent the original community, the definitive rule is astonishingly concise, compared to the preceding one: not even one-third the number of pages! The Gospel citations, which occur only to justify the religious obligations, are infrequent and abridged. For example, section 1, which requires the three vows of religion, states them very briefly, without any scriptural commentary, whereas the corresponding section in the preceding rule added thirteen lines of quotations from the Gospels.

The articles that govern admission to the order and the Divine Office are almost the same as those in the preceding rule, since they deal with canonical regulations that must be formulated precisely. The section that treats the subject of preachers, in the previous rule, took up two long pages, because Francis elaborated there on the *spirit* that should animate the friar who dedicates himself to preaching; this time, however, there are just a few lines. But care is taken to explain that the preachers will not venture to speak publicly in a diocese where the bishop forbids them to do so. The obligation to observe absolute poverty is firmly restated, with a special section forbidding the friars to accept money. This strict regulation, however, is mitigated somewhat: if it is a matter of bringing aid to sick friars, or to others who have no means of obtaining clothing, the custodians and the guardians ("but only they") are permitted to provide for their needs "through the mediation of spiritual friends"; similarly, if the friars are sent to distant missions where they will be exposed to severe cold weather, one may find some indirect way of buying the suitable clothing for them.

One new feature in this rule of 1223 is a section regulating the election of the minister general. Francis had gradually come to face the fact that he could no longer appoint a vicar to help him with the administration of the order, but would eventually have to give up his title and his role as minister general. Therefore, rather than see a malefactor of the order assume the position as his successor, thanks to a plot hatched by the innovators, he provides for a duly regulated canonical election. The entire paragraph is worth citing:

> All the friars are bound to have at all times one of the friars in their order as their minister general and the servant of the entire brotherhood: and they are firmly obliged to obey him. Upon his death, the provincial ministers and the custodians should proceed to the election of his successor during the chapter at Pentecost. At the chapter, the provincial ministers are obliged to assemble, in a place determined by the minister general.

This new text is often called "The Second Rule", but it is more appropriately referred to as "The Definitive Rule", since in the final analysis it is a question of the same rule in three successive versions. It has also been called the *Regula bullata*, because it was approved by means of a bull of Pope Honorius III dated November 29, 1223, *Solet annuere*:

> Honorius, Bishop, Servant of the servants of God, to our dearly beloved son Francis and the other Friars of the Order of Minors: greetings and Our apostolic blessing. The Apostolic See *customarily approves (solet annuere)* of pious plans and promotes the praiseworthy aspirations of those who make their appeal to it. Therefore, dearest sons in Our Lord, We confirm by Our apostolic power, and We corroborate by the authority of the present document, the rule of your order, which was approved by Our predecessor, Pope Innocent, of blessed memory. . . . Let no one, therefore, have the temerity to violate the terms of this, Our confirmation, or to contradict it. If anyone dares to attempt it, let him know that he incurs the indignation of Almighty God and of his blessed apostles, Peter and Paul.

It appears obvious that, in the eyes of Honorius III, this is indeed the same rule that had been approved fourteen years earlier by his predecessor: he himself is simply confirming the revisions, the definitive form of the document. And this definitive rule is the one that would rule the order of Saint Francis from then on.

5. The Third Order and the Crib

The year of the "first rule" of Saint Francis, 1221, saw the birth of an institute that was astonishing in a different way: the Third Order Franciscans. The first was the order of friars, the second—the order of nuns, and the third was the order of people living in the world.

Yet the idea for this institute went back much further. The decision itself to create a secular order—something of a contradiction in terms, which nevertheless would receive definitive canonical approval—was made by Saint Francis in 1212, shortly after the founding of the Order of Poor Clares, on that day during a preaching tour (in Cannara or in Alviano) when he had silenced a multitude of chattering swallows with a single command. Thus he was able to speak without interruptions, but his words were so fervent that the inhabitants of the town pressed close to him on all sides, asking permission to follow him. Obviously, Francis declined that unseasonable outburst of zeal, but he promised those new disciples that he would soon present to them an institute appropriate to their state in life. The *Actus beati Francisci* (a collection of reminiscences of the first companions, compiled by an anonymous friar) relates that, from that moment on, the father of the Friars Minor planned to found a third order.

The first rule of the confraternity, however, did not see the light of day until 1221, thanks to the collaboration of Saint Francis and Cardinal Hugolino, who once again understood the value of such a project and dutifully applied himself to making it a reality. No copy of this rule is extant. However, we have a partial copy of it, dating from 1223, which was discovered by Paul Sabatier in the convent of Capistrano in the Abruzzi region, and also the second rule, dating from 1228, which the same scholar found in 1901 in the National Library in Florence.

It is obvious that, when he founded this new "order", Francis of Assisi meant it exclusively for seculars—lay people—who were to continue the life that they were living before. The rule of 1228 is entitled: "Memorandum of a plan for the Brothers and Sisters of Penance, living in their own homes". Similarly, *The Legend of the Three Companions*, which seems to know of this rule, reports that "husbands and wives, who could not break the bonds of marriage, devoted themselves *in their own houses* (*in domibus propriis*) to stricter penitential practices, at the pious advice of the Friars (Minor)." We have also the testimony of Bernard of Besse, the secretary of Saint Bonaventure, in the *Analecta Francescana*: "The third order is similarly open to priests and lay persons, to virgins, widows, and married people. The vocation of the brothers and sisters of this order should be to live virtuously in their homes, to devote themselves to pious works, and to flee from worldly life."

It is clear also that between 1212, the date of the promise, and 1221, the date of the first rule, Francis enrolled in this institute (which did not yet have official status) a certain number of disciples who held positions of responsibility in the world. This was the case with Jacoba of Settesoli, whom Francis used to call his "Friar Jacoba" as a way of insisting on her membership in a religious institute. He had been acquainted with her since 1212; she became a widow in 1217, and until her death she continuously lavished her attentive care on the founder and his companions. Her portraits depict her in the penitential habit.

This is the case also with Count Orlando of Catanio, Lord of Chiusi. The ruins of the fortress on his former lands still loom over the Arno River. He was the nobleman who gave Saint Francis Mount La Verna, where he later received the stigmata. In the formal deed which the count's sons drew up to donate La Verna to the Franciscans in 1274, they recalled that their father had received from the saint himself the knotted cord that he wore around his waist as a sign of penance.

Besides these individuals whose names we know because of the special relationships that they had with Saint Francis, he also clothed in the penitential habit a multitude of men and women who will forever remain anonymous. Actually, the reason why the founder wrote a rule was not to raise up followers, but rather to determine their obligations. As early as 1221 fraternities of "penitent brothers" can be found everywhere: in Umbria, Tuscany, Romagna, and the Marches of Ancona. On December 16 of that year, Pope Honorius III promulgated a letter that enjoined the Bishop of Rimini to take under his protection the members of the Third Order in Faenza, who were being persecuted by the podesta [magistrate] because they refused to bear arms. Why? Their rule forbade it. This community, therefore, was powerful enough to resist the civil authorities; it could not have been formed within the few weeks that had elapsed since the existence of the rule was announced.

Obviously, the term *community* does not mean a gathering of individuals under the same roof, but rather a group of members scattered throughout the same city who meet regularly for devotions and charitable works. Indeed, chapter 7 of the rule deals with these meetings, which take place once a month; they consist of Mass, a sermon, and discussion by the members. And chapter 3 forbids them to bear arms.

The Third Order fraternities themselves became the source of other associations. In central Italy, such groups were devoted chiefly to promoting piety; in Perugia a tertiary named Bonaparte, with the help of Fr. Raynier, founded the Confraternities of a Happy Death. In northern Italy, the associations constituted a powerful political force with which the lords and senates had to reckon. By the year 1246, the confraternities of Lombardy formed a "congregation", that is, a federation having its own council and chapter meetings. In Flanders, where the Third Order was introduced at the end of the century, it was influential particularly among craftsmen and gave rise to the weavers' guilds.

One usually reads that the first community of penitents was the one at Poggibonsi in Tuscany, and the title of "the first tertiary" is awarded to the president of that fraternity, Luchesio. But that is because this fraternity was started by Saint Francis himself and because Blessed Luchesio was the first among the penitent brothers who received the habit from the founder's own hands to have his *cultus* approved. It happened in 1221 that Francis, who was passing through Poggibonsi on the way from Florence to Siena, met up again with that old friend who had resolved to change his life: formerly avaricious and careless about practicing his faith, he had become generous and pious. The ground was prepared. Francis had him put on the habit that would then be the uniform of all tertiaries: an ash-gray robe bound at the waist by a cord made of hemp. And a whole party of important people joined him in forming a fraternal association; among them were his wife Bonadonna, as well as Pietro di Colle, Bruno di Colle, and his wife. Luchesio spent the rest of his life caring for the poor at the hospital and cultivating his garden so as to sell the produce for the benefit of the needy; when the harvest was insufficient, he would beg. He was venerated as a saint immediately after his death, which occurred in 1260, and the church of the Friars Minor where he was buried was called San Luchesio from then on. Pope Paul III and Pope Urban VIII promulgated bulls, in 1547 and 1643 respectively, in which they confirmed the title of *saint* that was attributed to Luchesio —which does not keep the Friars Minor today from venerating that chosen soul, in the missal and the breviary, under the title of Blessed Luchesio (whose feast day is April 28). Pietro di Colle, on the other hand, was beatified by Urban VIII and May 31 was declared his feast day; but the Franciscan order neglected to reserve a place for him in the missal or the breviary.

Did the first tertiaries take vows, like religious? We find no trace of such a practice. One might suppose that in the early years, before the rule was composed, a certain number of them made a private decision, before God alone, to practice continence. We have one testimony to this effect in the *Actus beati Francisci*, where it says that, after preaching in Cannara, Saint Francis decided to found the order that was henceforth called "the order of the continent": *ordo qui dicitur continentium*. In support of that name, Celano relates that one day, when Francis was staying at the hermitage in The Cells, near Cortona, he received a visitor, a young woman eager to advance in the spiritual life; upon learning that she was married, he ordered her to go back to her husband, but to live with him in perfect continence.

In reality, the third order would be called the *Order of Penitents*, and Gregory IX would mention it in his letter of May 9, 1235, to Saint Agnes of Prague, a Poor Clare nun, under the name of *poenitentium collegia*. The virtue that would be particularly recommended in the Third Order was poverty, not only with respect to ownership, but also in one's way of life. Chapter 7 of the first rule establishes no customs in this regard, but leaves it up to the visitor—a religious belonging to the first order who holds delegated authority over the fraternity—to establish customs concerning clothing and hairstyles; excesses are to be punished, while obstinacy will result in expulsion.

Soon it was the turn of secular priests to join the Order of Penitents.

Bernard of Besse relates that, during the period before the rule was composed, one of these priests heard Francis' preaching and asked to become his follower; but Francis ordered him to remain in the service of his parish, while distributing his revenues to the poor. We are not told whether he gave him the rope cincture that symbolized membership. We also know of two thirteenth-century Italian saints who were parish priests and tertiaries: Davanzat (d. 1295), whose cult has not been approved by Rome, and Blessed Bartholomew ("Santo Bartolo") of San Gimignano, count of Mucchio, who became the curate in Pichena (in the Diocese of Volterra); afflicted with leprosy, he withdrew to the leprosarium in San Gimignano, where he served as chaplain and died twenty years later, in 1300. [In the early twentieth century], at the request of the Franciscans, who venerated him in their breviary as Blessed, Pius X approved his cult, which went back to time immemorial, but he had already been canonized by Alexander VI (1492–1503). His feast is celebrated on December 14. To these curates we should add the priest and canonist Giacomo di Castel delle Pieve, who was assassinated in 1304 to prevent him from pleading a just cause.

Among the Italian laymen, we cannot fail to mention Dante Alighieri, a Florentine tertiary who frequented the Franciscan convent of Santa Croce; his statue now stands in front of it, and the University of Florence grew out of the educational apostolate of the religious community there. Then, too, there was a naturalized Italian who came from the Languedoc region, Blessed Gerard (also called Blessed Gerard of Villamagne), who was a descendant of the counts of Lunel in the Diocese of Maguelonne: he began as a hermit near Pont du Gard, then boarded a ship for the Holy Land with his brother, but was cast up by a storm on the coast of Tuscany; he went to Rome, then to the Marches of Ancona; settling at Tolentino, he was received into the Third Order by the Franciscans and died in 1298. His body was transferred to Montesanto, near Loreto. Benedict XIV approved the title of *saint* by which he was honored in the Diocese of Teramo; the Diocese of Montpellier reveres him with the title of Blessed only; as for the Franciscan order, it has not even sought to make room for him in their breviary. This sort of mystical pilgrim prefigures another Franciscan tertiary, Saint Rock, the son of a viscount of Montpellier, who traveled about Italy half a century later, healing those who had contracted the plague; returning to his native land after his father's death, he was thrown into prison, where he died.

The reputation of the Order of Penitents, in the second half of the thirteenth century, extended as far as Brittany, where it captivated Ivo of Kermartin (Yves de Tréguier). It is true that he, as a student for thirteen years at the universities of Paris and Orléans, had had many opportunities to become acquainted with the Friars Minor. After becoming an official in Rennes, then a priest and curate of Trédiez in the Diocese of Tréguier, he became a friend of the Franciscan community at Guingamp and was enrolled in the Third Order. On May 9, 1303, he died as curate of Lannouec where, while practicing strict asceticism, he had devoted the better part of his time to the poorest of the poor. He was canonized by Clement XI.

The most extraordinary case of an individual tertiary living in the world, who was simultaneously a priest, scholar, and apostle, is that of Raymund Lull. At first, as seneschal of the king of Majorca, James I the Conqueror, he led a dissolute life and went so far as to pursue on horseback into the Cathedral of Palma a woman whom he desired. Christ called him; he made a general confession, distributed his goods to the poor, resigned from his post, and withdrew into solitude for nine years to pray and study. Then he traveled about the pagan world to convert it to the Gospel: we see him in Ethiopia, India, Turkistan, on the shores of the Baltic Sea, and especially in North Africa, where he was repeatedly thrown into a dungeon and subjected to flogging. This exhausting career did not prevent him from writing two hundred works of theology, philosophy, apologetics, and linguistics; founding a college for the propagation of the faith; and visiting popes, kings, and princes of the Church and of the world in order to solicit their aid. Finally, in 1315, at the age of eighty, while preaching on a square in Bejaïa [formerly Bougie], he was recognized, condemned to death, and stoned. He was beatified by Pope Leo X.

The rule of the Order of Penitents soon spread from the humble dwellings of central Italy to the courts of Europe. Actually it was not the tertiaries themselves who propagated their spirituality and their renown, but the Friars Minor who, from the dozen who had surrounded their founder in 1209, had increased to forty thousand when Saint Bonaventure was elected to the generalate in 1257, with convents in all the capital cities and wonderful preachers who were asked to speak in the presence of all the crowned heads of state.

The first king to wear the penitential robe from his youth was, it seems, Saint Ferdinand III, a gallant knight who combined piety with political wisdom and who, after uniting the kingdoms of Castile and León, seized all of southern Spain (except Granada), which had been held by the Muslims. He was followed by his first cousin, Louis IX, king of France, who hosted at his table the Franciscan Bonaventure and the Dominican Thomas Aquinas during the time when they were teaching at the Sorbonne, and who used to say, "If I could cut my body in two, I would give one half of it to Saint Francis and the other to Saint Dominic." Since he could not carry out that division, he chose Saint Francis, and he had a monastery of Poor Clare nuns built at Longchamp for his sister Isabel.

The arrival of the Franciscans in the court of Hungary came later, but the order may well have borne it most exemplary fruits there. It is certain that it occurred during the reign of Andrew II (1196–1235). A monarch of that ilk made very sure that he did not enroll in the Third Order: money-hungry, unscrupulous, and given to intrigues, he dabbled unceasingly in conspiracies and betrayals and was detested by the people and the barons. He was goaded on by his first wife, Gertrude of Meran (the blood sister of Saint Hedwig and Agnes, the third wife of Philip-Augustus of France and grandmother of Saint Louis), who eventually perished at the hands of an assassin. Of that baneful couple were born four children, who proved to be as praiseworthy as their parents had been contemptible: the second, Béla IV, king of Hungary from 1235 to 1270, a pious and just prince and father of the poor, entered the Third Order Franciscans. The third child, Kálmán, king of Galicia, married Blessed Salome of Poland and together with her, on their wedding night, made a vow of perpetual continence; when he died, she, a widow and a virgin, entered the Poor Clares in Krakow and became the abbess. The fourth child was Saint Elizabeth of Hungary (1207–1231).

It was not through her brother, King Béla, that Elizabeth became acquainted with the Third Order. She was four years old when she was engaged to young Prince Louis, the heir to the Landgrave of Thuringia, and sent to the castle in Wartburg. Louis succeeded his

ROYAL HOUSE OF HUNGARY

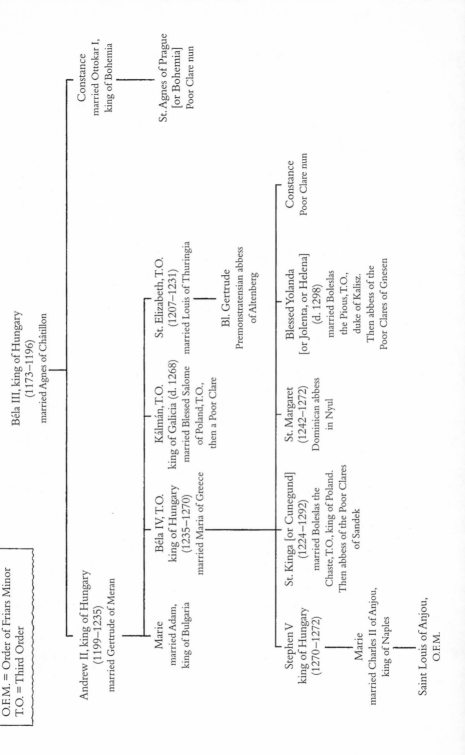

O.F.M. = Order of Friars Minor
T.O. = Third Order

Béla III, king of Hungary
(1173–1196)
married Agnes of Châtillon

Constance
married Ottokar I,
king of Bohemia

St. Agnes of Prague
[or Bohemia]
Poor Clare nun

Andrew II, king of Hungary
(1199–1235)
married Gertrude of Meran

St. Elizabeth, T.O.
(1207–1231)
married Louis of Thuringia

Bl. Gertrude
Premonstratensian abbess
of Altenberg

Kálmán, T.O.
king of Galicia (d. 1268)
married Blessed Salome
of Poland, T.O.,
then a Poor Clare

Béla IV, T.O.
king of Hungary
(1235–1270)
married Maria of Greece

Marie
married Adam,
king of Bulgaria

St. Margaret
(1242–1272)
Dominican abbess
in Nyul

Constance
Poor Clare nun

Blessed Yolanda
[or Jolenta, or Helena]
(d. 1298)
married Boleslas
the Pious, T.O.,
duke of Kalisz.
Then abbess of the
Poor Clares of Gnesen

St. Kinga [or Cunegund]
(1224–1292)
married Boleslas the
Chaste, T.O., king of Poland.
Then abbess of the Poor Clares
of Sandek

Stephen V
king of Hungary
(1270–1272)

Marie
married Charles II of Anjou,
king of Naples

Saint Louis of Anjou,
O.F.M.

father in 1217 at the age of sixteen, and it was not until 1221 that Elizabeth and he were married. A few years later, the Friars Minor established a community in Eisenach, the capital of the landgraviate. In 1226, the year of Saint Francis' death, Elizabeth chose as her confessor Father Konrad von Marburg, who clothed her two years later in the habit of the Third Order. Even before she was affiliated with the Franciscans, she lived a life of mortification, performing acts of charity for the disadvantaged and inspired by a great religious fervor. In 1227, as the widowed mother of four children, she was thrown out on the street by her brother-in-law, the new landgrave. This was the beginning of her mystical life.

Some tertiaries, as early as the thirteenth century, acquired the canonical status of hermit, for example, Blessed Novellone of Faenza or Gerard of Villamagna, or that of recluse, like Praxedes of Rome, Verdiana of Castelfiorentino, or Saint Margaret of Cortona. The tertiaries even went so far as to found actual religious congregations, with vows approved by the Church, such as the Beguines of Toulouse or the sisters of Angelina of Marsciano or those of Blessed Clare of Rimini.

It was around the time when the definitive rule was approved, in autumn of the year 1223, that Francis decided to reopen the theological school in Bologna for good. It was a memorable event in the Order of Friars Minor. The founder had intended and ordered that his friars would not be learned scholars. Certainly, he respected theologians and taught others to respect them, since they speak to us of godly things. Yet his order was not an order of theologians, like the Order of Preachers, which he admired, along with their founder Dominic. And he considered that owning books was contrary to the spirit of absolute poverty that was essential to his institute, and many times he had refused to give his friars permission, even if they were clerics, to keep even a breviary or a psalter in their possession.

But didn't these preachers have to learn doctrine in order to spread the Good News? Ever since the original rule it was understood, officially, with the approval of Rome, that the friars should preach *penance* to the people, in a very simple language, that is, the essential truths of the faith contained in the Creed, a concern for the Kingdom of God, love of neighbor, and submission to the Church. There was no need to study theology to give such talks: it could all be found in the

Gospel. Furthermore, praying and setting the example of a holy life was a surer way of converting people than giving long sermons.

However, since the approval of the original rule, many learned men had entered the order. Although certain individuals, like Gregory of Naples and Peter of Stacia, had taken advantage of their knowledge and tried to transform the spirit and the letter of the rule, others had demonstrated a profound humility and exemplary fidelity. In the early years of the community, scholars like Peter of Catanio and Caesarius of Speyer had won their father's confidence; better yet, they had helped him with their advice and had offered him their assistance in composing the rule itself. Then again, the friars no doubt had sufficient knowledge of doctrine to edify the people, but could they respond to the challenges of heretics? And resist heretical arguments themselves? The Church had come to realize acutely how poorly many priests knew their faith, and the Lateran Council in 1179 had decreed that there should be at least one theology professor in each archdiocese; but since then the decree had had little success. Faced with this serious scarcity, were not the Friars Minor called to fill those positions, thus combining knowledge and virtue?

Evidently this is what Cardinal Hugolino thought, who gravely remarked how much Francis was underestimating the importance of theology in forming religious and equipping them to preach. Besides, how could anyone ask the learned clerics not to make use of their knowledge when they spoke? To disregard, in their sermons about the Creator and the Savior, about priesthood and the Eucharist, the very foundations of those mysteries? Given the prodigious increase in the number of Francis' disciples, Hugolino was convinced that they would require schoolmasters to teach them sound doctrine. Furthermore they had already begun teaching at Oxford, urged on by circumstances, without having the time to refer the matter to a superior authority.

Bowing, therefore, to the will of the protector of the order (and knowing that he would one day become Pope), Francis ordered that the house of studies in Bologna should be reopened. Obviously, he did not put Peter Stacia (whom he had cursed) in charge of it. He knew that not far from there, in Montepaolo, there was a humble religious who had studied theology in Coimbra, Portugal, had amazed his listeners in Forlì, and was now living a life of prayer and penance in obscurity. That friar, in his teaching, would certainly be a faithful guardian of the spirit of the rule.

Therefore Brother Anthony was appointed, by the authority of the minister general, professor, and director of theological studies at the convent in Bologna. His renown spread far and wide, and he was called to teach in Toulouse and Montpellier. Then, when they saw heresies developing in Aquitaine, his superiors appointed him a preacher. He was prodigiously successful in Brive, Bourges, and Limoges, and throughout that province, where he constantly worked spiritual and physical miracles. Finally, after retiring to Padua, he died there at the age of thirty-six on June 13, 1231, less than five years after his spiritual father. In a unique display of favor, Cardinal Hugolino, who had become Pope Gregory IX, canonized him on May 30, 1232: less than a year after his death. The friar in question was Saint Anthony of Padua.

At the initiative of Saint Francis of Assisi, the year 1223 saw the creation of the Christmas crèche, which then became a custom in churches everywhere. That autumn, after a sojourn in Rome, where he found lodging in the back of Cardinal Brancaleone's garden, Francis went to the hermitage in Fonte Colombo to prepare for the Solemnity of the Nativity. He wished to see that precious anniversary celebrated by a larger gathering of people, but the hermitage was small and could not have accommodated a crowd. He decided to organize the celebration, not in the town of Rieti, which was only one league away, but in the market town of Greccio, three leagues to the north. In fact he had a devoted friend there, a layman named Giovanni Velita, who belonged to the local nobility and was numbered among the benefactors of the friars.

Two weeks before Christmas, Francis summoned Giovanni and informed him of his plans; the nobleman declared himself ready to comply. Here is the speech that Thomas of Celano places on the lips of Francis: "Signore Giovanni, if you want us to celebrate the next Feast of our Lord at Greccio, then diligently make the preparations that I will describe to you. . . . I wish to recall the memory of that infant who was born in Bethlehem and willed to undergo for us all the inconveniences of childhood. I would like to see him, with my fleshly eyes, lying in the crib and resting on the straw between the ass and the ox."

With ardent love, Giovanni went to the church in Greccio that his friend pointed out to him, and with the permission of the curate set up beside the altar a manger filled with hay. On Christmas Eve he led to it an ox and an ass, which neighbors gladly loaned him. Francis himself came to inspect these preparations and found them in keeping with his plans. Then, by means of proclamations that resounded in every corner of the market town, he summoned the populace to the midnight service. The entire town turned out, some brandishing candles, others with torches, so that the night was as bright as midday. They found a spectacle worthy of Bethlehem and, kneeling before the empty crib, Brother Francis, immersed in prayer, emitting deep sighs, his face beaming with celestial joy.

Then the celebrant processed in and Francis, wearing the deacon's dalmatic, accompanied him to the altar. After the Gospel, which he read in clear, cordial tones, to the great edification of all present, he also gave the sermon. Celano relates that it was yet another cause for rejoicing among the congregation:

> To speak about the birth of the King in poverty, he found words as sweet as honey. When he was about to mention Jesus Christ, he was inflamed with an immense love and called him "the Child of Bethlehem". He pronounced this name in the manner of a bleating lamb, more with his heart than with his mouth. And while he spoke of the Child Jesus, he passed his tongue over his lips, as though to savor the delicious taste of that name.

And behold, in the crib that was empty a moment ago, a baby was lying motionless, still asleep. Then Francis went up, with infinite tenderness, knelt down and venerated the Divine Infant, who woke up and smiled sweetly at him.

At the conclusion of that marvelous ceremony, those in attendance grabbed the straw from the crib, which they took with them as so many relics. They preserved it as a treasure, and it served to heal livestock that were suffering from disease.

PART FOUR

The Pure Path of the Soul's Journey toward God

Having arrived at the year 1223, which is the turning point in the history of the Franciscan order, let us dwell for a moment on the personality of its founder: a kind of photograph faintly superimposed over the action of the film as it unfolds. Francis was now forty-one years old; he was "in the middle of the path of his life", to use the expression of his disciple Dante at the beginning of the *Divine Comedy*. But his physical appearance had not changed; his portrait, painted in different places at different times in his life, is true to the description of Celano:

> He was of medium height, short rather than tall, with a joyful, kindly face, a round head, a low forehead, dark and innocent eyes, straight eyebrows, a fine, regular nose, and little ears that stuck out quite a bit. He had a keen and cordial way of speaking, with a voice that was simultaneously forceful and sweet. His white teeth were closely and evenly spaced, his lips were thin, his beard was sparse, his neck narrow, his arms were short, his fingers and nails long, his legs thin, his feet small. He had scarcely any flesh on his bones.

There had been no change in his personality since his conversion. Of course, he displayed some of the character traits that he had had previously: his amiability, charm, gentleness, natural eloquence, and poetic sensibility. But the dominant trait, for the past twenty years, was passion: his passion for Christ and his Gospel, his passion for his enterprise, which nothing could ever dampen, despite opposition, doubts, and distress. We must not rely on a superficial psychology and suppose that this passion engendered his spirituality, that his character gave rise to his love for Christ. It is just the opposite: the discovery of Christ and of his Gospel was what gave rise to this delirious attachment, this inextinguishable ardor. As a result, the psychological portrait of Saint Francis becomes his religious portrait, and the two things merge into one set of phenomena. What inspires him, what stirs and grips him, what incites all these feelings and drives him irresistibly in all his undertakings? It is this supernatural love; love defines his psyche, the supernatural defines the religious, but in him the two are inseparable. The *spiritual* portrait of a saint, of Francis, as of Bernard before him or of Augustine centuries before that, contains in a single word both meanings of *spirit*: the life of the mind and supernatural life, nature expanding under the influence of grace, or grace converting nature. In short: man relieved of original sin.

Therefore the reader should not be surprised to find here, as a spiritual portrait of the saint, the different aspects of his everyday passion, the colors of a unique prism through which the divine light radiates. The titles of the following short chapters converge to define the *spirit* of Francis and the path that his soul took on its journey toward God.

1. The Imitation of Christ

The sentiment that would carry Francis away and govern the founding of his religious order was, from the very first moment of his conversion, a delirious love for Christ. Not a contemplative love, which is satisfied with a perceptible, mental vision of the Savior, which dwells at length upon his words and his sufferings, but rather an active love. Of course, Francis habitually possessed that contemplative fervor, too, as all of his biographers assure us. Bonaventure writes: "He devoted such an ardent love to Christ, and his Beloved showed him in exchange such a familiar tenderness, that the servant of God had almost continually before his eyes the physical presence of his Savior."

And we find, in one of his prayers, the accents of all the great mystics: "Lord, I beg thee, let the burning, gentle power of thy love consume my soul and draw it far from everything that is under heaven, so that I may die for love of thy love, O thou who hast deigned to die for love of my love."

Furthermore, this is the desire that he expresses for Christians in general, in a sort of "encyclical letter" that he wrote entitled, "Letter to All the Faithful". To those who truly love Christ, he promises that they will be his spouses, his brethren, and his mothers:

> We are spouses when the faithful soul is united to Jesus Christ through the Holy Spirit. We are his brethren when we do the will of his Father who is in heaven. We are his mothers when we bear him in our hearts and in our bodies through our love, through the purity and fidelity of our conscience, and when we give birth to him by the performance of good deeds, which should be a light and an example for others. Oh, how glorious and holy it is to have such a Father in heaven! Oh, how holy, beautiful and amiable it is to have a Spouse in the heavens! Oh, how holy and precious, pleasing and humble, peaceful and sweet, lovable and desirable a thing it is, surpassing all else, to have such a Brother!

We find the same accents in the writings of Clare, the perfect disciple of Francis, for instance, in a letter to Agnes of Bohemia, who had become the abbess of the convent in Prague:

> Happy indeed is she to whom this is granted a place at the divine banquet, for she can cling with all her heart to him whose beauty eternally awes the blessed hosts of heaven; to him whose love gladdens, the contemplation of whom refreshes, whose generosity satisfies, whose gentleness delights, whose memory shines sweetly as the dawn; to him whose fragrance revives the dead, and whose glorious vision will render all the inhabitants of the heavenly Jerusalem blessed.

The 1221 rule had enshrined in its text the duty to belong to Jesus Christ:

> Let us not desire anything else, let us not want anything else, let nothing please us or give us joy except our Creator, Redeemer, and Savior, the one true God, who is the fullness of Good, the complete and total Good, the venerable and supreme Good, who alone is good, merciful and kind; who alone is just, truthful and right; who alone is beneficent, innocent and pure; from whom, through whom, and in whom is found all pardon, all grace, all glory for the repentant and the just, and for all the blessed who rejoice with him in heaven.

With Christ, Francis could give free rein to his poetic sensibility. But poetry is not good form in a canonical document, and so that exhortation was deleted from the definitive rule.

Now the love of Christ compels the soul and draws it into a service which is preferential, exclusive, and unconditional. Saint Bonaventure could write, "One word sums up all of Francis: faithful servant of Christ." As a servant, he was entirely subject to his master, as called for in the prayer that concludes his "Letter to the General Chapter":

> Almighty and ever-living God, just and merciful Lord, grant to us miserable creatures, for your own sake, that we may know what you will, and that we may always will what pleases you; so that, externally purified and illumined within and inflamed with the fire of the Holy Spirit, we may follow in the footsteps of your dearly beloved Son, our Lord Jesus Christ, and by your grace alone may arrive at our destination in you, O Most High, who in perfect Trinity and utterly simple Unity live and reign and are glorified, Almighty God, unto ages of ages. Amen.

To follow Christ is not only to serve him, it is not enough to do his will; it also means becoming like him. This love is a love that consists not only in doing, but in being; a love that thrives not only in activity but in the person. Francis, without having read the Fathers of the Church, follows their teaching in this: Origen, Athanasius, and Gregory of Nyssa demonstrate how the Son is the mediator of the Father: God created man in his image, in a state of perfection; original sin corrupted that image, and the Son, who is the perfect image of the Father, came both to reveal God to us and to teach us the way leading to the restoration of his image in us. Saint Francis adds, however, an original thought to this doctrine about creation: God the Father created us in his image with respect to our souls, and in the image of his Son, the Incarnate Word, with respect to our bodies.

The Friar Minor is someone who must put on Jesus Christ. The first rule states this explicitly: "The rule and the life of the Friars Minor consists of living in obedience, in chastity and without owning anything, by following the teaching and example of our Lord Jesus Christ." It adds, in the concluding admonition, "Our Lord Jesus Christ, in whose footsteps we must follow. . . ."

Now, Saint Francis himself is not content to call on his brothers in his rule and in his exhortations to imitate Jesus Christ: he proves himself to be his most fervent imitator. So much so that Saint Bonaventure, in the prologue of his biography, considers this fact an essential component of his master's personality:

> To all true lovers of humility and holy poverty, the grace of God our Savior has manifested itself in these latter days in the person of Francis, his servant, so that his example might present for their veneration the surpassing mercy of God in his regard, and might teach them to renounce once and for all the impiousness and covetousness of this world, to conform their lives to the life of Christ, and to yearn with an incomprehensible longing for Christ, our blessed hope.

Thus Francis calls his disciples to imitate Jesus Christ, and the disciples find in him the example of imitating the Divine Model. This is precisely the theme of the wonderful anonymous work composed by the friars who were closest to Saint Francis, *The Mirror of Perfection*. One of the chapters candidly declares, "Francis, faithful servant

and perfect imitator of Christ, felt that he had been completely transformed into Christ. . . ." And it concludes as follows: "Thus, having
spent twenty years in perfect repentance, on October 4 in the year
of the Lord 1226, Francis passed on to the Lord Jesus Christ, whom
he had loved with all his heart, with all his mind, with all his soul,
with all his strength, with the most ardent desire and most lively affection, following him to complete perfection, running eagerly in his
footsteps, and arriving at last in his glorious presence."

Francis claims to imitate Jesus Christ more especially in his lowliness and his suffering. This is the subject of one of his admonitions:
"Let all the friars consider the Good Shepherd who suffered death
on the Cross for the salvation of his flock. The Lord's sheep have
followed him in trials, persecution, and humiliation, in hunger and
thirst, in weakness, hardships, and all other sorts of misfortunes."

According to *The Three Companions*, a devotion to the Passion of
Christ was engraved on his soul at that moment in the ruined church
of San Damiano when the Crucified Lord spoke to him. "From that
day on, his heart was so struck and so profoundly wrenched by the
memory of the Lord's Passion that, throughout the rest of his life, he
harbored in his soul the memory of the wounds of the Lord Jesus."

He had composed an office of the Passion, along with a "prayer for
times of sickness", which has come down to us: "I give you thanks,
Lord God, for all my pains, and I ask you, my Lord, to send me a
hundred times as many, if such is your good pleasure. For I would
very willingly accept it if you did not spare me but overwhelmed me
with pain, since my submission to your holy will is for me a surpassing consolation."

And so the mystical gift of the stigmata was the answer to this
thirst for a practical union with the sufferings of Christ. A few moments before receiving it, he was praying to the Savior in these words:
"Lord, I ask you for two graces before I die: to experience in myself,
as much as possible, the sufferings of your cruel Passion, and to feel
for you the same love that drove you to sacrifice yourself for us."

Celano reckons that the manifest sanctity of Francis was the result
of the martyrdom that he received, not at the hands of the Muslims,
as he had hoped at first, but through the intervention of God himself:
"His perfection equaled that of the saints who had gone before him,
but his life shone with still greater brilliance. For our glorious father

was marked, in five places on his body, with the seal of the Passion and of the Cross, as though he had been crucified with the Son of God."

We find the same remark in the writings of Saint Bonaventure: "In order to arrive at the firm conviction that Francis, this messenger sent by the love of Christ for us to imitate, is the servant of God, it is enough to contemplate that perfection in his sanctity whereby he merited that he should be presented as a model for the perfect disciples of Christ. And what assures us of this is the irrefutable proof: the seal that made him into an image of the living God, Jesus crucified."

Love for Christ leads to love of the Eucharist—the living Christ offering himself on the altar for our salvation and reserved among us for our adoration. Francis left behind an exhortation on the Body of Christ that displays flawless doctrinal knowledge of this mystery:

Every day the Son of God comes to us under humble appearances; every day he descends upon the altar through the hands of the priest. And just as he revealed himself to the apostles in truly human flesh, so too he reveals himself to us now in the consecrated bread. They, when they looked upon him with their fleshly eyes, saw only his flesh, but because they contemplated him with their spiritual eyes, they believed that he was God. May we, too, when we see with our fleshly eyes the bread and wine, be able to see and believe most firmly that they are the most sacred Body and Blood of the living, true Lord. This, indeed, is the manner that he has chosen to remain always with those who believe in him, as he himself said: "Behold, I am with you until the consummation of the world."

In his "Letter to All the Faithful", Francis recalls the institution of the Eucharist and repeats the first words of the formula of transubstantiation. Then he comments: "The Son of the Father wants us all to be saved by him, and to receive him with a pure heart into a chaste body. . . . We must confess to the priest all our sins and receive from him the Body and Blood of our Lord. Anyone who does not eat his flesh and drink his blood cannot enter into the Kingdom of heaven."

At that time, the Church had not enacted very precise regulations for showing respect for the Eucharist, in particular for conserving the consecrated species, which were often left at random in some corner of a church or an oratory. Saint Francis denounced this scandal and urged clerics, his contemporaries, to venerate continually the Real

Presence of God under the appearance of Bread. The *Legenda antiqua* relates that

> Blessed Francis had a great respect and a profound devotion for the Body of Christ. That is why he had it written in the rule that the friars should surround the Eucharist with great care and a lively solicitude in the provinces where they were staying, exhorting and encouraging the clerics and priests to reserve the Body of Christ in a decent, suitable place; and that if they did not do so, the friars should do it in their stead. Nay, much more, he insisted on sending into the provinces friars who brought with them ciboria in which to reserve the Body of Christ.

We find an echo of this preoccupation in the "Letter to All Clerics on the Respect Due to the Body of the Lord". He calls to the attention of all the clerics who habitually surround the altar the sad state of the liturgical furnishings: chalices, corporals, altar linens; he notes that "many leave the Eucharist haphazardly, in dirty places, carry it through the streets unworthily and administer it indiscriminately." He, who was only a lowly deacon, ordered those to whom the letter was addressed that, wherever they found the Body of Christ in an unsuitable place, they should respectfully take it and find for it a worthy place. And then he allows his indignation to erupt: "And yet all these profanations do not move us to pity! Even though our Lord, in his goodness, abandons himself into our hands, and we hold him and our mouths receive him every day! Are we unaware of the fact that one day we must fall into his hands?"

In his "Letter to the General Chapter", the protestations give way to praise:

> Let mankind be seized with fear, the whole world should tremble and heaven rejoice, when Christ the Son of the living God is present on the altar in the hands of the priest! O wondrous majesty! O stupendous dignity! O sublime humility! O humble sublimity! That the Lord of the whole universe, God and the Son of God, should humble himself to the point where he hides under the form of a little bread, for our salvation. But you should keep nothing for yourselves, so that he who has given himself entirely to you may receive you entirely.

In another letter, "To the Rulers of the People", addressed to "magistrates, consuls, judges, and governors", Francis exhorts his readers, first, not to forget that the day of death is approaching, and that one must prepare for it by keeping the commandments, and second, to receive the Eucharist and to show great reverence for it.

His "Letter to All Superiors of the Friars Minor", on the other hand, takes up again the admonition that he addressed to the clerics concerning the Eucharist: "Ask the clergy with all humility to venerate above all the most sacred Body and Blood of our Lord Jesus Christ, together with his holy name and the writings which contain his words, those words which consecrate his Body." Furthermore he recalls the duty of all clerics to keep the Body of the Lord carefully reserved in a tabernacle, to administer it with discernment, and to remind the faithful in their sermons to receive Communion worthily.

2. The Gospel

What better place to find Jesus than in the Gospel? Before encountering him along the mystical way, in contemplation, and in union with his sufferings, Francis, as we have seen, heard his voice as it reverberated in the writings of the evangelists. At first with a simple devotion, like a well-informed Christian who receives these inspired texts with reverence; then, suddenly, beginning one year on the Feast of Saint Matthias, as a personal message. At that moment the Gospel became for him the book of life, the guide of his thought and action. Francis echoed this discovery in his "Testament": "When God gave me some friars, no one showed me what I should do; but the Most High himself revealed to me that I must live the life of the Gospel. I had someone write this down briefly and simply, and his holiness the Pope confirmed it for me."

Celano insistently records this constant preoccupation of his master:

His most resolute intention, his ardent desire, his ultimate purpose was to observe the Gospel in all things and always, and to follow the teaching and the example of our Lord Jesus Christ perfectly, applying himself to this task with all his vigilance, all his zeal, all his mind and all the fervor of his heart. Through assiduous meditation he always kept the Lord's words in mind, and through very keen contemplation he had his works continually before his eyes. He was especially concerned with the humility of his Incarnation and the charity that he showed in his Passion, and he could hardly think of anything else.

The original rule, approved by Innocent III, was made up almost entirely of passages from the Gospel. The rule of 1221, although purged of everything that did not seem useful to the canonists, still contains 175 verses (out of around eight hundred) taken from the Gospels. And at the very start, when Francis saw a few disciples coming to join him, he demanded nothing of them except to go and preach the Gospel.

However, despite the irritation that this excessively evangelical rule caused the learned doctors, and despite the pruning that it had to undergo, Francis continued to consider it, both in its spirit and in the few citations that it retained, as an indisputable guide proceeding from the will of Christ himself: "The rule is the book of life, the assurance of salvation, the marrow of the Gospel, the way of perfection, the key to paradise, the charter of the eternal Covenant."

One night he had a dream: he was gathering miniscule bits of bread on the ground in order to distribute them to his friars, who were faint with hunger; and when he asked himself how he was going to feed them with such a miserable pittance, he heard a voice from heaven: "Francis, with all these crumbs, make a host, and give it as food to those who crave it." That is why the definitive rule, which has deleted most of the Gospel citations, nevertheless begins with this important article, which expresses the whole mind, the whole will of the founder: "The rule and the life of the Friars Minor consist of observing the holy Gospel of our Lord Jesus Christ."

What was good for the Friars Minor was good for the Poor Clares. The preamble of the first rule, composed by Saint Francis, declares: "Since, by divine inspiration, you have made yourselves daughters and servants of the Most High and sovereign King, our Heavenly Father, and have given yourselves as brides to the Holy Spirit, in choosing to live according to the perfection of the Gospel. . . ."

At the end of his life, when he was prevented from attending the general chapter, Francis dictated for that occasion a long letter in which he declared, in particular: "I urge all my friars and I encourage them in Christ to venerate God's words wherever they may happen to find them in writing: to venerate them as much as possible and to the fullest extent of their competence. If they are not preserved properly or if they lie thrown about disrespectfully, the friars should pick them up and put them in a suitable place, thus honoring the words of the Lord who spoke them."

But this requirement does not apply only to religious, it is also valid for all the faithful. At the beginning of an encyclical letter that he addressed to them, he instructed them as to the meaning of his message: "Considering that because of my sickness and frail health

I cannot personally visit each one of you individually, I decided to send you this letter bringing a message with the words of our Lord Jesus Christ, who is the Word of the Father, and the words of the Holy Spirit, which are *spirit and life* [Jn 6:64]."

Just as he himself discovered his vocation through the words of the Holy Gospel, Francis subjects the conduct of all his friars to them. One chapter from the 1221 Rule, ten out of eleven lines of which consist of Gospel citations, enjoins them to apply literally the instructions that Jesus gave to his apostles when he sent them out on a mission. They must bring *nothing* with them on the way; in whatever house they are welcomed, they should eat and drink what is served to them; if someone strikes them on the right cheek, they should present the left; if someone takes their cloak, they should offer their tunic. Furthermore the friars are exhorted to go and preach to unbelievers, since the Lord said, "I send you as sheep in the midst of wolves."

Even if he does not exactly command his friars to preach the Gospel, Francis intersperses sayings from the Gospel throughout his advice. For example, when he speaks to his first disciples:

> God, in his mercy, has chosen us not only to bring about our salvation, but also to save many souls; let us go through the world and, by our example even more than by our words, let us exhort the people to do penance for their sins and to keep God's commandments. Trust in God who has conquered the world, for it is his Spirit that speaks in you and through you, in order to exhort all sinners to convert and to observe his precepts.

But this preaching, as ardent as it might be, had to be accompanied by humility. Celano has Francis delivering the following discourse:

> We must lament the preachers who sell their ministry for a farthing of vainglory. Why should you boast of the conversions of men, when my illiterate friars convert them by their prayers? Who is that sterile woman that Isaiah speaks of who brings many children into the world? It is my poor little friar who does not have the commission to give birth to children in the Church; but on the day of judgment, he will have given birth to many of them, because those whom he converts today by his secret prayers will be reckoned to his glory by the Judge.

3. The Church

What is remarkable about Saint Francis is that, in what he says and in his entire approach, Christ cannot be separated from the Church, nor the Gospel from ecclesiastical authority. For him it is not a question of fulfilling a necessary condition in obtaining approval for his order and his preaching, but rather a profound faith in the Church instituted by Jesus Christ, as the interpreter and extension of him, as his Mystical Body. Thus Scripture is not the property of the preacher; it is not even the property of the Church, who guards it as a deposit in trust so as to communicate it according to that very spirit in which it was handed down. In one of his admonitions, Francis declares, "The spirit of sacred Scripture gives life to those who do not claim each text that they know in the way that one possesses a physical object; to those who, by their example, acknowledge the ownership of the Lord Most High, to whom every good belongs."

Now the Lord manifests his authority by his Church. That is why, from the very first article, the first rule states his [Francis'] intention to be subject and to subject his friars to the head of the Church: "This is the way of life that Brother Francis asked Pope Innocent to authorize and approve. And the Pope granted it to him and approved it for him and his present and future friars."

The recruiting of religious is carried out according to their faith:

All the friars should be Catholics; they should live and speak as Catholics. If one of them strays from Catholic faith and morality, in word or in deed, and does not amend his ways, he will be definitively expelled from our fraternity. Furthermore, we must consider all clerics and religious as our masters, in what concerns the salvation of our souls and is not contrary to our rule; we must reverence their character, their office and their ministry in the Lord.

Having arrived at the end of his life, Francis recalls, in his "Testament", the conditions that he had been declaring since the foundation of the order:

> The Lord gave me and still gives me, because of their priestly character, such great confidence in the priests who live according to the law of the Holy Roman Church that, even if they were persecuting me, I would want to have recourse to them. And even if I had the wisdom of Solomon, and found some poor little priests living a worldly life, I would not want to preach against their will in their parishes. As for all the others, I want to honor, love, and revere them as my masters, and I do not want to examine the sin in them, because I discern the Son of God in them, and they are our lords.

The Mirror of Perfection records for us the rules that Francis gave to his friars during a time when they were making many new foundations, so that they could construct a convent in a town: "They should call upon the bishop of the town and tell him: 'Your Excellency, such and such an inhabitant of the town wishes to give to us, for the love of God and the salvation of our souls, enough land so that we might build a house there. We come to you first, because you are the father and master of the souls of the flock that has been entrusted to you. After all, we want to build with God's blessing and with yours.' "

Further on he added, "The Lord has called us to uphold the faith and to help the prelates and the clerics of Holy Church. Because of this, we are obliged to love, honor, and respect them at all times."

Here is another argument, which he makes in the "Letter to All the Faithful":

> We must be Catholics. We must make frequent visits to the churches and show our respect to the clerics; not so much for their own sake, since they can be sinners, but because of their office, since they are the ministers of the most sacred Body and Blood of our Lord Jesus Christ, which they sacrifice upon the altar, which they themselves receive and dispense to others. We should all know and firmly believe that no one can be saved, except by the Body and Blood of our Lord Jesus Christ and by the sacred Words of the Lord, which the priests preach, proclaim, and distribute, for the duty of distributing these things is theirs alone, to the exclusion of all others.

One of the exhortations of Francis that have been preserved in his writings takes up this theme again:

> Blessed is that servant of God who places his trust in the clerics who live uprightly according to the rule of the Holy Roman Church. And woe to those who hold them in contempt, because, even if they are sinners, nevertheless no one should judge them, because the Lord reserves judgment upon them for himself. Indeed, inasmuch as their ministry surpasses all others, since they are the ministers of the most sacred Body and most sacred Blood of our Lord Jesus Christ, which they receive and which they alone give to others, to that same degree the offense that one commits in sinning against them surpasses the offense that one would commit by sinning against all the other people in this world.

On his deathbed, the Father called Brother Benedict of Prato and gestured for him to write down his three last requests: "May the brothers always love one another as I have loved them and as I love them. May they always love and revere Lady Poverty. May they always prove loyal to the bishops and the priests of Holy Mother Church."

This reverence for the Church and for her clerics, this submission to the Church and to her laws appeared to Francis' contemporaries as one of the most characteristic features of his spirit, so much so that the author of his liturgical office gave expression to it in the first of all the proper parts for his feast, the first antiphon for the office of first vespers:

> *Franciscus, vir catholicus*
> *Et totus apostolicus,*
> *Ecclesiae teneri*
> *Fidem Romanae docuit*
> *Presbyterosque monuit*
> *Prae cunctis revereri.*

Which means: "Francis, a Catholic and entirely apostolic man, taught fidelity to the faith of the Roman Church and admonished [his followers] to revere priests above all others."

4. Prayer

A lover of Christ, completely devoted to the Gospel, and an obedient son of the Church, Francis was a man of prayer. Celano relates that "Francis, the man of God, was kept by his body far from the Lord, but by his spirit he strove to live in heaven: a fellow citizen with the angels, he was separated from it only by a partition of flesh. His entire soul thirsted for Christ."

The biographer is careful to point out that he saw with his own eyes what he goes on to relate next. It is therefore an eyewitness account:

> His every waking hour was like a holy rest during which wisdom dwelt within his heart. When visits from worldly men or business matters required his attention, he used to break off the conversations rather than complete them, so as to plunge again into the depths of his soul. He would make his way to some hidden place where he could converse with God, giving Him not only his soul, but also his members. When he was suddenly visited by the Lord in public, he made a screen of his cloak so as not to be without a cell. When he had no cloak, he would cover his face with his sleeve, so as not to betray the secret of the hidden manna. This he would do when he was in inhabited places. When he was praying in a forest or in a deserted place, he used to fill the woods with his groaning, water the earth with his tears, and strike his breast. In this more secluded retreat, he would speak with the Lord, answer the Judge, implore the Father; he would converse with the Friend and rejoice with the Bridegroom. Often his lips remained motionless, and then he was speaking interiorly; recollecting within himself his external senses, he allowed his spirit to soar to heaven. And when he concentrated his mind and his love in this way on the favor that he was asking of God, it was no longer a man praying, but rather prayer which had become man.

He was vigilant in setting aside all distractions, whether exterior or interior. If he lingered over some image that passed through his mind and thus disturbed his meditation or his prayer, he considered this weakness to be a sin and immediately went to confess it. One day, in order to keep his hands busy, he had started to fashion a vessel out of clay. During the office of Terce, afterward, his mind was engrossed by the memory of his vessel; when they were finished reciting the office, he went to fetch the vessel and threw it into the fire.

Frequently he went into ecstasy, and, even if he was traveling, he would lose the use of his hearing and his sight. Celano, again, relates a typical anecdote of this sort. One day he was supposed to travel through Borgo Sansepolcro, riding on his donkey, and news of this spread through the surrounding localities. The crowds surrounded him, touched him, sang his praises, and jostled him, cutting his tunic into pieces so as to make relics. He said nothing, saw nothing, heard nothing. Finally, when he had left the town far behind him, he came out of his rapture and asked, "Will we be arriving soon at Borgo Sansepolcro?"

Nevertheless, when he emerged from a state of prayer in which he had lost awareness of what was going on around him, he endeavored to behave in an ordinary way and not to let the flame that was still burning within him escape to the outside. He even made this the subject of a lesson he taught his friars: "When a servant of God receives some consolation from the Lord in prayer, he must, before ending his prayer, lift up his eyes to heaven, join his hands and say, 'Lord, you have sent me from heaven this consolation and this sweetness, although I am an unworthy sinner; I give them back to you so that you may keep them for me.' " Or on another occasion: "When a friar has finished praying, he must appear to others to be just as poor a sinner as if he had received no grace at all."

Saint Bonaventure, unlike Thomas of Celano, did not personally witness the life of Saint Francis, but he did interview the principal eyewitnesses of his life and confidently recorded the facts. This is what he says about his prayer:

> The servant of Christ, Francis, constrained by his body to wander in exile far from the Lord, although for love of Christ he had made that body impervious to earthly passions, strove to keep his soul always in the presence of the Lord by unceasing prayer, so that he was not deprived of the consolation of his Beloved. He vehemently declared that the grace

of prayer is what a religious must ask for above all other things. Convinced that without it nothing good can be done in the Lord's service, he urged his brothers to work at it with all their heart. He himself, whether walking or stopping, while traveling or in the convent, at work or at rest, applied himself to prayer to such a degree that he seemed to have devoted to it his whole heart and his whole body, his every action and all his time. He would never willingly have missed by negligence a visitation of the Spirit; when this occurred, he received him faithfully and tasted the sweetness that was offered to him for as long as that grace of the Lord lasted. When he was on the road and he felt the breath of the Spirit of God coming, he allowed his companions to go ahead of him and stopped in order to savor the sudden inspiration, so as not to receive the grace in vain. His contemplation sometimes lifted him so high that, enraptured and beside himself, he experienced what a man cannot experience and remained oblivious to all that went on around him.

Obviously, Francis considered the *Opus Dei*, the Divine Office, to be of primary importance. As Celano relates:

He paid to the canonical hours as much reverence as devotion. Although he suffered from failing eyesight and stomach, spleen, and liver problems, he would not allow himself, during the recitation of the psalms, to lean against the wall or the choir stalls, but always remained standing without his cowl, not letting his glance stray, and reciting the hours without omitting a syllable. When he was going about the world on foot, he would stop walking in order to recite the office, and when he was traveling on horseback, he would dismount.

Among his personal devotions, Saint Francis gave first place to the devotion that is due to our Lady, the Mother of Christ, whom he chose as the patroness of his order. Celano writes: "He sent up songs of praise to her, placed at her feet bouquets of fervent prayers, and offered her the outpourings of his heart."

The *Salutation to the Blessed Virgin* has come down to us, a prayer by Saint Francis that he liked to recite before her image:

> Hail, holy Lady,
> Most holy Queen,
> Mother of God, and
> Ever-Virgin Mary,

Chosen from heaven by the Father Most Holy,
O you, whom he consecrated
With his Most Blessed and dearly beloved Son
and the Holy Spirit, the Paraclete.

O you, in whom was and is
All the fullness of grace
And every good.

Hail, Palace of God!
Hail, Tabernacle of God!
Hail, Dwelling-place of God!

Hail, Garment of God!
Hail, Servant of God!
Hail, Mother of God!

Francis, as we have seen, had a special devotion to the Eucharist. Celano writes: "He burned with love for the sacrament of the Body of the Lord and remained dumbstruck before this mercy full of charity and this charity full of mercy. It would have seemed to him to be committing a serious sin if he had not at least attended Mass each day. He received Holy Communion often, so devoutly that his devotion was communicated to others."

Elsewhere, he writes, "He, more than anyone else, celebrated the Nativity of the Infant Jesus with ineffable joy. It was, in his own words, the feast of feasts."

He had great devotion to the angels as well, because "they fight at our side, they march with us in the midst of the shadows of death." But he fostered a lively devotion to Saint Michael in particular; he even prepared for his feast day by a forty-day fast, which started on the day after the Assumption.

About a dozen prayers composed by Saint Francis have come down to us. He used to recite one of them, which he called *Laudes* [praises], after all the hours of the Divine Office. Actually it is made up of two parts, one of which is a paraphrase of the Our Father, and the other a series of acclamations inspired by the Canticle of the Three Young Men (Dan 3:29–68) and by the Book of Revelation. Here are a few excerpts from it:

Our Father Most Holy, our Creator, our Redeemer, our Savior, our Comforter,

Thou who art in heaven, among the angels and saints, enlightening them so that they might know thee, for thou, O Lord, art light; inflaming them so that they might love thee, for thou, O Lord, art love; dwelling within them and filling them so that they might be blessed, for thou, O Lord, art the supreme good, the eternal good, from which all good comes and without which there is no good.

Hallowed be thy Name: may the knowledge of thee be made clear in us, so that we might know what is the breadth of thy benefits, the length of thy promises, the height of thy majesty and the depth of thy judgments.

Thy kingdom come: so that thou mightest reign in us by grace and bring us into thy Kingdom, where the vision of thee is manifest, the love of thee is perfect, fellowship with thee is happy, and the enjoyment of thee is eternal.

Thy will be done on earth as it is in heaven: may we love thee with all our heart, thinking always of thee; with all our soul, desiring thee always; with all our mind, directing all our intentions to thee and seeking thy honor in everything; and with all our strength, applying all our powers, all the senses of our soul and of our body to the service of thy love, and to nothing else.

5. Holy Poverty

Poverty has the reputation of being a specifically Franciscan virtue. Indeed, although all the saints have been attentive to its demands, sometimes in a heroic fashion, Francis of Assisi took it to extremes. Saint Bonaventure attempted to sum up this requirement in the following lines:

> Among the other graces that he received from God's generosity, Francis obtained the special gift of enriching the treasury of his simplicity by his love of extreme poverty. Noticing that this virtue, which had been the constant companion of the Son of God, had become the object of universal reprobation, he decided to take her as his wife and swore to her his eternal love. He was not content to leave his father and mother for her; he also distributed to the poor all that he could call his own. Never has a man been seen who was more jealous of his gold than he was of his poverty; no one ever watched over his treasure with more care than he lavished in guarding this pearl that the Gospel speaks of. Nothing so offended his eyes as to see among the friars something that was not in perfect conformity with poverty. The only riches that he himself had, from the beginning of his religious life until his death, were his tunic, his cord, and his drawers, and that was enough for him.
>
> It often happened that he would shed tears while describing the poverty of Jesus Christ and of his Mother. He found therein the explanation for the fact that poverty is the queen of the virtues: because of the splendor with which it shone in the King of Kings and in the Queen, his Mother. "Know, my brothers," he used to say, "that poverty is the privileged way of salvation, because it is the sap of humility and the root of perfection; its fruits, though hidden, are innumerable. It is that treasure hidden in a field, to purchase which one must sell everything; its [inestimable] value should impel us to disdain everything that can be sold."
>
> "Anyone who wants to reach the summit," he said, "must abandon not only worldly prudence, but also literature and learning; thus divested of what is still a form of ownership, he will proclaim the Lord's power

and will offer himself naked to the embrace of the Crucified. A person has not entirely renounced the world as long as he keeps in reserve in a recess of his heart some little treasure of self-will." He often cited the Gospel passage: "The foxes have lairs and the birds of the air their nests, but the Son of Man has no place to rest his head." From this he drew the lesson that the friars must build only small, lowly houses and not take up residence there as owners, but to conduct themselves as pilgrims and strangers in someone else's house.

Poverty was, in his view, the cornerstone of the order, the foundation of the building, which would stand firm as long as the virtue itself was solid and which would be destroyed if it were ever to disappear.

One day as Francis was traveling with a companion through Puglia, they saw a large purse full of coins abandoned at the roadside. The companion's first reaction was to suggest that they pick it up; not so as to keep the contents, of course, but to distribute them to the poor.

Francis was against the idea. "No, that purse contains a trap set by the devil. What you are proposing is not meritorious at all but is blameworthy, because that would be making use of money that does not belong to us under the pretext of giving alms."

But the good friar was not convinced. A little further on he restated his proposed plan again. "My father, are you not being indifferent to the plight of the poor?"

Annoyed, Francis, true to form, preferred to teach a practical lesson rather than elaborate on his reasons. He went back and found the purse again, which had not yet been taken by another traveler. "Pick it up", he ordered the friar.

The latter, noticing the unusual resolve of his superior, began to tremble. But after all, there was the duty of obedience. He stretched out his hand. At that, a long serpent slithered out of the purse and disappeared, dragging it along as it escaped.

And Francis calmly pointed out the lesson: "For those who serve God, my brother, money is the devil, or else a venomous serpent."

These anecdotes were obviously well known in religious communities, since their strictness and their picturesque details ensured that they would spread rapidly. Which still didn't prevent some of them from failing to learn the lesson. For example, one day a young friar saw a visitor, who had come into Santa Maria degli Angeli to pray, leave a fine silver coin at the foot of the cross as an alms. Spontaneously the friar picked it up and put it on a windowsill. When Francis came into the chapel and noticed the incongruous presence of the coin, he announced that the guilty one should accuse himself. The little friar immediately ran up to his superior.

"What?" the latter exclaimed. "You dared to touch that money with your hands? For your punishment, take that coin, hold it between your teeth, and go put it down on the dung of an ass."

The strictness of the religious poverty decreed by Francis, which applied to clothing, buildings, furniture, food, and of course money (which is so useful when traveling), was the main cause for the opposition of the innovators. It is understandable: they entered a new religious order, full of life and originality, and figured that it was quite simply a matter of following the customs of other orders, which sheltered their religious in vast, peaceful monasteries that sometimes resembled fortresses, where, despite the individual vow of poverty, collectively they had everything necessary for a flourishing community life. And they expected, in a *mendicant* order, to find the same facilities. Of course, they had not been present at the founding of this new order and had not understood that, in addition to being new on the scene, it was also new in its concept of religious renunciation. And so they dared to oppose the founder in the name of their own ideas.

But Francis did not yield; to all requests for mitigation, he would reply, "The friars must not keep anything except a tunic, a cord, and a pair of drawers. And shoes when absolutely necessary."

He was not sparing in his exhortations and admonitions, sometimes recalling the requirement of the rule.

> The brothers who serve as ministers hope to fool us, the Lord and me. But, even though all the friars know that they are obliged to observe the [counsels of] perfection from the Holy Gospel, I want it to be written at the beginning and at the end of the rule: "The friars are bound to observe strictly the Holy Gospel of our Lord Jesus Christ." And so that the brothers will have no excuse, I have proclaimed to them, and I proclaim to them now what the Lord has placed upon my lips, for my salvation and for theirs."

Occasionally it was in the form of an ironic rebuke. "You wish to appear in the eyes of men to be Friars Minor, and you value being thought of as observers of the Holy Gospel. In reality, you want to gather up full purses in return for your works."

It is true that the meaning of poverty goes much further than the ownership of tangible things, as Francis points out in an admonition on *The Spirit of Poverty*:

> Blessed are the poor in spirit, for the kingdom of heaven is theirs. Many are those who are diligent in their prayers and duties and impose fasts and mortifications upon their bodies, yet are immediately scandalized and troubled by a single word that seems to them like a physical injury or over some little thing that is taken away from them. People like that are not poor in spirit, because the person who truly has the spirit of poverty is the one who hates himself and dearly loves those who strike him on the cheek.

Unlike the innovators, the authors of the memoirs published after the death of Saint Francis emphasize his love of poverty and his vehement insistence on respect in the order for the obedience that was due him. The *Fioretti* tell of him saying to Brother Masseo along the road to Rome:

> Dear companion, let us go to Saint Peter and Saint Paul; let us ask them to teach us and to help us to possess this infinite treasure of most holy poverty. For it is such a precious and godly treasure that we are not worthy to own it. It is that heavenly virtue by which all that is earthly and transient is trampled underfoot, by which everything that holds the soul back is overthrown so as to permit it to unite itself freely with the eternal God. This is the virtue that allows the soul, while still earthbound, to converse with the angels. This was the virtue that accompanied Christ on the Cross, was buried with Christ, arose with Christ and ascended into heaven with Christ. . . . Let us pray to Christ's holy apostles, therefore, who were perfect lovers of this evangelical pearl, to obtain for us from our Lord Jesus Christ the grace of being true lovers, observers, and humble disciples of this most precious, most amiable, and evangelical poverty.

Bonaventure tells us that "Francis decided to take poverty as his wife." The language of Celano is quite similar: "As soon as he understood that the Son of God had made her [Poverty] his constant companion, he desired to be united with her by a perpetual and tender love. He became enamored of her beauty so as to become [with her] two in one spirit."

We are talking about the century of chivalry and courtly love. While he was still in the world, Francis' ideal was to become a troubadour and then a knight. Now he was realizing this ideal, in spirit: a knight of Christ for the conquest of the world of souls, he had found his lady, of whom he was ardently enamored, and he joined himself to her for a passionate marriage. This allegorical union delighted the Friars Minor who were faithful to the Franciscan ideal, and in 1227, the year after the death of Saint Francis, a little work was published entitled: *The Sacred Union of Blessed Francis with Lady Poverty* (*Sacrum commercium beati Francisci cum domina Paupertate*). The style in which it is written, clearly, is worthy of chivalric romances.

Francis is on a quest for his lady and does not know where to find her. He meets two old men, who might symbolize the compilers of the monastic rules or the Desert Fathers.

"Show me", he asks them, "where Lady Poverty lives, for I feel that I am swooning for love of her."

The old men explain, "This is where the lady lives: she has taken refuge on the top of that mountain. But in order to climb it, you must be naked and unburdened of any load. Therefore take with you some companions who will help you to make this difficult ascent."

Francis therefore chooses several reliable companions and makes his way to the top of the mountain. There, he arrives at the feet of the marvelous creature.

"Behold, our Lady," he announces to her,

we come to you because we know that you are the queen of all the virtues. Prostrate at your feet, we beg you to join us and to be the road by which we may come to the King of glory, for you were the road that he took when he came to rescue those who sit in the shadow of death. For, renouncing his royal abode, the King of the Most High sought you out—you, from whom all ran away—and, enamored of your beauty, he desired to wed you and you alone here below. You had prepared a throne for him in the poor, humble Virgin, a refuge in a miserable stable, and throughout his life you were his inseparable companion. Indeed, as a most faithful wife and a most tender lover, you never parted from him.

Francis then addresses a resounding prayer to the beautiful lady, to which she listens with ardent joy. She then tells her visitors her story, from Adam down to Jesus. After that, she does not fail to disparage her false lovers who abandon her, especially "those so-called religious who had promised to be faithful to me". Francis and his companions, moved to tears, then swear fidelity to the abandoned beauty, who joyfully consents to follow them to their hermitage.

As you see, this is not only the marriage of Lady Poverty to Francis, but also to his faithful friars. In contrast, Ubertino of Casale, one of the leaders of the "spiritual Franciscans" [as opposed to the innovators, who were called "conventuals"], places on the lips of Saint Francis alone the ardent "Prayer to Lady Poverty", which was published in his *Tree of the Crucified Life of Jesus* (1305):

> My sweet Lord, merciful Jesus, have pity on me and on Lady Poverty, for my love for her is in anguish, and I cannot rest without her. You know, O Lord, how much I love her. Behold, now she sits in sorrow, rejected by all, like a widow. The queen of all virtues is seated on the dunghill; she complains that all her friends have abandoned her and have become her enemies. Remember, Lord, that you came down from the abode of the angels to make this queen your spouse, and so as to have perfect children of her, in her, and by her. . . . It was in the close embrace of this spouse that you died, and she it was also who arranged your funeral rites, jealously watching to make sure that you would have nothing of your own, neither sepulchre, nor embalming, nor even a winding sheet, so that they had to borrow them. . . . Ah! Who, then, would not love Lady Poverty above all things? I ask you, therefore, O most sweet Jesus, as a special and perpetual privilege, to grant to me and to my confreres the grace of owning nothing under heaven, and of never having any more than a simple use of what belongs to others, as long as we shall be in this miserable flesh.

The first corollary of poverty is a mendicant way of life. If, indeed, Francis and his friars own nothing, and furthermore are not even allowed to use money, they must beg for a living. This custom, moreover, calls for the practice of two new virtues: humility in the one who begs, and charity in the benefactor.

From the moment when the first community was formed, the *Legenda antiqua* portrays Saint Francis giving this speech to his friars:

> Dearly beloved brothers, little children, do not be ashamed to ask for alms, for God became poor on earth for us. That is why we, following his example and that of his most holy Mother, have chosen the path of authentic poverty. . . . Go then and beg, full of confidence and in a

joyful spirit, with the blessing of the Lord our God. And you must ask for alms more freely and joyfully than a man who is about to give a hundred farthings for a gold coin; for you will be offering the Love of God to those from whom you will ask donations.

For his part, Bonaventure relates: "For the love of holy poverty, the servant of Almighty God much preferred alms that were begged from door to door to free-will offerings. If he was invited by important persons who had a more lavish meal prepared in his honor, he would first beg a few crusts of bread at the nearby houses and then went to table, rich in all his poverty."

And Celano explains: "He used to declare that being ashamed to beg is the enemy of salvation, while admitting that it is permissible to feel a holy bashfulness, provided that it does not make the beggar turn back. Thus he praised the blush that spread to the forehead of the young friar, but not the shame that confounded him."

Besides, the rule was there to encourage the friar to knock on doors. The Rule of 1221 says:

> When necessary, the friars shall go begging. Let them not feel shame; let them recall instead that our Lord Jesus Christ was poor and without shelter, that he lived on alms, together with the Blessed Virgin Mary and his disciples. Even if the people have put them to shame and refused to give them alms, they should thank God for it; for these affronts will bring them great honor before the tribunal of our Lord Jesus Christ. Let them be sure of this: the affront does not harm those who endure it, but those who inflict it. Almsgiving is the heritage and the right of the poor.

This praise of almsgiving reappears in the second rule—on a smaller scale, to be sure, but then the entire text of that rule was abridged in this way: "As pilgrims and strangers in this world, serving the Lord in poverty and humility, the friars will go begging confidently, without shame, for the Lord became poor for us in this world."

The second corollary of the virtue of poverty is love for the poor. If the mendicant way of life is the imitation of Jesus Christ, who lived in destitution and did not even have a place to lay his head, then love for the poor is an act of piety performed for Jesus Christ, who is recognized in the poor person. Celano asks:

What words could express the intense compassion that Francis felt for the poor? To be sure, this pity was innate, but it was enlarged by a heavenly grace. Francis' soul was moved by the sight of poor people; and if he could not help them materially, he showed his love for them. All the poverty and misery that he saw in an unfortunate soul he referred to Christ by a spontaneous reflection or a quick transposition. Although he had driven all feelings of envy from his heart, he could not do away with his jealousy of poverty. The sight of someone poorer than he aroused this jealousy and rivaled his own poverty, so that he feared that he would be beaten in such a contest.

One day, which traveling with one of his brothers, Francis came upon a poor wretch. He turned to his companion and said to him with a quavering voice, "This man's misery puts us to shame and sorely rebukes our poverty."

"How so?"

"I chose poverty for my wealth and for my Lady. Now, I see it more resplendent in this man than in myself. Do you not know that the news is traveling through the whole world that we have made ourselves the poorest of the poor for Christ's sake? But this poor man is proof that that is not the case."

One day, while he was at a hermitage, a poor, sick beggar came to ask for charity. After this encounter Francis was visibly moved, and so one of his brothers, no doubt without malice but rather to console his father, ventured to say, "Surely, that is a poor man. But after all, perhaps he is the richest of all in his desires."

Francis was indignant. He commanded the friar, "Go prostrate yourself at the feet of that man and beg his pardon for having shown contempt for him."

When the friar had done his penance, Francis explained to him, "When you see a poor man, you must see in him the one in whose name he comes, that is to say, Christ, who took upon himself our poverty and our infirmity."

6. Spiritual Joy

All the saints have been animated by a certain interior joy, and since the time of Francis de Sales it is commonly said that a sad saint is a sad excuse for a saint. Nevertheless, the praise of spiritual joy, not just as a Christian sentiment but as a necessary virtue, is still associated with the memory of Francis of Assisi.

Thomas of Celano seems to have plumbed the depths of this Franciscan sense of joy:

> The most successful defense against all the snares of the enemy, the saint used to say, is spiritual joy. Once the devil has managed to take joy from the soul of a servant of God, he has achieved his fondest hope. But when the heart is full of spiritual joy, in vain does the serpent try to inject his deadly venom. The devils have no hold on the servant of Christ whom they find full of a holy gladness. If, on the contrary, a soul is weeping, disconsolate, or vexed, it will easily allow itself to be invaded by sadness or to be driven toward empty joys. The saint endeavored, therefore, always to live with a joyful heart and to guard the unction of the spirit and the oil of gladness. He took the greatest care to protect himself from the dire sickness of melancholy, and when he noticed that it was creeping into his soul, he immediately had recourse to prayer.

We also have the testimony of the *Mirror of Perfection*:

> Besides the practice of prayer and the recitation of the Divine Office, Saint Francis constantly devoted himself to fostering a continual joy that was both interior and manifest. He especially valued it in his brothers, and he used to scold them when they showed sadness or ill humor. He would say, "If the servant of God takes care to acquire and to preserve, inwardly and outwardly, the joyful spirit that comes from purity of heart and is obtained by devotion and prayer, then the devils cannot harm him, and they will say, 'Since the servant of God is joyful in moments of disappointment as well as in times of contentment, we cannot find any way of entering into him and doing him harm.' And since a joyful

spirit comes from simplicity of heart and purity of perpetual prayer, you must strive, above all, to acquire these two virtues. Then . . . you will be able to have that interior and exterior joy which I summon up with all my heart and which I love to see and feel, in you as well as in me, for the edification of our neighbor and the confounding of the enemy. He and his followers deserve to be sad; it is for us to rejoice always in the Lord."

Francis occasionally had to reprimand brothers who were wearing a sad face. One day he spoke rather bluntly to one of them, "Why are you showing outwardly the suffering and the sadness of your sins? Keep that sadness between God and you. Pray that he will spare you in his mercy and will give back to your soul the joy of salvation that your sin has taken away from it. In front of the other friars, and in my presence, make sure that you always remain joyful; it is unfitting for a servant of God to show others a sad, discouraged face."

He himself was not content to maintain an interior joy; he frequently had occasion to display it outwardly. The originality with which he did so was not capricious, but rather the spontaneous expression of his poetical soul. The troubadour of yesteryear, full of zest and charm, was transformed into a juggler for God. In those moments of lyrical enthusiasm, he rediscovered what his biographers call the French language, which was in fact the dialect of Provence or Languedoc. Sometimes he would even take a stick and a wand, position the former under his chin like a violin and rub the latter against it like a bow; then he would amble through the woods, pretending to accompany his singing with an appropriate instrument. It sometimes happened, after that exaltation, that he would fall down on his knees in some remote place and give himself over to contemplating the heavenly mysteries that he had just celebrated in song.

Thus he showed to anyone who may have been watching that this ardent lyricism was not a jest, but rather an outpouring of religious fervor. Besides, he proscribed all joking, mockery, laughter, and witticisms, recalling that these things were nothing but vanity. Tradition has preserved an exhortation of his in which he declared, "Happy the religious who finds pleasure and joy only in the most holy words and works of our Lord, and who uses them joyfully to draw people to the love of God. Woe to the religious who delights in thoughtless, frivolous words and uses them to make people laugh."

The obligation to be spiritually joyful is written into the rule. There we find the words of Jesus in his prayer after the Last Supper: "These things I speak in the world, that they may have my joy fulfilled in themselves" (Jn 17:13), in union also "with the blessed who rejoice in heaven". The rule also says that the friars should "show themselves to be joyful in the Lord, cheerful and amiable as is fitting".

As is fitting: this brings us back to the contrast between true and false joy. And in another passage of the first rule, Francis again explains, "When we are undergoing various trials, when we have to endure in our body and in our soul all sorts of distress and tribulations in this world for the sake of eternal life, it is fitting that we should rejoice."

This is the lesson that he had already taught Brother Leo, "Write down what perfect joy consists of!"

7. Love for Creation

Of the original traits in the sanctity of Francis of Assisi, the one that is the most certain to win over his readers is his fondness for the divine work of creation and his familiarity with all creatures. We should beware, here again, of a misunderstanding: in the case of this spiritual man who was always anxious to render to God alone what is due him, it was not a question of a simple poetic love of nature, but rather of theological veneration, an act of glorifying the Creator of all things and of contemplating the Author through his works. Celano insists on this point quite explicitly:

> Although he was in a hurry to leave this world as a land of exile, this happy pilgrim found great consolation in the things of this world. When he considered the powers of darkness, the world in his eyes was a battle-field; but when he thought of God, it was a bright mirror of his goodness. In every work he glorified the artisan and sent up to the Creator the prayer of admiration that creatures inspired in him. He thrilled with joy at all the works produced by God's hands and, through these pleasing vistas, he saw the life-giving reason for them and contemplated the first cause. In the presence of all that is beautiful he acknowledged the supreme Beauty, and everything good cried out to him, "Our author is Goodness itself!"
>
> Thanks to the traces inscribed in nature, he walked everywhere in the footsteps of his Beloved, and everything served as a ladder by which he could ascend to the throne of God. He embraced all creatures in a devout and extraordinary love, speaking to them about the Lord and inviting them to praise him. He allowed torches, lamps, and candles to burn, refusing to be the one to extinguish that light which is the symbol of the eternal light. In the garden, he reserved a plot for sweet-smelling herbs and flowers, because they reminded those who saw them of the eternal sweetness. He removed insects from the road for fear that they might be trodden underfoot, and during severe winter weather he had generous portions of honey and wine brought to the bees to keep them

from dying of hunger. He called all animals by the name "brother", although he preferred those who are endowed with meekness.

Saint Bonaventure in turn recalls this pious affection: "By going back to the first principle of all things, he had conceived a lively friendship for them all, calling even the lowest creatures brothers and sisters, for he knew that he and they proceeded from the same principle. He was, however, inclined to have a greater fondness and tenderness toward those which, by their nature or through the teaching of Scripture, remind us of Christ's meekness."

On occasion he would ask others to purchase the freedom of lambs that were being led to slaughter, in memory of the most meek Lamb who willed to be led to death in order to redeem sinners. He had a particular affection for the crested lark, because it resembled his brothers.

"Sister Lark", he used to say,

wears a cowl like a religious. She is a humble bird that likes to travel a sure path in order to find a grain. When she flies, she sweetly sings the Lord's praises, like those good religious who are detached from the earth; their thoughts are always directed toward heaven and they praise God with fervor. Her plumage is like the earth; she sets an example for religious, that they should not wear fine or brightly-colored garments, but rather cheap habits that are the color of the earth, which is the lowliest of the elements.

He was not content to venerate living things; his devotion extended to inanimate objects. We have testimonies to this, such as this one from the *Legenda antiqua*: "When he washed himself, he chose a place where the water that he had used would not be stepped on. When he walked on rocks, he did so with fear and respect, for love of Christ, whom Saint Paul calls the Rock. He would tell the friar who gathered firewood not to cut down the whole tree, but to leave the stump."

To all of these insensate creatures, "he spoke with a great interior and outward joy, as though they were endowed with feeling, intelligence, and speech; moreover this was often the occasion for him to go into a divine rapture."

It was not enough that he had a devotion to the creatures of God; they responded with kind attentions and signs of affection. We have already seen how the wolf of Gubbio converted at the sound of his voice. During one stay in a hermitage, when he had neither bell nor companion to awaken him, he made an agreement with a falcon that nested nearby: it was to awaken the saint regularly when it was time to pray the night office.

At the Portiuncula, a cicada perched in a fig tree delighted the father's ears each day by its song. He called to it, "Sister Cicada, come to me." She left her branch to land on his hand. "And now, sing, my Sister, and joyfully praise the Lord, your Creator." She sang. And he, joining his voice to hers, performed a duet with her. Then he commanded her to return to her resting place, and she obeyed. But then, every time that Francis came out of his cell, she joined him and sang in his hand. Finally he sent her away; she disappeared and never came back.

One day when he was traveling with several friars in the vicinity of Siena, he passed by a meadow where a herd of sheep was grazing. He immediately greeted the animals courteously. They flocked to him, bleating joyfully. Even more charming is the story of a lamb that a devout person sent to him at the Portiuncula; it became attached to him and followed him everywhere. He then explained to it how it should behave: it was to participate in the Divine Office without ever disturbing the singing of the psalms. It obeyed. Whenever the community went into the church for a liturgical office, it followed them and took its place before the altar of the Virgin. During Mass, at the moment of the elevation, it prostrated itself devoutly.

During one of his stays in Greccio, someone offered him a young hare. The animal snuggled in his arms and gladly received his caresses. Finally, Francis made a speech in which he commanded it, above all, not to allow itself to be captured again; then he let it go. But in vain. It returned to its benefactor every time he gave it permission to run away. The biographers mention other similar cases: the one with the rabbit from an island on Lake Trasimeno, donated by some hunters; the one with the moor hen from Lake Rieti, given to him by a fisherman. These animals did not want to regain their freedom and became unfailingly attached to their friend.

What Francis marveled at in the spectacle of nature, therefore, was no longer simply its own charm, as in the days when he was the king of the golden youth, but rather at the same time the testimony that it continually gave concerning its author, the lesson that it never stopped teaching rebellious man. One of his exhortations reads: "Consider, O man, the excellence with which God has made you, since he created and formed your body in the image of his dearly beloved Son, and your soul in his likeness. Yet all creatures under heaven, each in its own way, serve and know their Creator and obey him better than you."

And then there was his sense of symbolism and his fondness for it, which were fostered by daily meditation on Scripture and which spontaneously made him see in creatures not only the goodness and power of the Creator, but also meanings that an ordinary person and even the average friar does not think of. Whereas a sheep suggested to him the Lamb of God immolated for our sins, flowers spoke to him of Christ, about whom it is said in the Song of Songs, "I am the flower of the fields, the lily of the valleys." He loved water because it symbolized "holy repentance, by which soiled souls are cleansed". He loved wood because it recalled the wood of the Cross upon which the Son of God redeemed us. He loved rocks, because Saint Paul writes that the Hebrews "drank from the spiritual Rock that followed them, and the Rock was Christ". He loved donkeys and oxen in memory of the Nativity, and he asked their owners to give them extra fodder on the Feast of Christmas. He even had a tender consideration for worms, because the psalmist said prophetically about the Savior, "I am a worm and no man."

We have seen how, on a road in Umbria, Francis preached to the birds and they listened to him. His most famous disciple, Anthony of Padua, addressed even less intelligent creatures: fish. Once when the Cathari of Venice refused to listen to his arguments, he went to the mouth of a river and began a fiery sermon. No sooner had he opened his mouth than a multitude of fish kept still, with their heads out of the water, as though to listen eagerly to his exhortations; he preached to them in a florid style, illustrated with examples from Scripture, congratulating them on the graces that they had received from heaven, beginning with their survival of the Deluge. This miracle drew an astonished crowd and led to an unexpected result: the heretics, who had also come running, made their act of submission.

Saint Francis had an enthusiastic fervor for the sun. It was, of course, as we will soon hear him sing, because it is beautiful and resplendent, but this aspect was an echo of the troubadour. His sense of the symbolic taught him something else: "Among all creatures," the *Mirror* reports, "he used to think and say that the sun is the most beautiful and furthermore can be compared with God, because in Scripture the Lord himself is called the Sun of Justice."

So it was that the famous "Canticle of Creation", which Francis composed in 1225 while sick and almost blind, was called at first "Canticle of the Sun", and certain manuscripts even refer to it as the "Canticle of Brother Sun".

> O most high, almighty, good Lord God,
>   to thee belong praise,
>   glory, honor, and all blessing!
>
> By thee alone, Most High, were all things made,
>   and no man is worthy
>   to speak thy name.
>
> Praised be my Lord with all his creatures,
>   especially Sir Brother Sun,
>   who brings us the day and brings us light.
>
> Fair is he and shining with a very great splendor;
>   he signifies thee, O Most High!
>
> Praised be my Lord for Sister Moon, and for the stars,
>   which he has set in heaven,
>   clear and precious and lovely.
>
> Praised be my Lord for Brother Wind,
>   and for air and cloud,
>   calms and all weather,
>   by which thou upholdest life in thy creatures.
>
> Praised be my Lord for Sister Water,
>   who is very serviceable and very humble,
>   and precious and clean.
>
> Praised be my Lord for Brother Fire,
>   through whom thou givest us light in the night;
>   and he is beautiful and joyous,
>   and very mighty, and strong.

Praised be my Lord for our Sister, Mother Earth,
 who sustains and keeps us
 and brings forth divers fruits,
 and flowers of many colors, and grass.

PART FIVE

The Sublime Path of Eternity

1. Stigmatization

Indignant at the insolence of the ministers, disappointed by the prudence of the Roman Curia, Brother Francis felt that he was losing control of his order. The work of fifteen years, which he had forged with so much love, was slipping out of his hands. Where was the Portiuncula now, that charming community that was once so innocent, spontaneous, fervent, abandoned to the will of God, and full of humble submission to the founder's authority? Those first friars, who still served as examples and continued to set a standard after his death, had had too many followers, and with the rapid influx of recruits, the younger friars had not received that education at the Portiuncula. Or maybe it was because of those learned scholars and logicians who had entered his religious institute, not with the humble intention of yielding to its discipline, but rather with their own opinions and their own notions. Francis felt like a stranger in his own family. There had been a time, after he had received papal approval and educated the first friars, when he considered himself useless and was planning to withdraw into seclusion. But when he asked Sylvester and Clare about it, they thought otherwise. Why had he not refrained from seeking their advice?! Why had he not followed his own inclination?!

While mulling over these disappointments and regrets, he had taken refuge in the hermitage at Poggio Bustone in late 1223. There, at least, he would be far from the impudent ministers, far from the cautious court of Rome, with a few devout and discreet religious; there he could abandon himself to Divine Providence. The religious were not so discreet after all, for they watched over his health, and his health was failing fast. He had mistreated his body, feeding it only a modicum of food (and sometimes spoiled food, at that, into which he mixed ashes) and covering it with nothing but a flimsy tunic in the dead of winter. Like many ascetics, he did not foresee, in his generosity, that one day he would be cared for by his confreres. To be sure, he used to temper the penitential ardor of his disciples, teaching them moderation in their mortifications, but he had not been able to moderate his own penances.

Therefore, far from being free in his daily routine, and especially in his diet, that winter he was very closely watched by confreres who were very concerned about him. They served him dishes cooked in fat, perhaps in lard. He protested, but he was not the guardian of the convent: he, who used to extol absolute obedience now had to bend and eat the delicacies that the cook devised for him. In the name of that same obedience he had to put up with a piece of fur that they sewed to the inside of his tunic so as to protect his stomach from the cold; he got his revenge by demanding another one just like it on the outside, thinking that it would have been hypocrisy to benefit from that amenity without others' knowledge.

Soon Francis left Poggio Bustone (because they were too attentive?) and moved to the hermitage in Gubbio. No doubt he took the opportunity to greet his friend the wolf. That spring, he went to stay in Greccio, then returned to his dear Portiuncula to preside at the 1224 chapter—his last general chapter. But he quickly left that cradle of his order; he had an entirely different plan in mind. He remembered that Count Orlando of Chiusi had made a gift to him not long before (while maintaining ownership as a legal fiction) of a solitary cliff at the very heart of his estates in La Verna (Alvernia), an uninhabited spot in the Apennine region. He remembered with emotion his visit to that rock. Why hadn't he decided before to take up residence in that solitude? No doubt that would be the best place in which to devote himself to contemplation. No one had built a convent there yet? Well, so what? Did he need four walls in order to seek the company of his Lord?

But first he wanted to make sure that he had the company of his friars. True ones: those whom he had taught in the initial enthusiasm of Santa Maria degli Angeli and who had remained faithful to his ideal. He chose six of them: first Leo, whom he had selected for his confessor and who could celebrate Mass at the desirable time; Angelo and Rufino, who with Leo would form the group called "The Three Companions" after the death of the father; Masseo, a practical man, whom he appointed guardian and who would manage the temporal

affairs; Sylvester, a consummate contemplative; and finally Illuminatus, his companion in the Holy Land, who had gone with him to call
on the sultan of Egypt.

The little band set out at the beginning of August. Francis intended to be there before the Feast of the Assumption, for the following day he began his customary forty-day fast in preparation for
the Feast of Saint Michael, celebrated on September 29. They had a
long itinerary, along the route of the highway that runs today from
Perugia to Ravenna: Bosco, Promano, Città di Castello, Sansepolcro,
Monte Casale, Chiusi. It was about a hundred kilometers, sometimes
on rocky, inconvenient roads, sometimes along the Tiber River on
a plain baked by a brutal sun; then there was the ascent of Mount
La Verna, a steep, narrow path that went on for twenty kilometers.
Once Francis had gladly made these stages of the journey, but now
he was exhausted, and each step became an ordeal for him. After a
few leagues his companions feared that they would see him collapse.
They decided to beg for a donkey. (Easy enough to do when you are
accustomed to a mendicant way of life.)

They entered a farmyard and found the farmer. "Do you have a
donkey to lend us? It is for Brother Francis, the holy preacher."

The peasant was astonished. "Brother Francis? The one that everyone talks about?"

"Yes, it is for him."

The good man insisted on personally bringing the animal to the
beneficiary; he wanted to make sure of the truth of these statements.
Might they not be false, calculated to force his hand? He arrived,
leading the donkey, and found himself in the presence of a poor little
friar who made a piteous impression, tottering, with sweat streaming
down his face.

"Are you really Brother Francis?"

"Yes, my friend."

"The one that they talk so much about throughout Umbria and
Tuscany?"

"That's me."

At this the peasant became stern. "In that case, Brother, try to live
up to your reputation. For there are many who have placed their trust
in you."

This rudeness pleased Francis: being addressed in those tones repaid his humility for the celebrity that seemed to impress the man. He knelt before the peasant and kissed his feet.

Now his confreres were reassured: they no longer had to fear that their father would collapse along the way and die in their arms. He, realizing that this congenial mount had become a necessity for him, did not protest. He was intent on arriving at Mount La Verna in good enough condition to observe Saint Michael's fast.

Once they had arrived at the estates of Count Orlando, the friars found that it was difficult to find the way. So as not to get lost, they looked for a guide. No doubt it was the owner of the donkey who had accompanied them that far. When they were half-way there, the man, who may have been accustomed to wetting his whistle while traveling, complained that he was thirsty. They stopped. The peasant continued to curse and swear. Then Francis, who never doubted God's mercy and who recalled the miracle of Moses in the desert, knelt and prayed, quite absorbed in the unusual request that he was making of God.

At last he stood up. "Turn a little to the right", he said quietly to his guide. "There you will find a spring."

The man hurried over. It was true. And even though pure spring water may not have been his usual beverage, he drank deeply of the delightful, clear, cool water that splashed over his hands and face.

They set off again. It was a difficult climb. This time they stopped beneath an oak tree. Francis dismounted to stretch his back and his legs. No sooner had he set foot on the ground than a fanfare of joyous song sounded: from all sides flocks of birds of various species and colors arrived and swooped down on the man of God, some of them fluttering around him, others perching on his head, his shoulders, and his arms. Francis, accustomed to this familiarity, let them be, speaking fondly to those "feathered brothers".

When the festival was over, he declared to his companions, "Dearly beloved, I truly believe that our Lord rejoices that we are coming to dwell on this solitary mountain, since our brothers the birds are so pleased at our arrival."

Count Orlando's men hastened to bring him the news: "My lord, Brother Francis and several of his companions are climbing Mount La Verna."

The next day he had his servants pack abundant provisions—bread, wine, and fruit—and then, surrounded by his valets and armed men, he in turn climbed the rock. When Francis realized this, he went to meet him and had a moment alone with him for a friendly conversation. The benefactor had already seen to the construction of a small platform with several huts made out of branches, which Francis had assigned to his brothers. But for himself, he had selected a more attractive spot, beneath a large beech tree, a hundred meters away, at the place where the chapel of Saint Mary Magdalen is now located. He asked the count to build a cell for him there. The count gave a few orders, and soon the valets had gathered the materials and built a rude cabin. Sir Orlando then left, stating that the friars should want for nothing while staying on his estates, and that they must not hesitate to ask for anything that they might need.

Then Francis gathered his companions and gave them orders for the duration of their stay. First of all the rule of poverty: however generous their host might be, they were not to take him up on his charitable offer.

Next, he justified the distance that he had decided to place between them and himself. "Look: I am approaching death. I want to live in solitude so as to recollect myself in God and weep for my sins. Brother Leo, when he deems it opportune, will bring me a little bread and water. But, please, do not let anyone come to me; if anyone speaks to you, it is up to you to respond."

The author of the little work, *Considerations on the Stigmata*, who was probably a disciple of Brother Leo, then relates: "From that moment on, Saint Francis began to taste frequently the sweetness of contemplation. He was often in such divine raptures that his companions saw his body lifted up in the air, and him beside himself in ecstasy. In these raptures, God revealed to him not only present and future things, but also the secret thoughts and desires of his brothers."

Here is one instance. Leo began to experience a strong temptation that was not carnal, the narrator explains, but spiritual. And so he wanted to have something written by his master. "If I had such a token," he thought, "I am certain that this temptation would go away."

Just then Francis emerged from his den. "Leo," he called to him, "come see me, and bring an inkwell, a pen, and some paper."

The friar hastened to obey. As the minutes passed, Francis covered

the page with his writing. Then he offered it to the beneficiary, saying, "Take this document, my dear brother, and carefully guard it
until your death. May God bless you and keep you from all temptation. But do not fear to be attacked by temptations, because the more
you are tempted, the more you will be the servant and the friend of
God, and the more I will love you. Truly, no one can suppose that
he is a perfect friend of God as long as he has not experienced many
temptations and tribulations."

However, when Leo took the scroll of paper away with him, every
temptation vanished from his soul. This document, one of the rare
autographs of Saint Francis that has come down to us, was preserved
as a priceless treasure and is still posted in the sacristy of the Sacro
Convento in Assisi.

When he returned to his hut, Leo unrolled the precious paper. On
one side he found, in Latin, a blessing framing the large capital Greek
tau (T), which recalls the Cross.

> May the Lord bless you and keep you,
> May he show his face to you and have mercy upon you.
> May he turn his countenance upon you
> And give you peace.
> May the Lord bless you, Brother Leo.

On the other side, in finer handwriting, but still in Latin, are the
"Praises of God", which were composed with incredible rapidity:

> You alone are the Holy One, Lord God,
> O you who work wonders.
>
> You are the Mighty One,
> You are the Most High,
> You are the all-powerful King,
> You, holy Father,
> King of heaven and earth.
>
> You are Three and One,
> The Lord God, all good.
> You are good, all-good, the supreme Good,
> Lord God, living and true.

You are Charity and Love,
You are Wisdom,
You are Humility,
You are Patience,
You are Security,
You are Rest,
You are Joy and Gladness,
You are Justice and Temperance,
You are all riches to sufficiency.

You are Beauty,
You are Meekness,
You are the Protector,
You are the Guardian and Defender,
You are Strength,
You are Refreshment.

You are our Hope,
You are our Faith,
You are our great sweetness,
You are our eternal Life,
The great and loving Lord,
God almighty, merciful Savior.

How many times, during the rest of his life, which lasted another fifteen years, did Leo—on his knees, sometimes exultant, sometimes sobbing—recite these litanies, which were for him like the last will and testament of his beloved father?

On Mount La Verna, the mystical phenomena continued. Leo took up his post at a short distance from Francis, who spent the greater part of his day in ecstasies. Levitation was a daily occurrence.

"During his raptures Francis was lifted up from the earth, sometimes to a height of three fathoms [18 ft.], sometimes four fathoms [24 ft.], sometimes as far as the top of the beech tree, sometimes carried up so high into the air and surrounded by so much splendor that one could scarcely see him."

When his body was within reach, Leo (who knew that the senses of a person in that state are suspended) would discreetly go over to him and kiss his feet. He was present at other spectacles, too, such as the dialogue between Francis and God. One day, seeing Francis on his knees, he came closer without making any noise and heard his prayer.

"Lord, after my death, what will happen to my poor family, which you, in your goodness, have entrusted to me, a sinner? Who will comfort them? Who will correct them? Who will pray for them?"

Several times he repeated this poignant complaint. And suddenly an angel appeared; Leo saw it. Then it spoke to Francis; Leo listened.

"I say to you on God's behalf: your order will last until the Day of Judgment. No sinner, however great a sinner he may be, will fail to find mercy with God, if in his heart he loves your order. And none of those who will persecute your order will be able to survive for long. Furthermore, no friar of your order, if he is very sinful and does not amend his life, will be able to persevere for long. Therefore do not be saddened if you see in your order bad friars who do not observe the common rule as they ought, and do not think that your order is in danger because of them. For there will be many who will observe perfectly the evangelical life of Jesus Christ and the rule in all its purity."

Now the Feast of the Assumption was near, and Francis, who knew that he was being seen and heard, if not actually spied on by his brothers, wanted to find a yet more remote and solitary place where he would not be seen or heard by anyone. In that way he would be able to observe the fast of Saint Michael in a still closer union with Christ the Savior. With Brother Leo's help, he looked for a place to which he could withdraw. And a little further south he found a cleft in the rock, wide enough to prevent anyone from jumping over it. If he took up residence on the other side, no witness would come to watch his supernatural conversations. Obviously, he first had to get to the other side. The friars found some solid planks that had been left there as material for building cells, and they positioned them over the gulf. It was hazardous, but eventually this improvised bridge was sufficiently wide. Francis asked the friars to build him a new cabin, which suited him. He then spoke to Leo, the only one who had permission to cross over (at his own risk) the chasm that separated the saint from the rest of the world.

"Brother," he said, "you shall come to visit me two times a day.

In the morning, to bring me some bread and water, enough for the day. And in the middle of the night, to sing Matins with me. But be careful: you will not go over this bridge without my permission. When you arrive at it, you will call out, *Domine, labia mea aperies* [the Invitatory of the Office of Matins: "Lord, open my lips."]. If I answer, you shall cross the gorge; but if I do not answer, you shall go away."

Leo understood: his master did not want to be surprised in ecstasy, as it had happened in the preceding days. Francis gave his blessing and went to take shelter in his new cell. For some time things went as the father had planned. But then one night, Leo called out, as usual, "*Domina, labia mea aperies*", and there was no answer. Should he go back, as he had been instructed to do? What won out over holy obedience? Curiosity, or the duty of coming to the aid of his revered master, if he should be sick or in danger? The *Considerations* state that Leo crossed the bridge "with a good and holy intention". That is quite possible, but we owe this statement to one of his disciples. We can surmise that there was a mixture of the two intentions.

By moonlight the friar advanced cautiously, went over to the cell and ventured to look in: it was empty. Where was he? A little further on there was a copse from which came bits and pieces of words. Padding very softly, taking care not to step on any twigs, Leo kept walking. Now he saw the saint, kneeling and speaking to God in a sorrowful, almost anguished tone of voice. "Who are you, O my God and Lord most kind? And who am I, despicable worm and useless servant?"

This monologue was repeated over and over again. Then, lifting up his eyes, Leo saw something in the sky like a large flame, burning brightly, that descended and came to rest over Francis' head. And a voice came from it, but Leo could not understand what it was saying. Then he felt that he had gone too far. Was he not there against obedience? He went back, slowly, reluctantly. Then, when he was about to cross the bridge again, he stopped. Now that he had started witnessing this mysterious scene, wasn't it right for him to stay so as to be present for the conclusion? But after a short dialogue, which was completely incomprehensible to him, he saw the flame depart toward the heavens. Then he went away slowly, feeling more joy than regret, but this time he did not take as many precautions. A twig snapped, making a sharp sound. He stopped. Had Francis heard it? He tried to steal away, but it was too late. Francis' voice resounded:

"Stop there, Brother. And don't move."

Leo stopped, his heart in his throat. Anguish gripped him. (Later on he confided to his companions, "I would rather have been swallowed up by the earth.")

Francis had seen his silhouette. He drew nearer. But this habit was the one worn by all his friars.

"Who are you?" he asked in a reproachful tone.

"Brother Leo, my Father."

The father was severe. "What?! Brother Leo, God's little sheep, did I not forbid you to come and watch me? In the name of holy obedience, tell me what you saw."

Leo repeated what Francis had said, then fell to his knees and tearfully acknowledged his guilt. Yet, as the close companion of this mystic for so many years, he asked him to explain the words that he had pronounced. Francis consented: he had seen clearly, in a twofold, splendid vision, the abyss of God's greatness, infinite wisdom, and infinite goodness, and the depths of his own vileness. And the flame? That was the sign of God's presence, like the burning bush before which Moses knelt.

And what did God say in the flame? He asked his servant for three gifts. The latter, although reduced to absolute poverty, had found them: they were the three religious virtues of obedience, poverty, and chastity. Leo was forgiven and sent back to the other side of the ravine, with instructions never again to disregard the order to stay there, unless he received an order to the contrary, as they had agreed on previously.

There was, however, another reason besides the daily bread and water that Francis called Leo over. Indeed, he wanted to know God's will. What should he do in order to conform to the designs of the Divine Master? For this purpose there was a method that he had used before: opening the Gospel book. Three times, in honor of the Holy Trinity. If the three texts obtained in this way were in agreement, then no doubt they expressed the will of God. Therefore Francis called Leo and asked him to bring the revealing book. Then he commanded him to open it three times in a row, and three times the Passion narrative appeared. Therefore the follower of Christ did not have to take any initiative: God was announcing to him that he was about to enter upon his passion.

He became even more firmly convinced of this when, on September 13, while he was praying in his cell, an angel appeared to him and said, "I exhort and warn you: prepare yourself and get ready, in humility and patience, to accept what God has decided to do to you."

Without fear, the hermit meekly replied, "I am ready to endure patiently whatever my Lord wishes to inflict upon me."

The following day, on the Feast of the Exaltation of the Holy Cross, expecting an extraordinary divine intervention, Francis arose before dawn and knelt down facing the East, toward the Holy Land, which had been the scene of the Lord's Passion. Abandoning himself entirely to him, he appealed to him with this loving prayer: "My Lord Jesus Christ, I beg thee to grant me two graces before my death: first, that for the rest of my life I may experience in my soul and in my body, as much as possible, the same pain that you suffered, O sweet Jesus, during the time of thy most cruel Passion; and second, that I may feel in my heart, as much as possible, the same love which inflamed thee, the Son of God, and led thee to suffer thy passion gladly for us sinners."

He remained in that position for a long time. As he repeated this prayer, he understood, without any need of a messenger, that it had been heard and granted. He no longer stirred. He desired to remain immersed, without any distraction whatsoever, in his intense meditation on the sufferings of Christ. Thus his communion with the Savior lasted a good part of the morning.

Then he saw a strange figure coming down from heaven toward him—a seraph, the biographers say, because he was endowed with six great and flashing wings: two were spread out over his head, two covered his body, and two were extended to fly, but his physical appearance was that of a crucified man. Slowly, this extraordinary being— half-angel, half-man, half-glorious, half-suffering—descended toward him. Upon seeing this vision, Francis himself was seized by a complicated feeling: a mixture of surprise, sorrow, and joy, intense joy at seeing this wingèd Christ coming toward him, a poignant sorrow at contemplating him nailed to the Cross.

At the same moment La Verna was suddenly all ablaze. It was not a fire, but rather an illumination like that of a glorious sunset, though a hundred times as intense; nevertheless, the shepherds in the valley earnestly believed that the mountain was in flames. The friars who witnessed this fantastic blaze related that it lasted more than an hour.

When it was over, Francis returned to his senses. He then felt a sharp pain in his hands, his feet, and his side, such as cold steel might produce. He looked at his hands: they were pierced through by heavy nails, with the round head against the palm and the point protruding through the back. He looked at his feet: they were pierced by similar nails, with the heads visible on the insteps and the points bent back under his soles. He opened his tunic: his side was bloody with a large, fresh, and gaping wound, as though he had been stabbed with a lance.

He tried to get up, but he could not stand on his feet without the points of the nails entering his flesh again. The blood that flowed slowly from his side was staining his tunic and his undergarment. What should he do? More importantly, what could he say? This was plainly a secret between him and God, but how could he conceal from his brothers for any length of time the nails in his hands? How could he account for the fact that he was unable to walk? How would he manage to wash himself and his blood-soaked garments without anyone noticing? The best thing to do was to consult a friar with a reputation for wisdom. He called Illuminatus and confided to him his predicament.

Illuminatus needed no time to ponder the problem; the answer was clear. He replied, "Brother Francis, if God sometimes reveals his secrets to you, it is not just for you, but also for others. If you keep hidden what God has manifested to you for the edification of the others, your conduct would be blameworthy."

Brother Leo was the one to whom Francis recounted the whole prodigious event. And Leo was the one responsible for taking care of the wounded man, the one who dressed his hands and his feet and applied a thick linen bandage to his bleeding side. He was obliged to attend to these duties every day, because the blood oozed continually, and he was afraid, moreover, that the wounds might become infected. Since he was dealing with the first stigmatist ever, he did not know what all the other similar cases have revealed: that these sorts of wounds, the effects of a supernatural cause, never become infected.

Thanks to the diligent care of his disciple, Francis managed to complete his fast and to celebrate the Feast of Saint Michael the Archangel at that spot. Then he decided that his stay on that hallowed rock had lasted long enough. The very next day, after hearing Mass, he left with Leo. Indeed, he was anxious to leave on Mount La Verna a little community, responsible for maintaining a continual presence at the place where the great miracle had occurred. Orlando had sent a servant with a donkey, a precious gift for the painfully wounded man. He gave brisk instructions to the friars who were remaining and slowly took leave of them. Before straddling his mount, he gave expression to his feelings: "*Addio*, my dear sons; live in peace. My body is parting from you, but I leave you my whole heart. I am going back now to the Portiuncula with Brother Leo, God's little sheep, and I will never again return to this place. Farewell to you all, and to everything here. Farewell, holy mountain; farewell, Mount La Verna; farewell, mountain of the angels. Farewell, dear brother falcon, who used to awaken me with your cry; many thanks for all your solicitude toward me. Farewell, Church of Saint Mary, and to you, Mary, Mother of the Eternal Word: I commend to you the sons whom I leave here."

Then the two travelers set out on the road to Borgo Sansepolcro. On the last elevation from which Mount La Verna was still visible, Francis asked Leo to help him dismount. He knelt on the ground and, facing the blessed site of his crucifixion, he pronounced his final farewells, "*Addio*, mountain of God, holy mountain. Adieu, Mount La Verna! May God the Father, God the Son, and God the Holy Spirit bless you! Live in peace. As for me, I shall never see you again."

The return was laborious and triumphant. Laborious, because not only did the stigmata prevent Francis from walking and using his hands, but his body was also overwhelmed by serious maladies: an infirmity of the eyes that rendered him almost blind, a stomach illness that allowed him to eat only a few foods, and complete prostration of his weary, mistreated body. To support this suffering, faltering flesh there was only one servant, Leo, who was at the same time guide, infirmarian, cook, and launderer. It was no small task for this religious, who did not have the strength of Masseo, to lift up his master's body after having walked for miles on narrow, stony paths, to lay him down carefully, to dress his wounds, and to provide all the care that his condition demanded, then to set out again, sometimes leading the donkey by the bridle. The biographers go on at length with their lamentations and cries of pity for Brother Francis, overcome with sickness and jostled by his mount; they likewise express their sympathy and admiration for Brother Leo, whose devotion and assiduous attentions were filled with boundless veneration for his holy master.

The return was also triumphant. The previous day people had seen Mount La Verna ablaze, and they already knew, by the sorts of rumors that are peddled from hamlet to village, that God had worked a great miracle on its heights. What had happened, no one knew, for Francis had forbidden Leo to reveal anything about it, and he himself carefully hid his sacred wounds. His fame was already great before this prodigy; now it burst forth on all sides. And, as the narrator remarks, the stigmata worked miracles, although they were concealed by the bandages.

Along the road leading to Sansepolcro a tearful woman stopped the head of the convoy; she was carrying in her arms her eight-year-old son, who had suffered from the dropsy since the age of four. His stomach was so horribly bloated, the narrator reports, that when he was able to stand up, he could not see his feet. Francis placed his pierced hands upon that shapeless mass, and the swelling disappeared instantly. The enthusiasm redoubled as they approached Borgo Sansepolcro. The occupants of the castle went out to meet the saint in a sort of procession, followed by peasants from the surrounding villages.

That evening they made a detour so as to stay overnight at the convent of Monte Casale. Upon their arrival, the travelers learned that a friar stricken with epilepsy had been isolated in his cell. The word does not appear in the account, but the description is eloquent: "Sometimes he threw himself bodily upon the ground, trembling violently and foaming at the mouth; sometimes all his members contracted, only to slacken again a moment later." The sick man was the subject of the conversation at table. Francis took pity on him. He took a morsel of his bread that had touched his hand, made the sign of the cross over it with that stigmatized hand, and ordered that it be brought to the sick brother. When that brother had eaten it, the sickness left him for the rest of his life.

Then Francis set out for Città di Castello, to the south. Even though the tom-tom was unknown in Italy, the villagers of the region had heard of his arrival, and a crowd was there waiting for him. As a circle formed around him, some of the villagers brought him a woman who disturbed the entire countryside by her fierce temperament. She was, they told him, possessed by the devil. A mental illness? This time it was no epileptic: she shrieked, uttered horrible cries, and howled like a dog. Those who were interceding so that she might be cured did not seem to pity her; she had become unbearable, and they wanted peace and quiet at last. Francis, held up by strong arms, managed to get down on his knees, and he prayed intently. Then he got up, made a large sign of the cross over the unfortunate woman, and said authoritatively, "Demon, I order you: leave this woman."

At that, the rage on her shriveled face gave way to a radiant smile. She looked around, calm and cheerful, and went back home with her relatives, just like all the other women.

News of the miracle made its way through the market town. As a result, the following morning a new group of villagers besieged the convent of the Friars Minor, demanding to see Brother Francis. He went out and found himself in the presence of a mother holding by the hand her young child, who suffered from a painful wound that would not heal. Francis had someone remove the bandage that covered it and noted the baby's affliction. Then he traced the sign of the cross three times over the wound and told the mother to put the child to bed. She let him rest until the following day. When she came to wake him up, the horrible wound had vanished; in its place there was nothing but a rosy spot formed by the new flesh.

Francis remained for a whole month at Città di Castello, whether because he was anxious to rest, or because he preferred to be in a fervent community for the Feast of All Saints, or simply because the inhabitants never stopped asking for the help of his prayers and miraculous powers. Now it was November, and it promised to be a severe winter. The peasant guiding the donkey, who no doubt was being paid by Count Orlando, insisted on going through with his mission. But one evening, probably because he was less familiar with this region, he discovered at nightfall that they were far from any shelter; it was no longer possible to find a place to sleep. They had to find a cleft in the crag that loomed over their route. The two religious, accustomed to life's inconveniences, did not complain about their lot. As for the guide, he did not lose his temper, at least, because he had too much reverence for his traveling companions to display his ill humor; but inside he was railing against them because of the freezing, windy night that he had to spend in a recess of the cliff. Now Francis knew about these feelings. As soon as his guide had stretched out, he touched him lightly, as the author of the *Considerations* notes, "with that hand that was inflamed and pierced by the seraph's fire". Then the good peasant felt a sweet warmth come over him, and he fell asleep, snug and comfortable. He related afterward that he had slept, in the midst of the rocks and the snow, more soundly than he had ever done in his own bed.

2. Death

Finally the trio arrived at the Portiuncula. The peasant went away again with his beast, edified and consoled. Francis and Leo were surrounded by a cloud of affectionate, enthusiastic gray friars. Francis, despite his fatigue and his sufferings, was radiant. He was home at last, in the cradle of his order, at the heart of the beloved place where he had gathered his first disciples in an incredible life in the shadow of the blessed shrine of the Mother of God.

Francis' first difficulty was to hide the stigmata. He was very anxious that no one, even among his dearest friars, should know about that favor, for he feared that the glory would be given to him and not to God. Of course, it was impossible for the precautions that he took to be completely effective. Even though he offered no explanation, there were many in his entourage who wondered about those constantly bandaged hands and feet, which were sometimes soaked with blood. The rugged mountain paths . . . really? Did the rocks of Mount La Verna cause lesions like that when you slept on them? And that tunic which was constantly purpled with blood and which was washed each day? The chances against concealing such a formidable thing were slim, since many suspected what had happened, and some evidently tried to verify it.

In order to keep the secret from most of the friars, Francis decided to ask just one of them to wash his garments, without revealing it to him. (He was deluding himself.) He appointed Rufino, one of his first companions. Rufino, although discreet, was no fool and quickly ascertained the reality of what he suspected, without guessing the supernatural cause. After washing his long undergarment, he put it on him and pulled it up past the waist, until his fingers touched from below the dressing on the wound on Francis' side. He noticed then that it was soaked with blood. But this maneuver did not go unnoticed by Francis, who upbraided his friend severely. Another time, while rubbing his master's back, he discreetly moved his hand forward to his chest; this time, however, his fingers went into the wound, as Thomas' fingers once probed Jesus' side. As a result the patient felt such a sharp pain that a cry escaped him.

He turned sorrowfully to his friend. "May God forgive you, Brother Rufino! But why did you do that?"

On another occasion, while Francis was handing his tunic to his launderer, the compress that covered his side was askew and left the wound visible. Rufino didn't even have to devise a maneuver in order to satisfy his curiosity. Little by little, Francis' stigmata became an open secret. And many of his sons piously sought to verify it. Some would ask to kiss his hand and took the opportunity to press slightly the bandage that covered it. Once word of the miracle had spread in this way, Brother Elias, asserting his authority as vicar general, demanded confirmation of the rumor that had reached his ears. He appeared, moreover, at the Roman court, and several cardinals traveled [with him] so as to command Francis to confirm it. Rinaldo Cardinal Conti, who had become Pope and taken the name of Alexander IV, declared in a sermon given to a group of clerics, among whom was Saint Bonaventure, "I saw, during his lifetime, the sacred stigmata of Saint Francis of Assisi."

For some time Francis remained quietly at the Portiuncula, and it seemed that he was already near death. He was extremely frail. It was not just the pain of the stigmata and the fatigue from the return trip that overwhelmed him, but his whole body, along with the approaching end of his life. Celano describes his condition as follows:

His body was wracked by various pains, more intense than before, because he suffered from several ailments, after having chastised his body so severely and reduced it to servitude for many long years. During the course of the eighteen years that he had just completed [as a religious], never or almost never had his flesh had any rest, for he ceaselessly went about the countryside to places near and far. He filled the whole earth with the Good News of Christ, visiting five or six localities on the same day—which sometimes meant five or six villages—announcing in each one the Kingdom of God, edifying his listeners by his example as much as by his words, and making his body a living sermon. But the law of the body and of the human condition requires that a man will start to fall apart day by day, even though he is renewed interiorly.

However, he could not be content with this state of inaction. He deemed that, as long as this body of his was still alive to submit to the rule, his earthly mission was not yet over. And so, one fine morning, he decided that he would start life over, such as it was, without worrying about his disabilities. Providence would make it possible.

"Brothers, let us begin! Until now, we have done little."

Despite the warnings of his most prudent friars, he decided in 1225 to take up preaching again. He could not walk, but so what? He had the use of a donkey. He preached. He even stopped by the leper houses, as in the old days, to attend to the needs of the most unfortunate of his human brethren. His physical handicaps were made up for by his reputation, which preceded him everywhere and disposed his hearers to listen reverently to his words. The saint was coming! Brother Francis was here! He was surrounded, served, cared for by the crowds. In certain towns, they even invited him to stay. What a blessing it would be for the inhabitants to have that chosen man of God die in their midst!

This renewal, however, lasted only a short time. One day, as he arrived in Foligno, Francis saw nothing at all. He was no longer visually impaired, but blind. The religious in that community alerted Brother Elias, who hastened to the monastery and ordered Francis to follow him to Assisi. To enter the city they had to pass by San Damiano. That was where the vicar general left the invalid, convinced that Clare and her sisters would know better than anyone how to take care of him.

They built for him a cabin close by the convent, devoid of comforts, according to his wishes. They had overlooked the fact that in the summertime rats infested the countryside and even certain lower parts of their house. They invaded Francis' cabin and even danced deliriously on his face as they scrambled about. He let them. Besides, could he have driven them off with his mutilated hands? Would his blindness, his suffering, his helplessness and the company of the hideous animals prevail over his cheerful mood? This was the time to practice the perfect joy that he had taught one day to Brother Leo. In that sordid hovel he composed his poetic masterpiece, which he later dictated to several of his companions: "The Canticle of Brother Sun". The nuns fervently listened to the still powerful voice of the former troubadour proclaiming in a graceful melody the beauty of creation, perhaps unaware that this was the joy of someone entering his final throes and that the charming voice was that of a dying man.

Francis counted on God to heal him, at least if that was his will. Brother Elias counted on men. Were there no physicians in Italy? There certainly were, especially at the papal court. Now at that moment, fearing the oppressive heat of the Roman summer, the papal court had just arrived at Rieti. It was a journey of thirty leagues, by bad roads; but after all, it was closer than Rome, which was almost twice as distant. Elias gave the order to depart for Rieti.

News of Francis' arrival had preceded him, even more than usual. The procession that came to meet him was made up of clergy and religious, with several cardinals walking at the head of it; among them, as was only fitting, was the bishop of Ostia, Hugolino. Along the way leading to the papal palace a thick crowd ardently acclaimed the saint at the top of their lungs. They brought him immediately to the Supreme Pontiff, who was anxious to receive him in an audience as soon as he arrived and reserved a few minutes to converse with him— a parenthetical note in the midst of the urgent affairs of the Church. Then, instead of letting the sick man rest in the cell that was reserved for him after his exhausting journey, the procession noisily and enthusiastically continued down the road to the bishop's residence. The Bishop of Rieti, instead of being at the Pope's side to welcome the saint, desired to receive him personally in his own palace. Furthermore he had obtained permission to shelter the sick man under his own roof.

When Francis was finally stretched out on the straw mat intended for him and had finally had a short rest, Hugolino, who had decided to take charge of Francis' treatment and consulted with Elias, sent him his own physician. Did he really believe in his efficacy? The good doctor himself perhaps no longer believed in it. Nevertheless he applied the usual remedies: bloodletting, cauterization, plasters. The sick man meekly resigned himself to it. But not one of these treatments was successful; and Hugolino had to admit that the science of men was not on a par with the power of God.

Francis scarcely had a moment to rest. People danced attendance to pay him a visit. And since he had not forbidden anyone to darken his door, his brothers, although uneasy, let it go on. For how does one forbid a cardinal of the Holy Church to enter the room of a mystic and miracle-worker in order to converse about the things of God? And if you cannot refuse a cardinal, how do you refuse a bishop or an abbot? And then a canon or a curate? And, of course, the leading townspeople. Were they going to stand in the way of a consul or a senator? But after all that, who would have the heart to send away the humble people, the ones whom Francis loved?

So it was that, even while lodging in a room in the bishop's palace in order to rest, Francis was subjected to a continual invasion of churchmen and laymen, to the point where his fatigue exceeded the limits of his endurance. Hugolino noticed it and, again in agreement with Elias, sent Francis to the place where they perhaps ought to have confined him from the start: to the hermitage of Fonte Colombo. Advent was beginning, so he could prepare himself there in peace and quiet for the Feast of Christmas.

No doubt it was there, however, that they administered the final treatment devised to cure his blindness (although some authors say that it occurred at Rieti or at Siena). Having observed the ineffectiveness of the Christian physicians, Hugolino sent his friend a renowned practitioner who was said to have been initiated into the science of the Eastern physicians, Theobald the Saracen. It may also be that the patron had delayed the appearance of this specialist on the scene because he was acquainted with the frightening aspects of his art. Indeed, the infidel carefully examined the patient's eyes and declared that it was necessary to have recourse to the most radical treatment: cauterization of the temple.

He calmly went to the kitchen, where he heated a small metal bar in the fire until it was red-hot. When he returned to the cell, the friars fled, horrified at the thought of the spectacle that was about to take place. Francis, for his part, was untroubled. When he saw the glowing rod brought to the level of his face, he made the sign of the cross over it and spoke to it affectionately: "Brother Fire, you are more noble and more useful than many creatures. You know that I have always been fond of you; and I will always be so, for love of him who created you. Therefore, I beg you, be gentle and kind to me; do not burn me more than I can bear."

Theobald then applied his instrument. The flesh sizzled. And the

few friars who had remained at the door trembled. When the operation was over, Francis calmly said to his torturer, "If you think that
that is not enough, you can begin again, for I felt nothing."

He had not felt anything, but he had not been cured, either. Therefore there was no more hope for the physicians of Rieti. Elias had
heard that there were some excellent doctors in Siena. Therefore he
ordered an immediate departure for Siena. Two hundred thirty kilometers, this time, via Terni, Narni, Orvieto, then Lake Bolsena. In
the dead of winter. What a terrible journey for that dying invalid!
Most of his confreres feared that they would see him die en route,
but the vicar general judged that the medical arts could still save him.
The patient did not protest. He, at least, knew that death was near.
But he let the authorities do with him as they would.

It was a long and painful road, then, about which we know very
little. Just one strange incident, not far from Radicofani, on an Apennine height. Celano relates that while the small cortege was making its
way down the road, three young girls appeared who were completely
alike: same height, same age, same face, same clothing. They stopped
in front of Francis and exclaimed in the same voice, "Welcome to
Lady Poverty!"

The travelers overtook and passed them, but then when they turned
around to look at them, they saw no one: the girls had disappeared. To
Saint Bonaventure these three gracious virgins represented the three
vows of religion: obedience, poverty, and chastity. Fine! It remains
to be seen why they greeted poverty alone, personified by Brother
Francis.

The little band was greeted, at Siena as everywhere, with enthusiasm. They did not take up lodgings in the city; the experience of
Rieti decided that. They went a little further north and stayed at the
hermitage of Alberino. Elias quickly found a famous physician who
immediately called on the renowned patient. He, too, was in favor
of cauterization, but his colleague had not operated at the right spot;
with his red-hot iron he pierced the two ears of the blind man. With
no result. Elias understood that it was useless to continue treatment.

All the more so since the father began hemorrhaging terribly one
night from the lungs or the stomach. This time, the friars thought, it
is the end. They all came to kneel around his straw mat and asked for
his final blessing, which he gladly gave them. Then, when he experi-

enced some relief, he asked Father Benedict of Prato, who served as his confessor, to fetch ink and paper, and he dictated what he thought would be his last will and testament: "I bless my Brethren who are in the Order, and all who shall ever come to the end of the world. As a sign of the blessing that I give them, and in memory of me, I leave them this testament: they should love one another as I have loved them and do love them, and they should always love and honor our Lady Poverty and remain faithful subjects to the prelates and clergy of holy Mother Church."

No doubt it was too much for his strength. He stopped. Then he blessed them again. They all wept. But in vain did they await the end: the hemorrhage did not recur, his strength returned, it became easier for him to speak. After a few days, he got up. His eyes (was it the postponed effect of the piercing of his ears?) began again to distinguish objects, although imperfectly. He even managed to resume the duties of religious life: meditation, prayer, exhorting the brothers. But they, after such an alarming turn, showed him the most attentive care. These attentions caused him to have scruples.

One day he stopped a friar and asked him the question, "Give me your opinion, my dear son, about a serious matter. My conscience unceasingly reproaches me for all the care that I am giving to my body. It fears that I may be falling into excessive indulgence."

The friar lacked neither spiritual experience nor a sense of humor. "My dear father," he asked in turn, "hasn't your body been generously obedient to the will of your soul?"

"Oh, I must admit that: it has always obeyed me well. My body and I have always understood each other perfectly in serving Christ our Lord."

"Well, then, my father, where is your generosity? Where is your sense of justice? Are you going to continue to receive the benefactions of this friend without giving him any in return? For the sake of God's service, your body was exposed to all sorts of dangers. And look: now that it is in need, you would refuse to come to its aid?"

"Blessed may you be, my son", exclaimed Francis. "You have answered wisely."

Then, addressing his body, he said, "Brother Body, rejoice, but I beg you, have a little consideration for me. From now on, I will do everything that you wish."

Thus the winter passed in the hermitage of Alberino. In the spring Elias decided to travel to Cortona; he had a certain partiality for the hermitage of The Cells, where he would one day die. But first, it was impossible to avoid stopping in the city itself, because the entire population, delirious with devotion to the friar who bore the stigmata, had gone forth to meet him and made him enter their gates in triumph. However, when he and his fellow travelers were about to go back outside the walls and head for the hermitage, the militia barred their way.

"We have orders", the officer explained, "not to let you leave."

Elias soon heard the explanation for this armed intervention. The consuls, having learned the state of Brother Francis' health, had concluded that he would not linger on before dying. It was expedient, therefore, to keep him within the city walls until his death, which would allow the town to claim his body. What glory, for the town, to harbor such a relic! What a boost for business, too, to host so many pilgrims! But Francis would have nothing to do with these plans. He declared that he was going to give a speech, and, seated on a rock, with more force than one would expect from his emaciated body, he spoke: "Noble townspeople, know that the will of God is that I live out my final days in the convent of Santa Maria degli Angeli in Assisi. But even though I depart, I leave you Brother Guido, to whom I commend you with all my soul. By the grace of God and by his merits, the town of Cortona and its inhabitants will be delivered from many evils."

After this speech, the municipal authorities had no alternative but to give the order to release their precious hostage. The stay at The Cells did not last long, however, because Francis decided to make his way to Assisi. By the usual route it was a relatively short journey: about fifty kilometers skirting Lake Trasimeno and passing through Perugia. But they had to make sure that the municipality of Perugia didn't seize the living relic instead of Cortona, for this time the magistrates would surely not let Francis go. Elias decided to make a grand tour to the north and the east, which would almost triple the distance, by way of Gubbio, Gualdo Tadino, and Nocera—there was no fear that any of those localities could launch such a bold surprise attack. And he was careful to send a messenger to the consuls of Assisi to warn them about the arrival of their saintly native son and the constant threat to his safety.

In fact, when the little band arrived at Nocera, an armed detachment from the militia of Assisi was waiting for them. And so eventually they entered Assisi, surrounded by servicemen. In keeping with his principle of submission to the Church and respect for prelates, Francis insisted on going first to call on Guido, who was still the bishop. The latter was deeply moved to see the saint whom he and his entire city venerated in such a pitiable condition. He considered the Portiuncula quite ill-suited to providing the care that he deserved; the lodgings and the food, along with the noise and commotion of the many religious, would hasten the death of this beloved son of Assisi. He officially assigned to him a room in his episcopal palace.

This was only common sense. The long journey on the back of a donkey, by rough roads, had undone whatever progress he had made in Siena and Cortona. The sick man, who could scarcely take any food now, was as thin as a skeleton. Nevertheless, he was perfectly aware of everything and was continually attentive to everybody around him. So in no time he found out about the ongoing public battle that pitted the bishop against the podesta over minor business matters. The bishop had excommunicated the podesta, and the podesta had forbidden his subordinates to have anything to do with the bishop. Tempers were still running high; the leading townspeople did not know which side to take, and the common folk were scandalized.

Francis was deeply troubled by the news, and he resolved to encourage the two adversaries to make peace. He taught two of his friars (Pacificus was probably one of them) a new couplet for the "Canticle of Creation", and when they had learned it, they announced that they were going to sing the Lord's praises that day and invited people to gather on the square in front of the episcopal palace. The bishop and the podesta maintained a prudent distance from one another, and all the magistrates of the commune followed suit. The crowd was pressing behind them, expecting to hear a brand new performance. The elders recalled how the young Francis, enamored of poetry, used to sing marvelous love songs. The friars stood in a circle in front of the listeners, leaving an empty place for the two cantors, who appeared and intoned the couplets composed by Brother Francis. Everyone joyfully and respectfully listened to the beautiful inspired song. Finally, when the performers had celebrated Brother Fire and Sister Earth, couplets with which the guests from the Portiuncula were familiar, they added an unknown couplet:

> May you be praised, my Lord, for all those who forgive their
>   enemies for love of you,
> and must endure injustice and tribulation.
> Blessed are they who persevere in peace,
> For they will be crowned by you, O Most High.

It was over. The two troubadour friars saluted the audience and rejoined their confreres. Then, in the profound silence that fell over the place, the podesta, in the grip of intense emotion, declared to those present, "Truly, I tell you, I forgive my lord the Bishop. I must and want to do so for my Lord's sake, and I am ready even to forgive the murderer of my brother and of my son."

Next he walked across the square, went up to the bishop and knelt before him. He then declared, "Here I am. I am willing to make reparation to you, in everything and as it may please Your Excellency, for the love of our Lord Jesus Christ and of his servant Francis."

Guido, touched and ashamed, lifted up his adversary and embraced him. "My office", he confessed, "requires me to be humble. But alas! I am naturally prone to anger. Forgive me."

They gave each other the kiss of peace with heartfelt affection. The friars raced to tell their father about this miracle of charity, and the whole town was abuzz with this event that brought peace to their society.

Guido had not given up hope of providing some relief for his guest, whatever the cost, and he summoned a renowned physician from Arezzo. His name was Bongiovanni, but since Francis had read in the Gospel that we are not supposed to call anyone "good" [in Italian *buon*], because only God is good, he referred to the doctor only by his nickname, "Bembegnato".

One morning the sick man, who had not yet received a heavenly revelation of when he would die, was anxious to know the approximate date, from a human perspective. He asked the practitioner of the medical arts, "Tell me, Bembegnato, when will I die?"

The other man, in a very worldly way, hastened to reassure the patient, "Oh, with God's help, your condition will probably improve."

Francis became stern. "I demand that you tell me the truth!"

This time, Bongiovanni gave in. "I suppose that it will be at the end of September or the beginning of October."

What joy for the sojourner! He extended his arms toward heaven and exclaimed, "Welcome, Sister Death!"

This was a sister who deserved a new stanza in the "Canticle of Creation"! He composed it spontaneously and called Leo and Angelo (which means that the latter had left Mount La Verna) to sing it:

> Praised be my Lord for our sister, the death of the body,
> from whom no man living can escape.
> Woe unto them who die in mortal sin.
> Blessed are they who are found walking by thy most holy will,
> for the second death shall do them no harm.

Angelo and Leo therefore warmed up their voices and sang the final version of the canticle for their delighted father.

This did not suit Brother Elias, who judged the singing to be out of place. People would hear it, because of the powerful voices of the singers, beyond the confines of the episcopal palace. And these troubadour friars even dared, at Francis' request, to celebrate with music in the middle of the night! And several times a night! The author of the *Mirror* carefully points out that it was for the edification of the lay people who were watching around the episcopal palace. But Elias, who didn't see it that way, burst into the poet's room and began scolding him. "My dear, dear Brother, I am consoled and edified by this joy that you are experiencing and which, in the midst of your ailments, you manifest to your companions. But really, now! Even though the inhabitants of this town consider you a saint, they know that in truth you are very close to dying. And then, when they hear these praises being sung night and day, I fear that they will wonder how anyone can show such joy when he is so near death?"

Francis, who was usually so courteous, reproved him sharply. "Brother, let me rejoice in the Lord and sing his praises in the midst of my sufferings; for by the grace of the Holy Spirit I am so united to my Lord that, by his mercy, I can rejoice in him."

For her part, Clare and her sister had learned that their father was staying a few hundred paces from their convent. Practically next door. The abbess sent him messages begging him to pay her one last visit; she did not realize how severe weakness, as well as the condition of his feet, prevented him from walking or making any effort. Without going into the reasons for his inability, he sent a friar to his friend to bring her a note and a verbal reply. The note contained a simple blessing; the verbal message was as follows: "Go see my lady Clare; tell her to banish all sadness and anxiety at not being able to see me again; she should know, rather, that before her death she and her sisters will see me, and they will receive great consolation from me."

And so the founder of the Order of Friars Minor had only a few days to live. It was surely a time of recollection and supernatural joy. It was also an opportunity to formulate his last will and testament, to save what could still be preserved of the original ideal of the fraternity, and to reconcile the divided brothers in obedience. This was when he dictated his "Testament", a work that is touching in its scope, which combines a recollection of the past with a concern for the future. There is a poignant lyricism in these pages associated with the last authoritative act of a dying master who does not want his work to perish.

> Here is how the Lord granted me, Brother Francis, to enter upon the penitential way. When I was still in sin, nothing seemed to me more hideous than the sight of lepers. But the Lord himself led me among them, and I performed works of mercy for them. When I left them, what had appeared bitter to me until then was changed into sweetness of soul and body. Shortly after that, I left the world. . . .
>
> Then the Lord gave me, and still gives me, such a great confidence in the priests who live according to the law of the Holy Roman Church, because of their sacerdotal character, that even if they persecuted me, I would have recourse to them. I want to fear, love, and honor them as my lords. . . . I act in this way because in this world I see nothing, physically, of the Most High Son of God but his Body and Blood which they receive and which they alone administer. . . .

After the Lord gave me brothers, no one showed me what I should do, but the Most High himself revealed to me that I should live according to the rule of the Holy Gospel. I had a document drawn up in a few words, and my lord the Pope approved it for me. Those who came to lead this sort of life gave to the poor everything that they might own; they contented themselves with a single tunic that was patched inside and out, along with a cord and breeches. And we do not want to own anything more.

We clerics recited the office according to the custom of other clerics. The lay brothers recited *Pater Nosters*. And we joyfully stayed in the churches. We were simple and subject to all. I, for my part, worked with my hands, and I want to work; and I firmly intend that all the other friars should dedicate themselves to an honest occupation. Let those who do not know how, learn, not out of a desire to receive payment for their work, but in order to set an example and to banish idleness.

The Lord revealed to me that we must greet one another with the words, "May the Lord grant you his peace!" Let the friars beware of accepting churches or small houses or anything that people may build for them, unless it is in conformity with the holy poverty that we have promised in the rule; they shall always dwell in those buildings as strangers and pilgrims. . . .

All the friars should be obliged to obey their guardian and to recite the office according to the rule. . . .

Let the friars not say: this is a new rule. No, it is a return to the past, an admonition and my testament. . . . The minister general, the other ministers, and the guardians [*custodes*] are bound by obedience to add or remove nothing from these words. Let them always carry this document on their persons, together with the rule. . . . I enjoin all my brothers, whether clerics or laymen, in the name of obedience, not to add any commentary either to the rule or to these words, saying, "This is how it should be understood." . . .

May whoever shall keep these commandments be blessed in heaven with the blessing of the Most High Father, and be filled on earth with the blessing of his dearly beloved Son together with the most Holy Spirit, the Paraclete, all heavenly virtues and all the saints. And I, Brother Francis, your poor little servant, assure you, insofar as it is in my power, of this most holy blessing at home and abroad.

From that moment on, after singing of Sister Death and making his last will and testament, Francis seemed to go through a short period of serenity, with some improvement of his general condition. He had abandoned himself to the will of God, and, recalling the lesson that one of the friars gave him about the proper care of the body, he made what we might call some capricious requests. One day, even though he could no longer swallow, he wanted to have some fish. Another time, in the middle of the night, he asked for parsley. After that, however, he bitterly asked himself whether he was guilty of provoking his brothers to the sin of irritation.

Brother Leo, for his part, was in anguish. The man who was his father, his counselor, his companion, the presence of God in his midst, was going to leave him. What was he going to do then? He often obtained permission to keep the night watch at the patient's side. If only he could have, as a lasting souvenir, some familiar object that had belonged to Francis! He looked toward the bed in the semi-darkness. Why search any farther? The most obvious thing, the most immediate reminder of his master's presence, was his tunic! But how could he dare to claim such an unusual favor, while the sick man lay there out of breath, at the end of his strength?

Now Francis, by a revelation, knew what he was thinking. At sunrise he spoke to Brother Leo. "My son, come here. I give you my tunic. It still clothes my body, but it already belongs to you. Consider it as your own. In a few days you will be the one that it clothes."

As those few days passed, Brother Elias judged that it was time for the founder to give his final blessing to his sons. He came into the room one day with many friars, who arranged themselves in a semicircle around the bed, and he himself knelt leaning against the bed, right beside the dying man. The latter stretched out his arms to pronounce a blessing. He placed his hand on Elias' head, but he could no longer see.

"On whom have I placed my hand?" he asked.

"On the head of Elias."

Then he collected his thoughts and declared: "My son, I bless you in everything and for everything. Just as the Most High has increased the number of my brothers and sons through your hands, so too I bless them in you and through you. May God, the Lord of all creation, bless you in heaven and on earth. I bless you as much as I can and more than I can. May the Almighty supply what I cannot; may he remember your labor and your works, may he hear your prayers and, on the day of reckoning, may your place be among the just."

Then he blessed the other friars. "Adieu, my dear sons. Preserve the fear of the Lord; remain always in Jesus Christ. Evil days are coming. You will go through a terrible trial. Happy are those who shall persevere in the work that they have begun! Some will go away because of scandals. As for me, I am going to God. I have served him devoutly and with all my soul; I leave this world with confidence. May the grace of the Lord be always with you!''

They arrived at the last days of September. The man of God was still alive. But they remembered Bongiovanni's prediction that he would die at the end of September or the beginning of October. So the decisive moment was drawing near. The sick man's whole attention was turned toward the cradle of his order, toward Santa Maria of the Portiuncula with its convent and its little chapel. Wasn't that the place where he ought to die? He could still be transported. And even if the move killed him, it would hasten his expiration by only a few days. Bishop Guido was departing on a pilgrimage. Therefore he would no longer be the dying man's guardian. Francis asked him for permission to leave, and he granted it.

With infinite care and a thousand precautions, the friars managed to transfer him from his straw mat to a stretcher. When news of this reached the consuls, they demanded that a guard should accompany the still-living relic and remain beside him until his death. Therefore the procession that accompanied the stretcher was immense: the friars, then the soldiers, the aediles, and finally the populace, who were unwilling to abandon this prestigious native son who, they hoped, would soon be canonized. He could not see. He heard the commotion, to be sure, but scarcely paid any attention: he was in God. The cortege passed through the Porta Maggiore, which is gone today, and made its way down the path that runs along the ramparts. Francis had taken this path so many times that, as the stretcher-bearers advanced, he knew at each step where they were.

And so, at one place he murmured, "Stop."

They stopped.

"Put down my stretcher."

They put it down.

"Turn my face toward Assisi."

They turned it.

He blinked his eyes, into which a dim light still entered. He probably sensed, to his left, a dark mass and guessed, without actually seeing it, that it was the Cathedral of San Rufino, where he had received baptism, and the Minerva, and the houses along the street where he had been born; and then, looming over it all, the remains of the Rocca Maggiore. Then he slowly raised his hand and made a sign of cross in the air.

"May you be blessed by the Lord," he said, addressing the city, "for he has chosen you to be the homeland and the dwelling place of all who acknowledge and glorify him in truth, of all who wish to honor his name."

Exhausted and suffering, he could say no more. The bearers took up the stretcher again.

The friars, who had been alerted to his arrival, were overwhelmed with joy that their father had been given back to them for his final moments and had built for him a little cell right next to the chapel. He would not see it, that dear chapel, for which he had such a tender devotion. But at least he would imagine it and would be happy to breathe his last sigh in its shadow.

After they laid him down on his new deathbed, Francis recalled Signora Jacoba of Settesoli; shouldn't she be present at his death, that cherished disciple, the only woman besides Clare whose face he had known after his conversion? He posed the question to the friar who was keeping watch at his side that day.

"My dear brother, I have only a few days of life left. It seems to me that if Signora Jacoba, that woman who is so devoted to our order, learned of my death without having been present, it would grieve her excessively. It is better to inform her right now, so that she can come to see me while I am still alive."

The friar agreed. "You are quite right, my father, for, given the great devotion that she has to you, it would be most unfitting if she were not here at the hour of your death."

Francis therefore commanded him to bring ink and paper, and he dictated a letter.

To Signora Jacoba, servant of God, from Brother Francis, little poor man of Christ: salvation and communion in the Holy Spirit and our Lord Jesus Christ. Be advised, dear friend, that the Blessed Christ, by his grace, has revealed to me that the end of my life will soon take place. Therefore, if you wish to find me alive, leave at once for Santa Maria degli Angeli. Bring some hair-cloth in which to bury my body, and the candles and the incense necessary for my burial. And I pray you, furthermore, to bring me some of the delicious dish that you made for me to eat when I was in Rome.

Now Jacoba had heard in Rome about Francis' final illness. She had immediately set out, together with a retinue and her son. It is difficult to determine the latter's age. He was probably already born in 1212, when his mother became acquainted with the saint, but was still an infant, since his mother was scarcely more than twenty years old. Now she was thirty-five or thirty-six, and he would have been fifteen or sixteen. The author of the *Considerations* says that she arrived at the Portiuncula "with her two sons, who were senators". The confusion arises here from the fact that her husband's family, the Frangipani, was a family of senators. Hence there were several of them by that name then in Rome, probably uncles or cousins of the boy. Therefore we should follow the account in the *Legenda antiqua*, which declares, "Signora Jacoba arrived from Rome, accompanied by her son and several high-ranking persons."

The ink of the letter had just dried, and the friar who was holding it had just left Francis' cell when he bumped into the visitor. He immediately went back to the sick man.

"My father, Jacoba has just arrived. What should we do? Is it not forbidden for a woman to enter our cells?"

"That prohibition", said Francis, "does not apply to our Brother Jacoba."

They opened the door for her right away, and she immediately fell to her knees at the foot of the bed. The *Considerations* tell us that "she held those most holy feet, marked and adorned with the wounds of Christ; she kissed them and bathed them in her tears with such great devotion that it seemed to the friars who were present that they saw Mary Magdalen at Christ's feet. And they could not separate her from them."

She had not forgotten, though, before leaving her palace, to prepare for her friend his favorite cake, a pastry that the Romans of that time called *mortariole* and soon afterward *frangipane*, after her family. The main ingredients were honey and almonds. But Francis, who no longer could take any food, simply brought this dainty to his lips. Jacoba remained at the Portiuncula until the funeral and was so piously devoted to that blessed city that she died there several years later and was buried in the lower church of the Basilica of Saint Francis.

On October 1, 1226, a Thursday, Francis—who despite his moribund condition was still completely lucid—summoned Brother Bernard. When the latter was kneeling beside his mat, he placed his hand on his head and declared: "The first brother that the Lord gave to me was Bernard. He was the first to put the Gospel into practice and to fulfill it perfectly by distributing his goods to the poor. For that reason and for many others, I must love him more than any other friar in the order. I wish and I order, therefore, as far as it is in my power, that the minister general, whoever he may be, should cherish and honor him as he would myself; and that the provincial ministers and the friars of the whole order consider him as my replacement."

Then, since news of this blessing had brought a certain number of friars to his side, he took the opportunity to admonish them briefly, "Cling with all your heart to holy poverty; always remain faithful to our poor little Portiuncula. This is the house of God and the gate of heaven."

Then, collecting his thoughts, he added, "I bless all the friars who are present, and all those who will belong to this order in the future."

Friday, while the religious were still gathered around him, he asked someone to read for him the Gospel about the Last Supper, which began, "Jesus, knowing that the Father had given all things into his hands, and that he had come from God and was going to God . . .". Then he asked Leo and Angelo to sing for him the "Canticle of Creation" in its entirety.

Finally, on Saturday, the third of the month, he knew that the last day of his life had arrived. He asked to be undressed completely and to be stretched out naked on the bare ground.

One friar exclaimed, "Dearest father, behold your sons, who will remain without a father and be deprived of the light of their eyes! Remember your orphans, whom you are abandoning. Forgive their failings, and give to them all the joy of your holy blessing."

In a weak voice the father replied, "Behold, my son: God is calling me. I pardon all their offenses and their faults, and, to the extent that I am able, I absolve them."

Then, as though gaining a second wind, the dying man powerfully intoned Psalm 142: "I cried to the LORD with my voice: with my voice I made supplication to the LORD."

And he continued until the final verse, which he managed to sing with one last effort, "Bring my soul out of prison, that I may praise thy name: the just wait for me, until thou reward me" [Vulgate; Douay-Rheims].

Night fell, and with it: silence. The friars who were nearest leaned over their father: he died while pronouncing those prophetic words.

At the same instant, in Naples, Brother Augustine, the minister of Campania, suddenly lifted his eyes toward heaven and began to cry out, "Wait, father! Wait for me! I want to go with you."

When his brothers urged him to explain the meaning of his words, he asked them, "Do you not see our Brother Francis, who is departing for heaven?"

At Assisi, as all this was taking place, the larks had gathered from every direction about the cell of their human brother. And as soon as he had breathed his last, they began to describe graceful circles in the air above him while singing joyously.

They opened the door of the cell for Brother Jacoba, who was waiting for the end. She threw herself down on her knees beside the emaciated body and kissed the pierced hands and feet with devotion.

The friars celebrated the funeral office privately. But on Sunday morning the inhabitants of Assisi, informed of the death of the man who was now becoming a national hero, came in throngs to the Portiuncula. The clergy of the city and the surrounding area wore their liturgical vestments, and a long procession formed, with each participant holding a lighted candle or an olive branch, while singing hymns and canticles.

So that everyone could behold the miracle of the stigmata, they had not buried the body of the deceased man in a winding sheet.

Celano relates that

Never had the witnesses read in Scripture, never had they heard tell of what they now saw with their own eyes. In this man was reproduced the image of the Cross and the Passion of the spotless Lamb who had washed away the iniquities of the world. You might have thought that he had just been taken down from the cross, with his feet and his hands pierced by nails and his heart as though wounded with a lance. They all gazed on that flesh which was once so dark complected, but now shone with magnificent splendor, presenting by its beauty a pledge of the blessed resurrection. His members seemed to have regained the suppleness and delicacy of innocent childhood. Who is there who would not have been moved to joy rather than to tears at the sight?

Fulfilling Clare's desire and keeping Francis' promise, the long cortege took the road that led to San Damiano, and the funeral bier was deposed in the church. The abbess and her sisters emerged from their cloister and huddled around this glorious body, in a moving scene that was subsequently illustrated by Giotto in the upper basilica. Despite everything, sorrow prevailed in their souls.

"O, father," Clare moaned, "what is to become of us? Why are you abandoning us, unhappy creatures that we are? Why are you leaving us in such desolation? Why did you not allow us to go on before you? O father of the poor, lover of poverty, who will help us in our trials, O holy man, who were tested yourself by so many temptations?"

Entering the city by the Porta Nuova, the procession stopped at the nearest sanctuary: the Church of Saint George, which was later replaced by the Basilica of Saint Clare. That was where they laid the venerated remains to rest. There his Funeral Mass was celebrated and the body was solemnly interred, awaiting the day when, as everyone expected, Francis would be canonized by the Church, and he would receive a more glorious burial place, one dedicated to him by name.

A few days later, Brother Elias wrote to Gregory of Naples, the minister of the order in France, a long letter in which he announced the news:

Before I begin to speak, I sigh, and not without reason. My sorrow springs up like an overflowing torrent, because the misfortune that I feared has befallen you and me. The one who used to console us is no more; the one who carried us in his arms like lambs has departed for the distant region. We must rejoice for him, but also weep for ourselves, who without him are wrapped in darkness and plunged into the shadow of death. We are orphans, deprived of the light of our eyes. . . .

And now I must announce to you a great joy, with an unprecedented miracle. Some time before his death, the friars saw our brother and father in the condition of one crucified, bearing in his body five wounds that were truly the stigmata of Christ. His feet and his hands bore holes that were pierced through and through by nails; his side, from which blood seeped, appeared to have been opened by a lance. He had no more beauty, so altered and consumed was his face by suffering. . . . But immediately after his death it became very beautiful again, with a dazzling whiteness. . . .

We are orphans. Now, it is written that the poor man is entrusted to the Lord, and that the Lord will come to the help of the orphan.

Let us all, then, turn to the Lord, my dear, dear brothers, and, after the destruction of this first precious vessel, let us pray the supreme Potter to give us another worthy of performing the same duty for our large family.

3. Canonization

All Italy, but especially Assisi, was now awaiting the official glorification of the humble saint whose earthly career had been so dazzling. We must not conclude, because of the lack of precision in certain historical accounts, that the *vox populi* was enough to proclaim a servant of God a saint. This voice of the people was an indication, an appeal that was brought to the attention of the official judge, who then proceeded to an investigation. This investigation had to establish that the dead person had worked miracles at his tomb and was thus worthy of being proclaimed a saint. This judgment was usually rendered by the bishop until the tenth century; then the pope became the official judge beginning in A.D. 993, when Pope John XVI canonized Ulric of Augsburg.

Therefore they were waiting for miracles: some of them because they were crippled and were counting on the deceased to obtain a cure; others for the praise of their compatriot and hence of their city; the majority for the glory of Francis himself, his order, and the Church. Miracles did not delay in coming; so plentiful were they that Thomas of Celano had to write, at the behest of the minister general, John of Parma, a *Treatise on the Miracles of Saint Francis*. We must be content with mentioning a few of those that were first listed chronologically.

The first miracle occurred on the very day of the interment. A little girl had a neck so twisted, probably from birth, that her head rested on her shoulder. The mother, who had attended the funeral, managed to bring this child up to the first row and pushed her under the catafalque where they had just laid out the stigmatized body. Immediately the child's head was righted, and she ran away in tears. The fact that she fled is understandable, because, given her tender age, she was afraid of the curiosity and the congratulations of the crowd; the tears are understandable, so great must have been her emotion. Her head had weighed so heavily on that frail shoulder that it left a hollow.

A man named Nicholas who lived in Foligno had an atrophied leg that was much shorter than the other; he could move about only with the help of crutches. He had spent all of his savings on doctors, who had not improved his condition in the least. Can a physician lengthen a limb? Quite to the contrary, their efforts ended up causing him acute pains, and sometimes at night he uttered such cries that he kept his neighbors from sleeping. He had heard Francis preach in his town, and he cherished the memory of that marvelous occasion. He had himself brought to the tomb. We can suppose that the neighbors who so often had been inconvenienced were very eager to be of assistance. He remained there for part of the night, deep in prayer. And suddenly he felt something inexplicable happen to his crippled leg. He got up, stirred by the emotion. The leg was the same length as the other. He went away, leaving his crutches behind.

A woman from the village of Ciaruccia had lost the use of all her limbs. She asked a charitable (and strong!) neighbor to transport her in a basket on his back to Assisi. He placed the basket against Francis' tomb. While she was praying to him fervently, she felt an influx of new strength run through her deadened members. She got up, climbed out of her "cage", and gesticulated. Her legs supported her, her arms stretched out, her hands could grasp objects. She had become a normal woman again.

Celano relates that for six years the beggar Bartholomew, an inhabitant of Narni, had had a leg so withered that one could cut it or burn it without any visible result. Limping along on a crutch, he arrived in Assisi and asked to see the bishop. The good Guido, friend of the poor, received him without hesitation.

"Here's the rub", the man told him. "The other night, while I was sleeping, Brother Francis appeared to me. He said, 'I pity you and I want to heal you. Go to Assisi, to such and such a place, and bathe in the water.' But I do not know Assisi, and so I can't find the place that he pointed out."

Guido took this story very seriously. He explained to the lame man how to find the stream indicated in the dream. The man made as much haste as his condition allowed, and once he was there, he waded into the water up to his waist. Then he felt something like a mighty hand that grasped his foot, and another that seized his calf; slowly, his leg slackened and regained its girth and strength. He was standing up without the crutch. He came out of the water: he was of sound body, walking at a good pace.

At San Severino, in the Marches of Ancona, a boy had contracted leprosy. The disease had made rapid progress through his lithe body; all of his limbs were starting to waste away, and he lost his ability to move around. Groaning on his bed, he continuously lamented his plight. His sorrowful parents were dejected.

One day the father said to him, "Son, are you willing to make a vow to Blessed Francis, who is presently working many miracles? Promise that, if he cures you, you will bring to his tomb each year a candle as tall as you."

The youth agreed. He folded his hands and invoked Saint Francis in a long and sorrowful prayer. And while he was praying, gradually, the leprosy faded away and new skin appeared. The big wax candle that was presented each year at the tomb of the miracle worker was, of course, very costly and quite heavy to transport, but it was less costly than the doctors and lighter than the poor little leprous body had been.

During that time period, two events renewed the religious life of the Order of Friars Minor. The first was the death of Honorius III. The Pontiff had been one of the great benefactors of the religious institute; he had entrusted it to the protection of Cardinal Ugolino, granted the indulgence to the Portiuncula, and officially approved the definitive rule. He commended his soul to God on March 18, 1227. The following day, the electors unanimously offered the papal tiara to the cardinal-bishop of Ostia, Hugolino of Segni. He was eighty-five years old. This was such an exceptionally advanced age in those days that everyone supposed that his pontificate would be extremely short. As it happened, he occupied the apostolic see for fourteen years and was almost a centenarian when he vacated it, having displayed, in both the internal and external affairs of the Church, a wisdom and a vigor that were praised by all. Within a few years of his election he canonized Francis of Assisi, Anthony of Padua, Dominic de Guzman, and Elizabeth of Hungary. The Franciscans were overwhelmed.

Another landmark for the order was the general chapter of May 1227. The participants had to elect the new minister general to succeed Francis at the head of the order. Brother Elias, the vicar general, counted on being elected; he had been appointed to his office by Francis himself and had administered his institute during his lifetime and during the seven months following his death. He had appointed a certain number of his friends to head the provinces. But the elders considered him a violator of the rule, and at any rate as an ambiguous character. Their influence was strong: the assembly conferred the generalate upon John Parenti, the minister of Spain, a former judge originally from Florence.

Now, the new Pope remained sympathetic to Brother Elias. Despite the express wishes of Francis, who had fought so energetically to allow his friars to build nothing but lowly convents, he commissioned Elias to build a great church to house the tomb of Francis—an edifice, unlike the Church of Saint George, his present resting place, in which he could be venerated worthily. The municipality of Assisi, which was won over to the project, made him a gift, by a notarized act dated March 29, 1228, of the hill that arose to the west outside the ramparts of Assisi, which was graciously yielded for this purpose by its owner, Simon Puzzanelli. The hill used to be called *L'Inferno*: Hell. Now they called it Paradise Hill. The document stipulated that the place was dedicated to the construction of "a convent, an oratory, a church, or any other building destined to house the body of Saint Francis".

Just then, in the spring of 1228, Gregory IX made a journey to Umbria, accompanied by the majority of the Sacred College of Cardinals. He stayed first in Rieti, then in Spoleto, and finally decided to reside for a while in Assisi. Before entering the city, he desired to make a stop at San Damiano, where he visited Clare and her community, who welcomed him with a very special reverence. When he left the convent, the whole city was waiting for him, with the bishop and the clergy in the lead, then the secular authorities, the long line of religious and the populace. Thus, in pomp and splendor, he entered the city of Francis, the Poverello.

Once he had settled in, he issued a decree enjoining all those who, since the death of the saint, had benefited from any sort of miracle to come and testify before a commission of cardinals appointed for that purpose. Deeming that this commission was working conscientiously, he went for a time to Perugia with a few selected collaborators. There he heard the news that the findings of the cardinalatial commission were conclusive. He then called a consistory which, after hearing the report of the commission, decided that it was licit to proceed to the canonization. It was scheduled for Sunday, July 16, and the news of it was brought to Assisi.

On that day, when Gregory IX arrived in the city, it was all festively decorated and illuminated. In the tiny Church of Saint George there was no room for the crowd. The nave was just large enough to accommodate the clergy (bishops, abbots, canons, sons of Saint Francis, and clerics of all sorts) and the dignitaries (princes, counts, podestas, governors, and consuls). By way of exception, a papal dispensation had been granted to Clare and her community to leave their cloister so as to be seated in the first rows, beside the general of the order and the provincial ministers. When the Pope entered, preceded by the cardinals in white miters, a profound silence fell over the assembly. With deep respect they watched the nonagenarian Pontiff enter, almost overcome with emotion himself. He took his place in the choir, on the throne reserved for him, and spoke, beginning with a verse from the Book of Ecclesiasticus: "He shone in his days as a morning star in the midst of a cloud, and as the moon at the full. And as the sun when it shineth, so did he shine in the temple of God" [50:6–7].

He then started to give the customary eulogy for Brother Francis, but his love did not allow him to compose rhetorical flourishes; while recalling his friend's beginnings in penance, poverty, and charity, he burst into sobs and had to break off his speech. Thomas of Celano, who had already been chosen as the saint's official biographer, saw the tears run down the Pontiff's face. And so, dispensing with a longer discourse, the latter handed the proceedings over to the cardinal-deacon Ottaviano Conti, who punctiliously read the list of the forty miracles accepted by the commission of cardinals. A number of those who had been miraculously cured were present, attentive, nodding their heads and weeping. Finally, Gregory, who had calmed down, stood up and forcefully declared the words of the solemn act: "For the glory of Almighty God, Father, Son, and Holy Spirit, of the glorious Virgin Mary, of the blessed apostles Peter and Paul, and

for the honor of the Roman Church, intending to venerate on earth
the man whom God has glorified in heaven, having consulted Our
brothers and other prelates, We declare that there is good reason to
enroll blessed Francis in the catalogue of the saints. His feast day will
be celebrated on the anniversary of his death."

The Holy Father then intoned the *Te Deum*, which was taken up
by all the clerics and religious. The bells of Saint George, then all
the bells of the city, rang out in a joyful concert. During this time,
Gregory descended into the crypt, where the shrine [*châsse*, i.e., case
containing the relics] of the new saint had been placed, and kissed it
with touching affection.

When he had returned to the ground level, Brother Elias informed
him that the work of excavating and leveling Paradise Hill was now
completed, and that it was his, the Supreme Pontiff's prerogative to
position the first stone of the basilica that they were going to erect
on that spot. He accepted the invitation and put off the ceremony to
the following day, so that it would be more impressive; indeed, he
dedicated Monday, July 17, to that ceremony. On Tuesday he went
to his palace in Perugia. There he composed a papal bull, *Mira circa
nos*, telling the Christian world what his emotions had not permitted
him to express in the Church of Saint George.

That was still not enough. On February 20, 1229, he published a
new encyclical ordering that the feast of Saint Francis be celebrated
throughout the universal Church; all archbishops and bishops were
obliged to include this celebration on the fourth of October on the
liturgical calendar.

In order to celebrate this feast worthily, there had to be a liturgy
suited to its originality: a special office and Mass praising the particular
virtues of Saint Francis and the unprecedented graces that he received
from the Lord. Prominent churchmen were eager to contribute to the
composition of them. Gregory IX himself insisted on writing several
of these proper prayers, for instance, for the sequence of the Mass,
the hymn for first vespers, the florid eighth response at matins in the
eighth tone, and the antiphon of the *Benedictus*. Cardinal Thomas of
Capua composed two hymns, a response, and an antiphon; Cardinal
Rainier of Viterbo wrote a hymn.

It is difficult to get a sense of the liturgical office of Saint Francis
that was composed by his contemporaries unless you actually have

the manuscripts in your hands. The texts and the melodies, in comparison with those of earlier centuries, are in a completely new style, which goes to extremes in the liberties taken by the poetry and music of the thirteenth century. Apart from the psalms and the readings, which are all drawn from the Bible, the authors of the texts give free rein to their imaginations. Antiphons and responses, in keeping with a new fashion that was unknown in classical poetry, are rhymed, and sometimes go on at great length. The antiphons for lauds and vespers, made up of six verses each, are sometimes clumsy, due to the fact that they are obliged simultaneously to rhyme and to follow the account of the saint's life. The antiphons of the Magnificat are endowed with fourteen to sixteen verses, that of the *Benedictus* has sixteen, written according to an involved metrical scheme. Here is an excerpt from the first antiphon of the Magnificat:

O stupor et gaudium,	O wonder and joy,
O judex homo mentium,	Though man, a judge of minds,
Tu nostrae militiae	You, the chariot and driver
Currus et auriga.	Of our militia;
Ignea, praesentibus	In the presence of your brothers
Transfiguratum fratribus,	This fiery chariot carried you
In solari specie	Transfigured,
Vexit te quadriga.	Radiant as the sun.
In te signis radians,	Upon you, resplendent with miracles,
In te ventura nuntians,	Upon you, announcing future events,
Requievit spiritus	Rested the double spirit
Duplex prophetarum.	Of the prophets.
Tuis adsta posteris,	Stand by your unhappy sons,
Pater Francisce, miseris;	O Father Francis,
Nam, increscunt gemitus	For the moaning of your sheep
Ovium tuarum.	Grows louder.

Even though one senses throughout these verses and these melodies an admiration, devotion, and love for the departed founder, the composition seems too contrived, and the hymns are a far cry from the sweetness and delicacy characterizing those of the two preceding centuries.

Be that as it may, the liturgical office for Saint Francis was a fervent homage to the saint of Assisi, who at that moment became a saint of the universal Church through an alliance between the devotion of his sons and the authority of the common father of all Christians. The second tribute was the biography written by Thomas of Celano. Gregory IX requested it of him as a justification for the canonization, so as to acquaint the world with the life and virtues of the new saint. Composed during the year 1228, it received papal approval on February 25, 1229. The minister general Crescentius of Jesi, however, deemed that this glorification of the founder was inadequate, and in 1244 he ordered that all the surviving disciples of Francis should send him their memories. Based on this collection of new documents, Celano composed a new biography, published in 1247, which is known as the *Vita secunda*.

Lastly, the third tribute was the basilica in Assisi. From the moment when he was charged with responsibility for this construction project, Brother Elias did not waste any time. He maintained cordial relations with the German Emperor Frederick II. The latter sent him a renowned architect from northern Italy, Jacopo. He was unacquainted with Franciscan spirituality, the deceased friar's love of poverty. They asked him to honor a great saint, and he wanted to do so in the grand style. With the consent of Elias, who also wanted to offer a grandiose tribute to his spiritual father, he designed the building with three levels: the crypt, where the tomb would be enshrined; a lower church, somber and meditative, a symbol of Francis' interior life; and an upper church with a high ceiling and flooded with light, a symbol of his glory. In April 1230, two years after the first stone was laid, the lower church was finished.

Having been informed of this, Gregory IX published on April 22 a bull, *Is qui Ecclesiam*, in which he spared the friars the embarrassment of owning such a building by declaring that the basilica was his and that it would henceforth be the mother of all the churches of the order. This was contrary to the will of Francis, who had repeatedly said that Santa Maria degli Angeli would forever remain the mother church of his order. But, after all, Gregory IX was the Pope.

The consecration of the basilica was scheduled for May 25. The Pope was detained in Rome, so he delegated the minister general, John Parenti, to represent him. The ceremony lasted a long time;

THE SUBLIME PATH OF ETERNITY

indeed, it was twofold, consisting of the solemn translation of Saint Francis' body from the Church of Saint George to its new resting place, and the dedication of the "patriarchal" basilica, so called after the patriarch of the Friars Minor. Rumor had it that the richly embroidered cloth that covered the coffin had been sent by Queen Blanche of Castile, the mother of King Louis IX.

The translation ceremony had a strange ending, which the Pope's absence only facilitated. The civil authorities in Assisi were still afraid that a neighboring town (Perugia, for example) would make off with these sacred remains, which were now their glory. As the pallbearers were approaching the church, the archers of the municipal militia charged on and dispersed the crowd, seized the coffin, and locked themselves up with it in the crypt. They remained there until they had hidden the remains in a place that accomplices had prepared for this purpose. When both groups emerged, no one knew any more where the body of Saint Francis was. Those who had plotted this scheme died without divulging their secret.

This hiding place remained unknown for six centuries. In 1824 Leo XII, at the request of the minister general of the Friars Minor Conventual, who resided in the Sacro Convento, ordered an investigation. The work was carried on secretly for fifty-four nights, at the end of which the catafalque of Saint Francis was brought to light and moved to a place where it could be venerated by all the pilgrims. In memory of this event, the Pope permitted the Friars Minor to celebrate the feast of the Invention (*inventio*, in Latin, means discovery) of the body of Saint Francis, which is celebrated each year on December 12.

Prayer of Thomas of Celano to Saint Francis

Behold, our Blessed Father, we have striven, in the simplicity of our zeal, to praise your marvelous life to the best of our ability, and to record, for your glory, some of your unforgettable virtues. We know, of course, that the words that we employ are inadequate to reflect the splendor of your merits, and that they will always be incapable of expressing such perfection. We ask you, and those who will read about you, to consider not so much the resulting work as our love and our intentions. Who, then, could imagine and make others understand the ardor of your soul, O greatest of the saints? Who could conceive of that ineffable love for

God which arose continually from your heart? Nevertheless, charmed by the sweetness of your memory, we have written your life, and for as long as we live we will strive to make it known to others, although we can only stammer.

Draw us to yourself, O venerable father, and make us run after you in the odor of your ointments [cf. Song 1:3, Douay-Rheims], although you see that we are lukewarm, careless, slothful, and languishing. Our weak eyes cannot endure the brilliance of your perfection. Grant us renewal of life, you who are the mirror and the type of all the virtues. Do not suffer us to be unlike you in our conduct, since we are like you by our religious profession.

Chronology

ca. 1140   Bernardo Moriconi, nicknamed Bernardone, a cloth merchant from Lucques, settles in Assisi.

ca. 1150   Birth of his son Pietro (Pietro di Bernardone).

ca. 1180   Pietro marries Pica, a woman from Provence.

1182   (September 16?) Birth of Giovanni, son of Pietro, later nicknamed Francis.

1198   Election of Pope Innocent III.

1202   War between Perugia and Assisi; the army of the latter is defeated at the Bridge of Saint John [Ponte San Giovanni]. Francis is imprisoned until 1203.

1204   Sickness. Disillusionment with the world.

1205   The vision at Spoleto. Francis leaves to rejoin the army of Walter of Brienne in Puglia but returns to Assisi.

1206   Called by the crucifix of San Damiano. The journey to Rome.

1207   Francis renounces his inheritance.

1208   Repair of the Portiuncula.

1209   Called by the Gospel at the Portiuncula. The first eleven or twelve disciples. The original rule. Approval by the Pope.

1209–1211   First preaching tours.

1211   The community settles definitively at the Portiuncula.

1212   (March 19). Francis gives the habit to Clare and her first companions. Journey to Rome; friendship with Jacoba of Settesoli.

1213   Journey to France and Spain.

1215 (Pentecost). First general chapter in Assisi.
Fourth Lateran Council. Meeting of Saint Francis and
Saint Dominic.

1216 Honorius III grants the indulgence of the Portiuncula.

1217 Missionaries depart for France, England, and Germany.

1218 The rule of Saint Clare.

1219 Mission to Egypt.

1220 Francis steps down as head of the order and appoints
Peter of Catanio. Martyrdom of the first five friars in
Morocco.

1221 Death of Peter of Catanio. Brother Elias becomes
vicar general. Composition of the First Rule Cardinal
Ugolino becomes protector of the order. Foundation of
the Third Order.

1223 Composition of the second rule (the definitive rule) in
Fonte Colombo.

The Christmas crib at Greccio.

1224 (September 14). Francis receives the stigmata on Mount
La Verna.

1225 Returns to San Damiano. Composes the "Canticle of
Brother Sun".

1226 (October 3). Dies at the Portiuncula. Funeral. Laid to
rest at Saint George.

1227 Hugolino becomes Pope Gregory IX. John Parenti is
elected minister general.

1228 Canonization of Saint Francis.

1230 (May 30). Translation of the body to the new basilica
built by Elias.

1232 Elias is elected minister general. Canonization of Saint
Anthony of Padua.

PART SIX

The Paths
By Which Saint Francis Is Known

1. The Written Works of Saint Francis

Speaking about the writings of Saint Francis of Assisi sometimes surprises people, and even arouses suspicion. Saint Francis, an author?! The very thought seems inconsistent with the way in which he is usually pictured. He is above all a preacher and a singer. He makes use of his voice, not of his pen. He himself declares in his "Letter to the General Chapter", "I am ignorant and unlettered." But this statement is nevertheless made in a letter.

Did he dictate that letter? That is what many authors did: they had secretaries. And it is perfectly normal. First, because this method is more convenient; the man of action does not have to be bothered with a writing desk and all the implements in order to write a page that is deemed important when the occasion presents itself. Second, because after the age of forty-five or fifty, one's eyesight becomes weak. Before the invention of eyeglasses, even the best authors needed to dictate their works, and these bear their name and not the name of their secretary. Francis, who died at the age of forty-four, did not wait that long to have recourse to the help of an intermediary. The blazing sun of Italy and Egypt had ruined his eyes, and he could make use of them only with difficulty. We know that a good number of the "writings" of Saint Francis came from the pen of Brother Leo, and the *Speculum perfectionis* portrays him dictating his testament to Brother Benedict of Prato.

This does not mean that Saint Francis did not *know how* to write. On Mount La Verna, when Leo yearned to have a keepsake written by his master, he knew what was possible. And when Francis commanded him to bring paper and ink, he did not dictate the "Praises of God" to him; he himself wrote them down. Despite his painful eyes, he produced more than thirty lines of studious penmanship, which we can still decipher today. Thus there are manuscripts in Saint Francis' own handwriting, as well as more numerous writings in another

305

hand, which are nonetheless his compositions since the hand was only the docile instrument of his word.

The ensemble of his works was compiled imperfectly, yet significantly, as early as the seventeenth century by the erudite Franciscan friar Lucas Wadding. At the beginning of the twentieth century, in 1904, other specialists, applying the methods of textual criticism, simultaneously published a collection of writings attributed to Saint Francis. These scholars were Böhmer, who edited them under the title of *Analekten*, and the Franciscan Fathers of Quaracchi (near Florence), under the title of *Opuscula*. The latter collection was translated several times into French: first by Fr. Ubald d'Alençon in 1905, then by Fr. Gratien of Paris in 1935, and finally, twenty years later, by the Friars Minor of the Parisian Province, a precious bilingual Latin-French edition, accompanied by scriptural references, notes, and tables. This 350-page volume is still available from the French publishing house, Éditions Franciscaines.[1] We will follow this edition in presenting the various "writings" of Saint Francis, in the order in which they appear there (which is, in any case, arbitrary).

The first part is composed of twenty-eight admonitions. They are from a venerable source: a manuscript from Assisi dating back to 1245 —less than twenty years after the author's death. They are composed on the same scale, on the whole very short. The longest one is the first: two pages about the Body of Christ.

The second part is devoted to the rules. The primitive rule, obviously, is not printed, since it is not extant. Traces of it can be found, however, in the following version, called the first rule (1221), which to a great extent adopts the same wording and elaborates upon it. Indeed, its prolixity was one of the reasons that it was called into question by the Roman Curia. Then there is the composition of the definitive rule, which comes next. We have, next, two short texts of the rule of Saint Clare; more precisely, the first of them is the prologue of the original rule; the second a paragraph from the definitive rule. Then we find the "Testament" and the bylaws for hermitages.

The third part contains Saint Francis' letters, or at least those that

---

[1] *St. Francis of Assisi: Writings and Early Biographies: English Omnibus of the Sources for the Life of St. Francis*, edited by Marion A. Habig, O.F.M. (Quincy, Ill.: Franciscan Press, Quincy College, 1991).—TRANS.

have come down to us, for it is likely that he dictated a larger number of them, given his extensive dealings [with communities throughout Europe]. The anthology includes eight of them. The first, "To All the Faithful", about a dozen pages long, is a sort of summary of the ordinary preaching of Saint Francis, presenting the principles of Christian life to the listeners: reliance on the Gospel, the Eucharist, prayer, confession, and penance. The second letter, "To All Clerics", deals specifically with the respect and veneration due to the Eucharist. The third letter, almost eight pages in length, is addressed to the general chapter in order to recall the practice of the virtues of religious life.

The fourth part is a collection of prayers. The longest is an "Office of the Passion", which Francis used to recite especially during Holy Week. Nevertheless, it reveals very little about him: all in all it is a series of psalms, systematically arranged and separated by an antiphon —always the same one—of which Francis is the author: "Holy Virgin Mary, there is no one like you among the women born into this world: daughter and servant of the Most High King, the heavenly Father; Mother of our most holy Lord Jesus Christ; spouse of the Holy Spirit. Pray for us, with Saint Michael the Archangel, all the virtues of the heavens and all the saints, to your most holy and dearly beloved Son, our Lord and Master."

The "Laudes" [Praises], which Francis personally added to all the hours of the Divine Office, are likewise his composition, although they contain many borrowings from Scripture. They begin with a commentary on the Our Father, as we have seen in the excerpts printed above as part of our discussion of Saint Francis' prayer life. They continue with acclamations drawn from the Book of Revelation and from the Canticle of the Three Young Men [from Chapter 3 of the Book of Daniel]. "Holy, holy, holy, Lord, God almighty, who is, who was, and who is to come. Let us praise and exalt him above all forever. . . . Worthy is the Lamb that was slain, to receive power and divinity and wisdom and strength and honor and glory and blessing. Let us praise and exalt him above all forever", etc.

Next we find prayers in poetic form, such as the one that he gave to Brother Leo on Mount La Verna, and the "Salutation to the Blessed Virgin Mary", both of which are reproduced in previous chapters. A completely original prayer is the Salutation of the Virtues:

Hail, Queen Wisdom, may the Lord preserve thee,
with thy sister, holy and pure Simplicity.
Holy Lady Poverty, may the Lord preserve thee,
with thy sister, holy Humility.
Holy Lady Charity, may the Lord preserve thee,
with thy sister, holy Obedience.
All of you most holy virtues,
may the Lord preserve you,
from Whom you proceed and come.

In conclusion, the collection presents the famous "Canticle of Creation", which has the great advantage of appearing in its original Umbrian, the dialect that Saint Francis spoke.

Finally, the sixth part offers various texts attributed to the saint, all of them short. Among them is the letter to Jacoba of Settesoli, and the last "Testament" ("Write that I bless all my friars. . ."), which are cited above in the chapter on his death.

All of these notes are quite brief, but the present book is intended as a biography, not an anthology. The present [French] edition of the *Works of Saint Francis of Assisi* (Éditions franciscaines) is 330 pages long. This short chapter is only an introduction.

One final remark, however. The very widespread and very popular prayer that begins, "Lord, make me an instrument of your peace", is usually entitled "Prayer of Saint Francis" or is followed by the note, "Prayer attributed to Saint Francis".

In fact, it is not by Saint Francis, and over the course of the centuries it was never attributed to Saint Francis. It quite frankly dates back to the twentieth century and was composed by an anonymous author, one who was no doubt familiar with the saint's life and writings. It appeared for the first time in 1912 in a simple bulletin in Normandy, *La Clochette*, and then was reprinted several months later in a magazine, again in Normandy, *Les Annales de Notre-Dame de Tinchebray*, obviously without a by-line. In January of 1916, while war was ravaging Europe, the directors of a lay association, le Souvenir Normand, went to Rome to present this text to Pope Benedict XV for the cause of peace, under the title of "A Simple Prayer"; again, without naming an author. Until that time, therefore, no one thought of attributing it to Francis of Assisi. Now, at around that same time (1916? 1917?), a Capuchin father from Rheims, Fr. Étienne [Stephen], reprinted the prayer on the back of a holy card depicting Saint Francis, without in any way suggesting that it was his composition. But some of those who had copies of this image spontaneously interpreted it in this sense: on the back, the text; on the front, the author. And the multitude followed.

2. Sources for the Life of Saint Francis

Thomas of Celano

Thomas, a native of Celano in the Abruzzi region, received the habit of a Friar Minor in 1215 from the hands of Saint Francis himself. In 1221 he took part in the mission to Germany and, as the number of convents there increased, was appointed *custos* [guardian] of the Rhineland in 1222, and then the provincial minister of Germany the following year, succeeding Caesarius of Speyer, who devised the plan to set out for the land of the infidels. After returning to Italy, he witnessed most of the deeds and accomplishments of Saint Francis, which prompted Gregory IX to entrust to him the project of writing the first biography of the new saint.

No doubt the author applied himself zealously and conscientiously to the task. He writes in his prologue:

> Taking truth as my guide and mistress, I have attempted, with a pious devotion and constant effort, to write the life of our blessed father, Saint Francis. Since no one can recall in their entirety all his actions and teachings, I have striven, at the command of our glorious lord, Pope Gregory, to report as accurately as possible, albeit in a very imperfect style, the words that I heard from his mouth and the accounts that I have received from experienced and trustworthy witnesses.

This is how Saint Gregory the Great had proceeded in writing the life of Saint Benedict; although he had not known his subject personally, he diligently interrogated all the surviving eyewitnesses of his life.

This biography would have sufficed to immortalize the founder. But rivalries were rocking the order, and the various factions cited the examples and words of Saint Francis to justify their positions. This prompted the minister general, Crescentius of Jesi, to request in 1244 a new anthology of recollections, which would complement the first. He assigned the work to Thomas, who had very honorably acquitted himself of his first task. At the general chapter of Genoa that same year, however, he asked all the friars who had known Saint Francis personally to send him their contributions in writing. Three of Francis' first companions did so—Leo, Angelo, and Rufino—and perhaps others whose names have not gone down in history. Equipped with these source materials, Thomas completed his task rapidly—so much so that it was ready in spring of 1247 and was approved at the general chapter of Lyons.

The new work, much thicker than the first, deemphasizes the biographical events, which nonetheless are the subject of thirteen short chapters. Instead, in 166 chapters it develops a spiritual portrait of the saint, made up of words and anecdotes; an inexhaustible mine for all the subsequent biographers.

This account paid little attention to the miracles, in which the readers of this sort of literary work were usually most interested. At the command of the new minister general, John of Parma, Thomas took up his pen again and in 1253 produced the manuscript entitled *Tractatus de miraculis* (English edition: *The Treatise on the Miracles of Saint Francis*).

We should also explain that in 1230 (that is, two years after the *Vita prima*) the same author had composed a *Legenda chori*. The word "legend" here, as in other works of that period bearing this title, should not be taken to mean that it is a legendary account in the sense that we understand today, but rather as a text that is "supposed to be read" (which is the Latin meaning of the word). Under the circumstances, these few pages were designed to be read in monastic choir during the office of matins from 1230 to 1266.

We should also add that Celano is very probably the author of the famous sequence, *Dies irae*, which in the eighteenth century was incorporated into the Requiem Mass. This author, after serving his order so meritoriously, retired to become the chaplain of the Poor Clares of Tagliacozzo, where he died around the year 1260.

Derivative Biographers

The renown of Saint Francis was so great that other authors decided to edify the public by publishing biographies that were more or less inspired by the work of Thomas of Celano.

Julian of Speyer, O.F.M., a German religious who had once served as choirmaster of the French royal court but then entered the order during Saint Francis' lifetime, wrote two works between 1232 and 1240. The one is a *Vita*, the other a large-scale liturgical composition intended for recitation in choir, the *Officium rhythmicum*.

Henri of Avranches, a cleric of both Norman and Germanic ancestry who was endowed with the title of poet laureate [*archi-poète*], composed a *Legenda versificata* after the canonization; this is an enormous poem consisting of 2,589 verses, to be sung in the courts and at public meetings.

On the other hand, Bernard of Besse, the secretary of Saint Bonaventure, produced a charming treatise in verse, *De laudibus beati Francisci*.

Saint Bonaventure

In spite of so many edifying testimonies, the two camps within the Friars Minor continued to tear each other apart. The "spirituals" found in Celano and the "Testament" the confirmation of their positions in favor of absolute poverty and living in hermitages, whereas the "conventuals", disciples of Elias and Gregory of Naples, derived from the definitive rule their justification for a mitigated poverty and residence in large urban convents. At this point, in 1257, the general chapter met to choose a successor to John of Parma (who favored the spirituals); the friars elected Brother Bonaventure, a lecturer at the University of Paris, the most famous scholar in the order. Since he was a saint, the spirituals hoped in him; since he was an intellectual, the conventuals believed in him.

The order had undergone an unprecedented development and now numbered around forty thousand members, belonging to only thirty-three provinces, which were subdivided into custodies. The ministers of the foreign provinces were not attuned to the subtleties and passionate convictions of their Italian confreres. To the great majority, who were equally tired of the turbulent reformers and the minimalists, Bonaventure appeared to be a conciliatory candidate, combining holiness and intelligence and thus capable of finding solutions that would be acceptable to both camps.

The first expedient devised by the new general was to write a biography that would portray Saint Francis as being favorable to one camp as well as the other. An arduous and ultimately an illusory undertaking, for he had to prune away from this life an abundance of significant deeds and words—a selection process that considerably impoverished the founder's personality. He threw himself nevertheless into this work, which must have been a ruthless project, because of his veneration for such a saintly master and his acquaintance with such a rich life. His biography, therefore, is expurgated but precise in all the facts that it does report. Begun in 1260, the delicate work was not completed until 1263, when it was immediately approved by the general chapter. But the wrangling continued, and the recalcitrant partisans continued to claim for themselves the authority of the previous biographies. Therefore the chapter in 1266 decided on a radical measure: it commanded all the friars, in all the convents of the order, to keep only the official biography composed by Bonaventure and to destroy all the others. As a whole, the ministers and the guardians sorrowfully complied. The spirituals refused to obey the order and carefully concealed the other source materials, in view of the fact that they constituted the principal witness for the legislation and the spirituality of their order.

This work by Bonaventure was called *Legenda major*, to distinguish it from the *Legenda minor*, the collection of readings that were read at the office of matins. In effect, it replaced the *Legenda chori* by Celano, which was consigned to the flames.

The Compilations

Fortunately for the historian and the devotee, and fortunately for the Church as well, many owners of the forbidden writings not only treasured them but also had their imitators, who wanted to own the precious writings of the early friars, too. Indeed, the written testimonies that had been requested by Pope Gregory and the minister general Crescentius, and which had assisted Celano in composing his biographies, remained in circulation. Many convents wanted to possess copies of them. But, depending on the tastes of the copyist, or perhaps on the amount of time at his disposal, these transcriptions were often partial. In general, they consisted of selected excerpts: the copyists devoted themselves to making compilations that regrouped chapters from different manuscripts.

Especially during the first half of the fourteenth century, about a hundred years after the death of Saint Francis, these transcribing friars dedicated themselves to this work in their hermitages. We must not suppose, however, that the texts themselves dated from that period; they are contemporary with Saint Francis. Furthermore, many of the religious who appear at the beginning of the fourteenth century are disciples of the founder's companions and report their observations.

There were certainly many manuscripts of this type in central Italy. Unfortunately, they vanished over the course of the centuries. In the nineteenth century, which was par excellence the century of historical research, well-qualified and zealous researchers, who have been called "Franciscanizers" [*franciscanisants*], rummaged around all the places where one might find remnants of this process of textual replication, both in the municipal libraries and in those of monasteries and convents. And they gleaned manuscripts that, although disappointingly few, soon provided a basis capable of revising Franciscan history. Incidentally, the *Vita secunda* by Celano, even though it was the official text of the order, was itself not discovered until 1798, and the first printed edition is of an even more recent date, 1899.

When Crescentius of Jesi asked the first companions of Francis to send their memoirs to Thomas of Celano, three friars, who were close to the founder and close friends themselves, joined forces to commit to writing the many charming events that had changed their lives. They were Leo, Angelo, and Rufino. Even though these pages passed through Celano's hands, they were still preserved by the spirituals as well and used by them for polemical purposes. Thus it was possible to reconstruct a *Legend of the Three Companions* (*Legenda trium sociorum*), which is made up of only the beginning of the memoirs (sixteen chapters) and the conclusion (two chapters on the death and canonization). Nevertheless it is a very beautiful account, full of tenderness, fervor, and simplicity, which conveys the sentiments of the early community even more than the memories of it. A manuscript of this work was discovered in the eighteenth century, since it was published by the Bollandist Suysken in 1768.

Another, more complete version of this text—including many chapters that fall chronologically between the beginnings of the order and the founder's death—had been published in Venice in 1504 under the title, *Speculum vitae sancti Francisci et sociorum ejus* [*Mirror of the life of Saint Francis and his companions*]. But because of the authority of the Bollandists, it was the incomplete edition that became popular and has been translated recently into modern languages. In 1855, Franciscan Father Melchiorri received another version of *The Three Companions*, this one in Italian; it had been translated from a Latin manuscript in 1577. Melchiorri published it in 1856, and in 1862 it was reprinted in French by the Abbot of Latreiche, but without much success. A fourth version, more complete than the *Legenda* but less so than the *Speculum vitae*, was discovered in the library of Perugia and published in 1962 by the Bollandist, Van Ortroy.

The *Mirror of Perfection* (*Speculum perfectionis*) was discovered in 1894 by the Protestant scholar Paul Sabatier in a sheaf of Franciscan documents that he found in a volume dated 1509. He published the work in 1898, noting Brother Leo as its author. It is almost certain, however, that the account is of a later date and was composed by Leo's disciples, who attributed it to him as their source.

In 1922 A. G. Little published a manuscript that he discovered, again in the library in Perugia, and which he named the *Legenda antiqua*. The text is quite similar in many passages to Celano's *Vita secunda* and the *Mirror of Perfection*. The textual critics even conjecture that certain chapters were written in Leo's own hand.

The most popular of all the Franciscan compilations, however, is the *Fioretti*, a collection of marvelous texts composed in Italian in the first half of the fourteenth century, which is actually made up of six works:

The *Fioretti* or *Little Flowers of Saint Francis* properly so-called,
      which is the largest, having fifty-three chapters;
Considerations on the Holy Stigmata (five chapters);
The Life of Brother Juniper (fourteen chapters);
The Life of Blessed Giles (ten chapters);
The Sayings of Blessed Giles (eighteen chapters); and
The Additional Chapters (twenty chapters).

The main source for this impressive collection seems to have been a somewhat earlier Latin work, *The Acts of Blessed Francis and his Companions*, for which we know at least one of the authors, Ugolino di

San Giorgio, a confrere of Brother Leo's disciples, who learned the facts from them.

The Chronicles

The Chronicle of Jordan of Giano, published in 1870, relates the history of the Franciscan order from the conversion of Saint Francis in 1207 until the year 1238. It is a treasure-trove of anecdotes concerning the foundations of the Franciscans in the [Middle] East, in Hungary, and in Germany.

The Chronicle of Thomas of Eccleston (compiled in the years 1264–1270) tells of the arrival of the Franciscan foundations in England.

The Chronicle of Salimbene, dictated around the year 1287, attempts to collect all the major events of the Franciscan order from its origins down to that date.

The Chronicle of the Twenty-four Generals not only reports on the work of the first [two dozen] ministers general of the order, but also describes many important personages from the early years: Bernard, Giles, Leo, and Masseo.

The Annals of the Order of Friars Minor (Annales ordinis Minorum) by Lucas Wadding (1588–1657). A very learned man who entered the order at the age of sixteen, Wadding was a professor of theology at Salamanca, then the general procurator of the order in Rome. He published this vast eight-volume work during the years 1628–1657. His account covers facts from the years 1208 to 1540. It is an incomparable gold mine for the first three centuries of Franciscan history.

Bibliographical Note

Some of these sources have been published in English. The following are now in print or can be found in a good Catholic seminary or university library:

St. Francis of Assisi: Writings and Early Biographies: English Omnibus of the Sources for the Life of St. Francis. Edited by Marion A. Habig, O.F.M. Quincy, Ill.: Franciscan Press, Quincy College, 1991.

St. Francis of Assisi: First and Second Life of St. Francis with selections from the Treatise on the Miracles of Blessed Francis. Thomas of Celano.

Translated with introduction and footnotes by Placid Hermann. Chicago: Franciscan Herald Press, 1988.

St. Francis of Assisi, His Holy Life and Love of Poverty: The Legend of the Three Companions. Chicago: Franciscan Herald Press, 1964.

St. Bonaventure's Writings concerning the Franciscan Order. St. Bonaventure, N.Y.: Franciscan Institute, St. Bonaventure University, 1994.

The Little Flowers of St. Francis: An Entirely New Version with Twenty Additional Chapters; also, *The Considerations on the Holy Stigmata; The Life and Sayings of Brother Giles; The Life of Brother Juniper.* Garden City, N.Y.: Image Books, 1958.

The Little Flowers of St. Francis. The Mirror of Perfection. The Life of St. Francis. London: J. M. Dent; New York: E. P. Dutton, 1938.

Clare of Assisi: Early Documents. Edited and translated by Regis J. Armstrong. New York: Paulist Press, 1988.

3. His Followers

As early as 1219, as we have seen, the marvelous edifice constructed by Saint Francis was already beginning to creak in places. The rule that he wrote, which was entirely spiritual and not canonical, made up of Gospel citations and outbursts of sentiment, had governed the fervent community for ten years. But it was designed for saints, for an elite. As numbers increased, it became impractical, or rather, it was put into practice badly, for the application of the rule to everyday life was not spelled out but was left to the generosity of each religious. While he was present, Francis could teach the members of the early community each day, set them an example, communicate his spirit to them. But the friars recruited in other places, in southern and northern Italy, in France, Germany, and the East, would not have the founder as their spiritual master. They would obey this loosely defined rule (which left room for all sorts of enthusiasm and all sorts of weaknesses) as they themselves interpreted it, with a vision of consecrated religious life that would always depend upon their life in the world.

The first friars were humble of heart. They were not interested in grumbling, quibbling, discussing, or debating. But when Francis realized that he could not be everywhere and began to delegate his authority to ministers, many of whom were well-educated clerics, trained in law and acquainted with the monastic rules, they deemed that this little cloth merchant was incapable of governing a large-scale order, or of devising a discipline that could be applied throughout Christendom. And they interpreted the rule as broadly as possible. Hence the rebellion of little Brother Stephen, who went all the way to Egypt to notify their common father of this betrayal.

This laxity that prevailed in many convents pained Francis. But he was aware that he could not put a stop to the trend. That would have required two contrasting orders: one small, ardent, unyielding, which followed the Gospel to the letter and perpetuated the folly of the Portiuncula; the other one broad-based, sedate, reasonable, which would approve modifications to the rigorous rule. But such a solution would be madness: How could he tear in two this seamless garment? Would it not be better to expel the unworthy friars? But how would he manage to sort them out?

The order was in this disarray because Rome, in a conciliatory spirit and out of understanding for human weakness, sided with the ministers. Certainly not so as to contradict and find fault with the founder, but in order to make it more feasible to obey the rule. The first two rules had been written for the desert fathers, and the time of the desert fathers had passed. Francis understood the reasons given by Hugolino and Honorius, but he could not adopt them as his own: that would have been to deny his whole mission. He preferred to hand over responsibility to a friar who would preserve his spirit and who might be more acceptable to the learned and wise members of the community. He chose Peter of Catanio.

We must understand the situation that Francis was in, torn between the Christ who was calling him to live according to the Gospel in all respects, and the Church of Christ, which objected that the rule was impracticable. With difficulty he came to recognize that, although the marvelous mission presented by the crucified Christ of San Damiano and subsequently approved was indeed his own, it was not the mission of all his brothers. Furthermore he realized that by imposing upon the friars a rule that, although still very difficult, was not the one that he himself had chosen, the Church was not betraying Christ; she was making it possible to reconcile his will with the vocation of many men who could not follow their leader to the very end. The solution, in effect, was for him, along with an elite group of disciples, to obey Christ himself, while allowing the majority to obey a mitigated rule. This is what Saint Robert (1029–1111) had done when he left Cîteaux to return to Molesmes under orders from Rome. It was an awkward solution; not only did it ruin the mission undertaken by Francis, but it also divided his order, which soon was prey to factions. In the final years of his life he already heard the learned friars expressing disdain for the little brothers who could not read and the simple brothers accusing the learned ones of treason. What would happen to them after his death?

Indeed, their common father, who was called to be conciliatory, had been unable to unite the faithful friars and the challengers during his lifetime, and his death was the signal for an even more bitter struggle. The group consisting of the original friars and their disciples, who were nicknamed *zelanti* (zealots), claimed that only the original rule was valid, as explained by Francis' testament. The innovators, citing Rome as the sole judge in the matter, declared that the 1223 rule was still too indefinite and strict, and that the Curia should further mitigate it. At the chapter in 1227, the year following Francis' death, the election of John Parenti as minister general was quite reassuring to the zealots: he was a religious with integrity and zeal for the implementation of the rule. The lax friars wished that Elias was still vicar general; during the year that he had governed the order he had granted all requested permissions and all absolutions for infractions of the rule. Those were the good old days. They let Parenti govern for three more years, since the rule did not provide for terms of office. In 1230, in a show of force, even though they were in the minority at the chapter, they rejected John Parenti and proclaimed Elias the new general, carrying him off in a triumphant procession.

The conflict shifted. It was no longer the innovators against a narrow-minded general, but rather the rigorists against a general who was too broad-minded. Gregory IX, however, was satisfied with this reversal. Elias—in his eyes the man who was both the builder of the basilica of Assisi and the astute leader capable of commanding respect for the definitive rule—established his authority over the entire order. He burdened the friars with a combination of tyranny and caprice, which to his mind was a suitable revenge for the disdainful treatment that he had previously put up with. Salimbene, author of a chronicle that demonstrates his thorough knowledge of the order at that time, lists the most serious grievances against the general:

1. *Lack of education*. In Cremona, while seated in front of a roaring fire, he once received the podesta without standing up or removing the fur cap that he was wearing.

2. *Lack of discernment in admitting men to the order*. He welcomed without distinction sincere postulants and those without a vocation.

3. *Lack of discernment in selecting ministers*. He appointed ministers and guardians from among the lay brothers who were uneducated and unqualified.

4. *Lack of rigor in observing customs.* He allowed free rein to the imagination in matters of garb.

5. *Lack of regular visitation.* The general remained in Assisi, without ever traveling to the convents to supervise their observance of the discipline.

6. *Mistreatment of the ministers,* whom he used to humiliate in order to assure his own authority.

7. *Luxurious tastes.* Ignoring the rule that forbade riding horseback, he used to travel on one of his chargers. He hired a lay domestic staff, who dressed in livery and served him with reverence, especially a cook who was responsible for preparing a fine cuisine for him. He called frequently and obsequiously on the German Emperor and other high-ranking dignitaries.

Against his adversaries, he conducted a reign of terror. He had them incarcerated and treated like criminals. The ones who suffered most were Bernard of Quintavalle (whom Francis, while he lay dying, had blessed as the elder brother of the order), Andrew of Spello, and especially Caesarius of Speyer, who had been one of Saint Francis' closest co-workers and had won his confidence. Andrew was imprisoned for several years in a dungeon. Bernard endured a similar incarceration but managed to escape and find a safe place in which to hide until the general fell from power. As for Caesarius, he found the convent door open one day and took the opportunity to go for a walk in the fresh air, whereupon his guard, a merciless lay brother, clubbed him so severely that he died from the blows.

The general's tyranny shocked even the moderates, who opposed the *zelanti* but still advocated strict obedience to the definitive rule. A conspiracy was formed, headed by two professors from the University of Paris, Aymon of Faversham and Jean de la Rochelle, with the collaboration of Jordan of Giano, the provincial of Germany. At the general chapter of 1239, the conspirators were supposed to overthrow Elias. He was informed of the plot, however, and summoned lay brothers armed with clubs. Now the grand penitentiary of the Pope at that time was a Franciscan, Brother Arnoul; he sent orders to all the suspects to remain in their convents. Foreseeing the storm that was going to break during the chapter, Gregory IX insisted on presiding over it in person. Acknowledging the truth of the accusations brought against the general, he deposed him. The moderates, who were in the majority, elected as his successor Albert of Pisa, the provincial of England.

Albert died six months after his election. During his short time as general, and during the terms of his successors, Crescentius of Jesi and John of Parma, the more prudent friars—both spirituals and partisans of Elias—came to accept the authority of the Holy See as well as the spirituality of Saint Francis. These living arrangements were not easy, but they were necessary only at the provincial level, and not locally. The spirituals dwelled in isolated hermitages, often in the mountains, whereas those who followed the rule lived in large urban convents (hence the name, "conventuals"). The equilibrium, if we understand this to mean the establishment of the moderate position, was the work of the intellectuals, notably those at the University of Paris. They had instigated Elias' downfall, and thereby won the confidence of those who had been wavering and of the less adamant spirituals. The moderate position triumphed in 1257, when the Franciscans elected Saint Bonaventure to the generalate. (Anthony of Padua, their glory, had been dead for twenty-six years and was already canonized.)

A spiritual giant. His baptismal name was Giovanni Fidanza, and he was born in 1221 at Bagnorea in Tuscany. He was four years old and seriously ill when news arrived that Brother Francis was passing through the market town. The mother hurried to present the boy to the saint with the stigmata, and he blessed him. Immediately cured, the child began to run about, and the astonished mother exclaimed, "*Oh, buona ventura!*" ("What good fortune!"). The name stuck, and as an adolescent he kept it when he received the habit in the order of his benefactor: he became Brother Buonaventura, in Latin *Bonaventura*. Endowed with keen intelligence and deep piety, he was sent to the University of Paris, where he studied under Alexander of Hales, who greatly admired his young disciple as both a mystic and a genius, and arranged for him to succeed him in his professorial chair. He was thirty-six years old and revered by the entire Franciscan Order when he became its minister general, and he remained in that post for seventeen years.

He was the one who brought about unity, which had been thought impossible just a few years before. So successful was he that he was later described as "the second founder of the Franciscan order". He put his plans into effect as much by his meekness as by his firmness.

He even managed to impose a uniform religious habit: an ash-gray tunic, which was quite an accomplishment in an order of forty thousand men, many of whom dressed as they pleased, so that one was just as likely to find a burlap sack reminiscent of the Desert Fathers as a flattering, bright-colored bourgeois robe. To those who objected to the learned friars on the grounds that Francis had forbidden books, he replied: "As for the use of books, the rule gives you the answer, for it obliges the friars to say the office and to preach. If the friars are not to tell fables but preach the word of God, which they can know only by reading, and if they cannot read it unless they possess it in writing, then clearly it belongs to their state of perfection [i.e., religious life] to have books."

To those who claimed that only small houses were permitted for the friars, he replied:

> Our convents are spacious because it is an indispensable requirement. Indeed, we have to have a cloister, a chapel, annexes [outbuildings] for the friars, the guests, and the sick; a garden so that the infirm can recuperate and those who are well can preserve their health, and so that those who are devoting themselves to intellectual study can have recreation. All of this is necessary so that those who live in the cloisters might know where to be quiet, where to speak, where to pray, or work, or read, or write. Otherwise each one could drink, eat, work, and rest in any place he wanted. That would be the end of order, discipline, recollection, and piety.

These explanations show that Bonaventure had gained experience that Francis had not had while living a Bohemian life in nature with brothers like himself, without organization or strict discipline. In 1274 Pope Gregory X rewarded the merits of this great theologian, who was nicknamed the Seraphic Doctor (and who had been his own teacher) and gained a reputable counselor by appointing Bonaventure cardinal-bishop of Albano. The latter died a few months later at the Council of Lyons, where he had just convinced the representatives of the Church of Constantinople to enter into union again with the Church of Rome. As early as 1282 Pope Martin IV (Simon de Brie, formerly a minister to Saint Louis, king of France), canonized him.

Thus, at the end of the thirteenth century, the Order of Friars Minor experienced a great surge of fervor and, generally speaking, conformity to the rule. In the early fourteenth century, however, a wind of laxity blew again. Many friars petitioned Rome, not for amendments to the rule, since the matter was settled, but rather for personal exemptions that would grant them the right to inherit property or to hold public office. Many obtained prelatures in this way, contrary to the solemn warnings of the founder. During the century that followed his death, there were no fewer than 568 Franciscan bishops. A few dozen, to be sure, had been chosen to serve as diocesan ordinaries, but most of them were decorated with episcopal titles *in partibus*, without a flock to shepherd, enjoying a title, a palace, revenues, and a life of luxury. The ministers general of that period, having as their subordinates provincials who were not inclined to be strict, were outflanked.

It is understandable that this period was the new golden age for the spirituals, an era of compilation in which the strictness of Saint Francis and the perfection of his first brothers were exalted, along with the importance of the "Testament" and the duplicity of Brother Elias. It was also the period during which extraordinary individuals rose up, among the spirituals, from the ranks of the disciples of Brother Leo and Brother Angelo. The leaders of this little flock of rebels, who rejected the authority of the minister general and regarded the popes as heretics who had falsified the rule, were Angelo Clareno from Fossombrone in the Marches of Ancona, and above all Ubertino of Casale (d. 1338), from Tuscany, who composed *The Tree of the Crucified Life of Jesus* while in exile on Mount La Verna. This is simultaneously one of the most admirable defenses of the Franciscan ideal and one of the most distressing pamphlets for those who practice the virtue of charity.

In the midst of these two extreme positions the Observance was born. In 1334 Jean de Valle received permission from the general, Gerard Odon, to withdraw to the convent in Brugliano and to live there a life of perfect poverty, within a community that had been won over to his plan. His project was continued by Gentilis of Spoleto, then by Paul of Trinci (d. 1390), who extended this reform to fifteen other convents. The general, Enrico Alfieri, observing the homogeneity of these communities and the praiseworthy spirit of their members, appointed Brother Paul the general commissioner of the convents of the Observance. The movement subsequently spread to Spain and then to France and was prodigiously successful at the beginning of the fifteenth century thanks to Saint Bernardino of Siena, a renowned preacher, and his ardent disciples, Saint John of Capistrano, Saint James of the March [of Ancona], and [Blessed] Albert [Berdini] of Sarteano. Within a few years the Observance grew to the point where it numerically equaled the rest of the order. It became necessary to legislate so as to give the Observant Friars the share in the administration that was their due. It was understood that the heirs of the moderates, who assumed the role of the conventuals, would elect the minister general, whereas the Friars of the Observance would be represented in his council by two general vicars, one for the Cismontane family (consisting of Italy and central Europe), and the other for the Transmontane family (western Europe).

The Observant Friars, however, having formed entire provinces, continued to grow until they held an absolute majority. They complained then about the role that was allotted to them in the government of the order. In 1517, Pope Leo X approved of their claims and divided the Franciscan order in two. By the papal bull, *Ite, et vos*, he recognized the Observance as the sole heir of the religious institute founded in 1209 by Saint Francis, and reserved to it the title of Friars Minor and the election of the minister general. He joined to this order three reformed branches of lesser importance: the Colettines, disciples of Saint Colette, a reformer of the order of Saint Clare; the Amedeans, founded in Portugal around 1460 by Blessed Amadeus of [Portugal, or João Mendes de] Silva; and the Discalced Franciscans, instituted in Spain around 1500 by Juan de Guadalupe. Soon the last-mentioned branch, which kept its own statutes within the order, was made illustrious by a new giant of asceticism, mysticism, and preaching, Saint Peter of Alcantara. The Conventuals formed a separate order, headed by a master general; they have persevered to this day, under the name of the Friars Minor Conventual, especially in Italy and in Slavic countries.

Several years after the bull of separation, however, a new spiritual movement appeared within the bosom of the Observance. Certain religious desired to return to the primitive life in three respects, namely, by abandoning the large urban convents in favor of hermitages, by discontinuing theological studies, and by modifying the habit imposed by Bonaventure. In 1525, Matteo di Baschi, a Friar Minor from the Marches of Ancona, obtained permission from the Pope to attempt this reform. He succeeded in erecting a certain number of hermitages, and he requested that these be separated from the Observance. Pope Clement VII granted his request in 1528, but subjected this new religious family to the general of the Conventuals. Since it had drawn up for itself constitutions that were quite different from the statutes that ruled the Conventuals, it requested autonomy. It did not receive it until 1619, but then it could elect its own minister general and govern itself. This religious family has grown considerably and lasted to this day; because of the distinctive, pointed cowl adopted by these religious, they are called the Friars Minor Capuchins. By the end of their first century of religious life, however, they had abandoned the other two causes that motivated their secession: now they pursue serious theological studies and own large convents in cities, even though they have kept the custom of wearing a beard that was conceded to them as hermits.

During this time three other religious families took root and developed, without leaving the bosom [or ambit] of the Observance: the Recollects, established in France in 1590; the Reformed, who were organized in Italy in 1526 and then spread to Austria and Poland; and the Discalced who, under the leadership of Saint Peter of Alcantara, adopted their own constitutions in 1555. These, too, were movements of returning to the origins, while at the same time they were practitioners of forms of asceticism forbidden by Saint Francis, such as perpetual abstinence from meat. In 1897 Pope Leo XIII combined these four families into one, under the name of the Order of Friars Minor.

As for the Poor Clares, they experienced vicissitudes as well. Their rule was extremely strict. Two princesses obtained permission from the Holy See to follow a mitigated rule: Saint Agnes of Prague, the daughter of Ottokar I of Bohemia, who erected her monastery in the very city of Prague, and Blessed Isabel of France, the sister of Saint Louis, who established hers at Longchamp and thus, thanks to a bull issued by Urban IV in 1263, founded the branch of the *Clarisses urbanistes*. The decadence that set in during the fourteenth century provided Saint Colette of Corbie (d. 1477) with the opportunity to reform and found monasteries ruled by very strict constitutions. A century later, Maria Longa founded the Capuchin Poor Clares, with statutes similar to those of the Colettines.

Although we have devoted a short chapter to the development of the order of Saint Francis, the order that was his life's work, it is not possible to add to it a history of all the individuals who have rendered it illustrious by their sanctity (around three hundred saints and blesseds), their learning, their preaching, and their missionary work in distant lands. That would require several supplementary volumes.[1]

It is appropriate to note here, however, that Christ has kept thus far the promise that he made to Saint Francis: the little seed that he planted has become a great tree, with many branches, which continue to grow and to produce abundant fruit.

---

[1] A source for recent information might be *New Saints and Blesseds of the Catholic Church*, volume I, which includes chapters on Saint Maximilian Kolbe and several other Franciscan saints and blesseds who were raised to the honors of the altar in or around the year 1982, the centennial of Saint Francis' birth.—TRANS.

Index